"An insightful look at where our food comes from and how it is brought to the dinner plate. Silbergeld brings us face to face with the harsh reality as she explores ways we can go forward in feeding the world."
—*Food, Inc.*'s CAROLE MORISON

"A powerfully original exploration of the problems of industrial-scale animal agriculture that touches on public health, the environment, and worker safety. No one else has written so thoughtfully or vividly about the 'chickenization' of the agricultural industry around the world and what it means. Silbergeld has written an important, informative, and excellent book."
—TOM PELTON, host of *The Environment in Focus*, WYPR

"This is a must-read for anyone interested in our food system—how we got here, why it doesn't work, and how we move forward."
—FEDELE BAUCCIO, CEO, Bon Appétit Management Company

"Listen to Ellen. The dangers that she reveals are real, but so are the opportunities to do better. As a lifelong farmer, producing over 50 million chickens annually with no antibiotics or drugs, I know that a superior— and safer—model can be successful."
—SCOTT I. SECHLER, owner, Bell & Evans

"It takes a tough professor to write a book that takes on the proponents and opponents of the industrialization of agriculture at the same time. Ellen Silbergeld's approach is based in public health: how to make sure all people are able to access nutritious and safe food. She writes with data, humor, and passion. This is a critical contribution to discussions about our global food supply."
—JOSHUA M. SHARFSTEIN, MD, former Principal Deputy Commissioner of the U.S. Food and Drug Administration, Associate Dean, Johns Hopkins Bloomberg School of Public Health

CHICKENIZING FARMS AND FOOD

CHICKENIZING FARMS & FOOD

How Industrial Meat Production Endangers
Workers, Animals, and Consumers

ELLEN K. SILBERGELD

Johns Hopkins University Press • Baltimore

Johns Hopkins University Press
2715 North Charles Street
Baltimore, Maryland 21218-4363
www.press.jhu.edu

Library of Congress Cataloging-in-Publication Data

Names: Silbergeld, Ellen K., author.
Title: Chickenizing farms and food : how industrial meat production endangers workers,
    animals, and consumers / Ellen K. Silbergeld.
Description: Baltimore, Maryland : Johns Hopkins University Press, 2016. |
    Includes bibliographical references and index.
Identifiers: LCCN 2015041797| ISBN 9781421420301 (hardcover : alk. paper) |
    ISBN 9781421420318 (electronic) | ISBN 1421420309 (hardcover : alk. paper) |
    ISBN 1421420317 (electronic)
Subjects: LCSH: Food—United States—Safety measures. | Food supply—United States—
    Safety measures.
Classification: LCC RA601 .S58 2016 | DDC 363.19/26—dc23 LC record available at
    http://lccn.loc.gov/2015041797

A catalog record for this book is available from the British Library.

*Special discounts are available for bulk purchases of this book. For more information, please
contact Special Sales at 410-516-6936 or specialsales@press.jhu.edu.*

CONTENTS

Preface

I came to the issues of industrialized food animal production unexpectedly, like much of my experiences in science. In 1999, my department chair at the University of Maryland Medical School asked me to sit in on a seminar being given by a faculty recruit because the room was sparsely filled. I asked, "What's the topic?"

"Drug-resistant infections in the hospital," he said.

"I know nothing about this," I said rather brashly, and, having reached that self-satisfied point in my career where I could make such ridiculous statements, I added: "I have no interest in this topic." But he persisted, and eventually I acceded.

Dr. Anthony Harris turned out to be an excellent and engaging speaker, so as I slumped in the back of the lecture room, I became interested despite myself. At one point, Dr. Harris mentioned—almost as an aside—that many drug-resistant infections came from eating food. That woke me up: at the time, I knew what most people know, that you can get sick from *Salmonella* if the chicken salad is left out too long in the sun. But why were some of these illnesses drug-resistant?

At the small reception and lunch following the talk, I sought out a colleague, Dr. Judith Johnson, and asked her that same question, "Why are they drug-resistant infections?" She hardly paused and said, "Oh, that's because they feed chickens antibiotics." I will never forget my immediate and unspoken reaction: *That seems like a really bad idea!* More than fifteen years of research and engagement in national and international policy debates have not changed my opinion.

I want to bring you along to the same poultry and hog farms and the same slaughter and processing plants that I have visited and in which I have conducted research over those years. I will rely on this firsthand experience as well as the more distant gaze of the scientist. This book will also take you into the kitchen, not to recommend what to eat or where to buy your food, but to introduce you to the real events and real people that move food from farms to plates, affecting workers, consumers, and environments. So this book may differ from others about food and agriculture, for I do not separate these events. In many ways, we have the agriculture we deserve, because we don't see these relationships clearly.

Changes are needed, but not the changes most commonly advocated in the debate on food and food production. This book reports on the process of research and questioning that has led me to consider pathways of change that do not cause collateral damage, that do not increase the cost of food or make it more difficult to access food. This book likewise takes seriously the welfare of workers who make our food possible. I am a scientist deeply engaged in research on many of the topics in this book, and I know that the basis of science is to make progress from incomplete to more complete knowledge, and thus from more incorrect to less incorrect decisions. Making the case for change does not, however, require us to assume that those who made decisions in the past were utterly wrong.

One of the most striking lessons I learned in my own progress to this realization was a chance meeting on a mountain hike in Colorado with the granddaughter of an expert who had served on the US government committee that approved the use of tetraethyllead in gasoline in 1927. This decision has been held out by distinguished historians of science as a paradigm of wrongheaded thinking, all the more wrong because it was made at a time when it still would have been possible to avoid this path forward to the age of the automobile. (By implication, this interpretation of history is that those who rejected the eloquent testimony of Alice Hamilton, one of the founders of environmental health in the twentieth century, must have been either stupid or venal.)

As we talked on the mountain path, my new friend told me how pleased her grandfather had been when the Environmental Protection Agency (EPA) began the process of removing and reducing lead in gasoline in the early 1970s. When I asked why in 1927 he had joined the majority of the committee in approving lead as a gasoline additive, she insisted that he—along with most of the other experts—had no doubt of the hazards of lead. So why did they approve it? Because they did not think that there would be so many automobiles that it would make a difference. Such difficulty envisaging the future explains a great deal. But an equally important lesson from science is the danger of continuing past practices, without further examination, just because it is what we have always done.

Some have argued that the ancient alchemists were not wrong but only less right in their concepts of chemistry in their quest to turn lead into gold. But their fault was not a result of incomplete knowledge of chemistry by modern standards but rather a persistent belief in their theories of trans-mutation of the elements in the face of continued failures to make gold from lead. This is when proto-science trips over into belief or ideology, when practices that no longer work start to impose limits on change. The allegiance to past practice is strong in agriculture, given traditions of fa-milial involvement over generations, which I observed more than I realized from helping out my maternal grandparents on their farm when I was a little girl. They farmed much as their grandparents had farmed, and the question "Why?" was not likely to elicit much of an answer from them. This book has connected me back to my family's history of farming and to a little girl feeding chickens and collecting the cows on her great uncle's farm. These connections do not make me any more of an expert on the sociology of farming, but they have served to remind me of the reality of farming during my research with communities, workers, students, and others on industrial food animal production in several countries and inten-sive discussions of economics and policy with politicians, industry leaders, and advocates.

The past can be a prison in technology, much as it is in politics. The fu-ture is to the nimble, not to the steadfast, in the face of changing knowledge and unanticipated circumstances. This is the condition of industrial food animal production today, a failure to reconsider methods and practices that have been accumulated over some eighty years since Arthur Perdue began to reorganize poultry production in Maryland. I am a scientist, but before I was a scientist I studied history. Attention to history, if not to a particu-lar historical perspective, prevents one from wishful thinking. What hap-pened, after all, has happened, and if we are concerned enough to change the present realities, it may be wise to start from what has been delivered to us from the past. I have started from the assumption that decisions in the last great revolution in agriculture—that of industrialization—were based, at the time of their making, on some coherent calculations of benefits and risks, most clearly demonstrated in the history of using antimicrobial drugs in animal feeds. These calculations have in many cases turned out to be inaccurate, but that is true of most human predictions of benefit and loss. There are those who see such calculations and the profit motive as inher-ently evil, and capitalist systems as conspiratorial, but they would write a very different book.

What can we say of the present? This book begins and ends with the proposition that change is needed. Necessarily, then, this book deals with changes in our estimation of the benefits and risks of industrialized agriculture in light of increasing knowledge. Much of this knowledge has arisen from understanding the extent of unintended events inside and outside what we define as agriculture, just as we had to enlarge our vision to deal with the environmental impacts of pesticides, beyond their risks and benefits to crop production. We still mostly think about food and its problems in terms of nutrition; it is a new thing to think about food production as a driver of diseases unrelated to the constituents of food itself. We worry about consumer choice—both quantity and quality. It seems to be less common that we think about how workers and animals are affected by the making of our food. We note the ecological impacts of agriculture, but we ignore many of the dangers of the industrial nature of agriculture.

Throughout this book, I acknowledge that the successes of the industrial model are important, and that they have in many ways transformed and improved daily life for millions. Arthur Perdue will emerge as an impressive figure in this book, which may surprise some, not least his grandson, Jim Perdue, who now runs the family company. The benefits of more productive agricultural systems are real and important. Increased productivity in agriculture has stimulated social growth and improvements in individual welfare for millennia. And the work of agriculture has also improved over the millennia. The old ways of agriculture were in many ways degrading to the humans involved as well as to their animals. Agricultural labor has involved slavery, peonage, and economic indenture for thousands of years. Traditional agriculture was damaging to ecosystems, cruel to animals, and profligate in the consumption of natural and human resources. Only the size of human populations at the time prevented greater damage from these older methods, but there are examples where lack of knowledge on the part of ancient agriculturists of the environmental impacts of their practices resulted in the collapse of ecosystems and societies, such as on Easter Island, as described by Jared Diamond in his 2005 book, *Collapse*.

I was stunned when I first learned that food was a major source of drug-resistant infection. Over the next few months, I asked more questions and learned more about the use of antimicrobial drugs in animal feeds and how chickens are raised under direly unhygienic conditions that result in drug-resistant bacteria in poultry products. I was informed that these risks were confined to food, but no one seemed unduly or specially alarmed by this fact. I began to think more about it, and, as usual, tried to link these new ideas with things I did know.

A step back by way of explanation: my training is in environmental engineering, so I have a natural tendency to think about things in a systematic way, that is, not only in terms of production and consumption but also disposal of the by-products of production. Some years before Dr. Harris's seminar, I had worked on the problem of harmful algal blooms that had suddenly appeared in the Chesapeake Bay and its estuaries. Harmful algal blooms involve the rapid growth of algae, aquatic microorganisms that, like larger plants, live by photosynthesis. Some of these organisms can produce natural toxins that can harm fish and affect humans as well.

Starting in the late 1990s, a severe and as yet not fully understood outbreak of both fish kills and human health complaints were reported up and down the Chesapeake Bay region from Delaware to North and South Carolina. The general wisdom was that excessive land disposal of animal waste—from chickens and hogs—resulted in overloads of nutrients, termed *eutrophication* by ecologists, sufficient to stimulate the overgrowth of these toxic microorganisms in the estuarine streams and rivers of the bay as well as Pamlico Sound in North Carolina. As a professor at the University of Maryland Medical School, I had been recruited into several studies of this episode. So after the seminar on food safety, I began to think about chicken waste again. If disposing poultry wastes on land had caused this ecological problem as well as food contamination, then the waste itself should be a very big problem beyond eutrophication of surface waters, and environmental releases of human pathogens could be an unrecognized risk for human health, as much if not more than *Pfiesteria*, a toxic phytoplankton, that seemed to suddenly appear. I mentioned these thoughts to my chairman. He gave me the look that scientists give earnest laypeople who claim to have figured out the cause of cancer. "No," he said, "it's a problem of food contamination." Never one to let ignorance get in the way of my thinking, much like Nobel Prize winner Sidney Brenner, I could not shake the idea that exposures other than food, such as environmental releases and workers in direct contact in farms and slaughterhouses, could be part of the problem. It led me to spend as much time thinking about fields and watersheds as about farms and consumers.

In another chance event, I took the place of a friend's wife in attending the annual banquet of the Public Justice Center of Maryland, a nonprofit legal advocacy organization founded in 1985 that uses litigation to achieve significant impact on a law or practice that has widespread effects on the citizens of Maryland. The honoree of the year was Patrick Harmon, a chicken catcher representing a small community group called the Delmarva Poultry Justice Alliance. Social justice runs deep in my blood, by both nature and nurture from my parents and my heritage. The gears began to turn, and I thought, "We need to do a study of chicken workers and their exposures to antimicrobial-resistant infections."

I began my work at the University of Maryland, a large land-grant university with a distinguished medical school and a distinguished college of agriculture. But I could never have finished this work at Maryland; after all, its School of Poultry Science was named for Arthur W. Perdue and many of its faculty advise the poultry industry. As my research gained notice and some notoriety among the industry, pressures mounted, and those at Maryland who had generously introduced me to the realities of poultry production began to distance themselves (one junior professor at the College of Agriculture, who had boldly invited me to speak at the Perdue Department, quit her job after resisting the pressure to disinvite me). For this and a variety of other reasons, I jumped back to Johns Hopkins University, where I had received my doctoral and postdoctoral training. There, a very different atmosphere prevailed.

Dr. Patricia Charache, then head of the Hopkins Hospital pathology lab, assisted me in establishing a microbiology lab to study antimicrobial resistance. Her generosity and support were extraordinary; when I thanked her for the third time, she said, "I have always been concerned about this use of drugs in animal feed. You are the one to take this seriously." Dr. Charache was essential to the beginnings of my work, as was Lance Price, another refugee from the University of Maryland, who came with me to Hopkins. Lance was an extraordinary young scientist who had left behind a highly productive career as a research associate in molecular microbiology in Arizona. He was bored by his work on commercializing a probiotic approach to preventing sepsis and was quickly seized by the same excitement and dedication that motivated me. He started from a position of infinitely more knowledge of the field, but we shared a commitment to the importance of a problem that no one else seemed to be interested in or take seriously. Lance is now an international leader in cutting-edge research on antimicrobial resistance, never forgetting his original focus on agriculture.

Even at Hopkins, my road was not initially very smooth. At my first seminar, which concerned chickens, as most of my conversations did at the time, one of my colleagues asked, "But how important is this anyway? I've never heard of it," referring to antibiotic resistance. In fact, before I came back, no one at Hopkins had ever done any work related to the largest private-sector industry of the state. The most senior member of the faculty, a man who had nurtured my early training in engineering, replied before I could, "My grandson is across the street having surgery for an infection by drug-resistant *Staph aureus*. This is one of the most important issues in public health today."

Why did I write this book? The push came from my belated realization that industrial food animal production is now the globalized model—"The Chickenization of the World," in the words of the US Department of Agriculture (USDA). With no apologies, this book focuses on the United States because the industrialization of food animal production began here with poultry, and this is where the industrial model first began to displace traditional methods and economic organization in poultry and then in pork production. It began in Maryland and in Georgia and in Arkansas. Why these states were the cradle of change is a story in itself, which opened my eyes to the origins of many persistent problems. By now, industrialized methods have largely supplanted traditional animal husbandry in countries such as Brazil, China, and Indonesia, and they are making inroads in Africa and the rest of Asia and the Americas. Even in Mongolia, the first industrial swine operation has been established to feed the growing urban population of Ulaanbaatar, bringing the benefits and the problems of modern technology.

This is not a book about food in the usual sense of focusing on diets and nutrition. The USDA schematizes food production as "from farm to fork"; this book focuses on the first part of this process, from the farm to the packages leaving the slaughter and processing plant. It follows the transport of packaged meat and poultry into the wholesale and retail systems to assess how well we control the problems that begin on the farm, and what this means for the safety of what we eat. Many books on agriculture give little space to industrial agriculture, as if to say that the industrialization of farming could not happen, even though it already has. It is the dominant system that we must deal with. Unless we engage these stages and these methods, we constrain our options as individuals and as societies. We may also fail to consider how the ways in which we produce our food affect domains other than our own diets and consumer choices. This book particularly brings the workers—those whose hands touch our food, in the memorable words of Carole Morison of the Delmarva Poultry Justice Alliance—into the discussion.

Finally, a note on the tone of this book. It is intended to open doors, not to push readers through them. I also hope to avoid the reactions that I have sometimes seen in groups to whom I have given talks on this topic. I know I have failed when I can sense a ripple of reaction that includes disbelief, shock, rejection, and (once) actual doubt as to the truth of what I was saying. Doubt is usually expressed by industry persons and scientists as well as corporate executives. I have also experienced doubt from outside the industry, as if the audience cannot accept that any business would engage in such behavior. There are others who find it difficult to accept that government agencies have refused to change policies if—and here is the escape ladder— the evidence is so strong. It is easier for them to doubt the evidence than to doubt that the public and private powers of our society have permitted and encouraged the current state of hazards in industrial agriculture. This is not the reaction I want, because it gets in the way of any mobilization of broader public engagement.

If in 1905 the readers of *The Jungle* had thrown the book across the room in disgust and disbelief, Upton Sinclair would have failed. He was in fact dissatisfied with the lack of response to his book's shocking description of the workers' conditions in the meatpacking industry. I am determined to carry his message, all of it, forward. And not to be discouraged myself. I aim to avoid eliciting this reaction from you. How you respond to the last chapter will be a measure of my success. If we do nothing, then we truly have the agriculture we deserve.

Acknowledgments

First of all, I am deeply and forever indebted to my parents, Joseph and Mary Kovner, for the example of their integrity and unwavering commitment to social justice. To my mother's family I owe my first experiences in agriculture and to all of them—from my grandfather and his family and later to poultry grower Carole Morison and to the slaughterhouse workers and the leaders and members of the United Food and Commercial Workers union—I owe incalculable debts for their patience, their strength, and their honesty. I hope I have honored them with this book, which, in its faults, remains my own.

I also acknowledge inspiration and encouragement from many at Johns Hopkins who kept me going during the years when we were alone in our research, especially Professors Reds Wolman, Alan Goldberg, Ken Nelson, Ruth Faden, Robert Lawrence, and Dr. Patricia Charache; Joachim Otte and Pierre Gerber (formerly) at the Food and Agriculture Organization of the United Nations; Fedele Baucio of *Bon Appétit*; and many colleagues at the US Centers for Disease Control and Prevention (CDC) and the US Food and Drug Administration (FDA). Funding from CDC, the FDA, and the National Institutes of Health along with foundations and internal sources at Johns Hopkins (particularly the Center for a Livable Future) covered the lean years before federal agencies provided funds for my students and research projects.

To my students who have contributed their brilliance and determination to much of the research on this topic, I am eternally grateful: Dr. Lance Price, Dr. Jay Graham, Dr. Jessica Leibler, Dr. Leora Vegosen, Dr. Jub Hinjoy, Dr. Amy Peterson, Dr. Meghan Davis, Dr. Yaqi You, Dr. Kimberly Leahy, and Dr. Ricardo Castillo. Meghan Davis also saw to the proper format for the illustrations in this book. I also thank many of the people who attended seminars and lectures I have given on this topic over the past ten years; your comments and questions sharpened my own thinking and first stimulated me to the possibility of a wider audience for this work, most particularly the International Women's Forum in Bologna.

My work on this book was supported by a fellowship from the Rockefeller Foundation, which supported a month in the wonderful environment of Bellagio, where I began to make progress. I was also supported by the generous appointment to a visiting professorship at the Johns Hopkins School of Advanced International Studies in Bologna, where Dean Ken Keller provided me an office, a place to live, and, most importantly, the intangible benefits of stimulating colleagues in fields outside public health. Michael Plummer, now dean of the Hopkins School of Advanced International Studies in Bologna, walked me through the reports on agricultural economics that he had coordinated while at the Organisation for Economic Co-operation and Development, and I benefited from the many intellectually curious students at the school. My thanks to Kathryn Knowles and Erik Jones of the Bologna Institute for Policy Research for welcoming me into their midst. I thank the Food and Agriculture Organization in Rome for inviting me for a week's participation in a meeting and also the opportunity to test out ideas with their impressive experts, especially Tim Robinson and Pierre Gerber. Long before even the idea of this book arose, Erica Schoenberger "baptized me"—with incomplete success—into the challenges of writing outside my comfort zone, for which I thank her. I learned much from her recent analysis of the origin of environmental problems. Publication was also made possible by a generous bequest from the Mauss family in support of my research in environmental health.

I thank my editors at Johns Hopkins University Press for their patience and encouragement throughout my struggles with "plain talk." I thank my children, Sophia and Nicholas, for tolerating bouts of what they call "public health tourism" (the Rome trash dump wasn't all that bad, was it?) and those friends who listened to my exclamations over new knowledge with unfailing enthusiasm, particularly Alan Goldberg, Ann Stiller, Elaine Richman, and Richard Kagan. Whatever is valuable and worthwhile in this book is thanks to all of the above, while all the mistakes and inadequacies are my responsibility alone.

CHICKENIZING FARMS AND FOOD

INTRODUCTION

This book is not about food. This book is about how we got the agriculture we now have, with a time line that begins in the 1920s in the southeastern United States—so, relatively recently and very quickly on the scale of agricultural history. From small beginnings, this new agriculture—new in methods, animals, feeds, work, food, economic and social organization—has transformed agriculture globally. The US Department of Agriculture, which facilitated the transformation, calls this process "chickenization," in recognition of the primacy of modernizing poultry production, although the process is not limited to production of poultry.

This book is about everything that happens before we buy and consume our food and how we make animals into our food, a process that has changed everything in agriculture. This book is about how it happened. This book is about the people who form a largely unacknowledged chain engaged in making our food—the "heart" that Upton Sinclair lamented when he said, "I aimed at the public's heart and by accident hit its stomach," the heart that was missed by the public when they read and reacted to *The Jungle* in 1905. This response fueled the public demand for a better food safety system, but not much was improved for the people who produce our food by growing animals and working in slaughter and processing plants. The lives of farmers have gotten harder, by most accounts, and the lives of workers in meatpacking and poultry processing are much the same as they were at the turn of the twentieth century. "When was this book written?" demanded Keith Ludlam, president of the local union representing these workers in Tar Heel, North Carolina, when I gave him a copy of *The Jungle*. When I told him, he replied, "Nothing has changed! Nothing has changed at all!" In contrast, a lot has changed for the worse for animals since 1905, with a boomerang effect on our health, which is a main topic in this book.

This book is not about food. This bears repeating, because there have been many books on food in America over the past decade, most of which are about what we eat and what we should eat. This book is about agriculture, specifically, the production of animals for our food. Agriculture has been changed fundamentally over a relatively short period of time from a mostly agrarian to an industrial model of production. "Industrial" is not a bad word in itself, but industry without the constraints of other social goals can cause and has caused great damage. In this industrial age of agriculture, we live in a time of resistance to change. Resisting change is nothing new. Every earlier change in technology, not only in agriculture, has elicited social and ethical concerns and resistance from those whose livelihoods have been based on older ways of working within an existing social order.

In chapter 1, I consider how debates about agriculture are confused by our individual perceptions and experiences as well as the manufactured images of agribusiness. Why is it so difficult to talk about agriculture? Largely, it is because we don't perceive the reality of agriculture and making food; our vision has been clouded by a carefully selected and fostered set of cultural memories. We see things that are no longer there, like images of traditional family farms, and we trust in things that no longer exist, such as the bucolic life of animals in natural settings. The creation of this manufactured reality is deliberate, and it works to hide the problems of food animal production: its impacts on the dignity of workers and animals, on our shared environments, and the same health we share with animals. "One health," a concept developed by veterinarians and public health practitioners, emphasizes the interrelatedness and similarities between the health of animals and that of humans. A major task of this book is to open all of our eyes at last so that we can reject the false comfort offered by a fictional past and false present.

Chapter 2 examines the process of agricultural industrialization over the past ninety years within the history of agriculture. Industrial agriculture is different but not separate from the entire history of agriculture, which is a series of technological revolutions from the Neolithic period to the present. Agriculture has always been a domain of technology, and, as a stage in technological development, industrialization does not have to be bad so long as we pay attention to it. "Industrial" refers to the technological, economic, and social structures that have characterized other areas of human economic activity since the seventeenth century, starting in the West. It is more accurate as a description of agriculture today than the terms used by our government and others, such as "concentrated" or "confined" or "intensive." Some of these terms are actually misleading, as I discuss in chapter 6.

Chapter 3 describes how raising animals for human consumption (and, along with this, growing crops for animal feeds) changed in the twentieth century. This chapter focuses on the United States because that is where it all began, starting in Maryland with the production of "broilers," a new breed of chickens that could be quickly cooked by frying or broiling rather than stewing or boiling.

In chapter 4, I discuss how what happened in poultry production prefigured the transformation of producing other animals for food as well as the crops for animal feeds, which set the road map for the rapid industrialization of food animal production worldwide. Chickenization has rapidly increased as these practices spread internationally, not through the reach of globalized industries but through national policies. This chapter describes the greatly speeded-up history of agricultural industrialization in China and Brazil, now the global leaders of pork and poultry production, respectively, and in Thailand and India. While there are country-specific particularities in these histories, the main drivers of industrialization are similar.

In both chapters 3 and 4, I spend a good deal of time on this history because the industrialization of food animal production is a revolution as profound as anything that has happened in the history of agriculture since our hunter-gatherer ancestors became cultivators of plants and domesticators of animals. Despite its profundity, this latest agricultural revolution has been hardly noticed by historians of agricultural and social development. Whether we notice it or not, the dominance of industrial food animal production across the globe has transformed agriculture as much as did the introduction of the plow. Like the plow, industrialization of animal husbandry was a response to social change, and it now both drives and supports the continuation of change in a loop that has characterized all steps in agricultural development. My perspective is not universally shared. There are those who consider that agriculture is privileged, distinct from other modes of production, in being impossible to industrialize. The adoption of industrial methods and organization is described as a dead end, "a mistaken application to living systems of approaches better suited for making jet fighters and refrigerators." I don't accept this as a matter of fact because agriculture has already been industrialized, which is why I have tried to depoliticize the word *industrialization* and to recapture agriculture as a technological endeavor of humanity over the millennia to the present.

With chapter 5, I turn to the adversities that have come along with the industrialization of agriculture. I focus first on one of the most critical issues in this area in terms of our health, the use of antimicrobial drugs in animal feeds that began seventy years ago. The history of how drugs got into animal feeds is something of a mystery, and I have recorded my unraveling of this mystery as I experienced it, from deconstructing the accepted accounts to actually testing the claims of industry in support of this continued practice. As this is one of the most important impacts on human and animal health, it deserved its own chapter.

Chapters 6 and 7 focus on the environmental adversities of industrial food animal production, starting with a consideration of the term *confinement*, which is considered to be one of the defining characteristics of industrial methods. The image of a screen seems appropriate. What do you see when you look at a screen: the holes or the lattice? Either way, a screen is not much of a barrier.

Chapter 7 considers the evidence for large-scale ecosystem damage related to industrialized agriculture. Part of this damage is the expansion of environmental reservoirs of drug resistance that now flow among bacteria, including pathogens, contaminating our food and sickening us with illnesses that are increasingly untreatable by the drugs we have relied on for nearly eighty years. To date, there has been widespread reluctance to connect these health effects to chickenization. Most of these problems are largely due to willful neglect rather than unavoidable aspects of industrial technology, just as we have learned that chemical plants and oil refineries pollute the environment only when we let them.

In chapters 8 and 9, I look at the impacts on the people who work in producing food from animals and those who consume animal products as food. Like Upton Sinclair, I consider these topics to be intrinsically related, that unsafe workplaces result in unsafe food. I found a disturbing flaw at the heart of food safety systems in the United States, a flaw that unravels whatever flimsy protection remains in food regulation in most countries. In the United States, as a result of deregulatory policies starting thirty years ago, this web of protection is dangerously close to nonexistent.

In chapters 11 and 12, I consider but reject the argument made by many for a return to the agriculture of the past, which was hard on farmers and limited the availability of food for consumers. Instead, I offer a path forward, explicitly accepting that two obligations must be met in proposing changes to current practices in industrialized agriculture and in evaluating its alternatives. The first obligation is the paramount importance of ensuring safe and affordable food, and the second is the charge that we must feed the world. I emphasize these issues, which both relate to public health, over many other critically important issues because these two obligations are why we have agriculture and why it is so important to us. My allegiance to the importance of safe and affordable food is not trivial, and more than anything else it compelled me to reconsider many of the assumptions I brought to writing this book. Safe food is a constant challenge, and the industrialization of agriculture has not solved this challenge; in many ways, it has made things more difficult. Affordability is the most problematic and the least directly acknowledged issue in much of the current writing about food and food systems, which is often directed—consciously or not—at a small segment of the population that can afford extraordinarily high prices for the products of older methods in an era of cheap food. I do not accept this solution, and I do not write this book exclusively to the audience that can accept these costs. In response to the notion of "feeding the world," which has many meanings, I begin with the obligation to avoid solutions that continue or exacerbate unequal burdens in terms of access to food.

The call to feed the world is in many ways a diversion. The world has never been adequately fed; within countries, not all citizens have been fed. Even within my city of Baltimore, not everyone is fed. As others have argued, feeding the world may be more a social and political issue than a technical or agronomic issue. There is considerable evidence that the mass of food disposed of in some countries, if evenly distributed, would be sufficient to feed the world, but it is not trivial to distribute food, just as it is difficult to ensure drinking water in arid regions. In the absence of solving all these problems, we have to consider the need for increased agricultural production. In looking for the answers to many of these questions, I found signposts in the history I uncovered, pointing to the solutions I offer in chapter 12. I found that if you accept the necessity of feeding the world—rich and poor, meat eaters and vegans—there is no path back to the past. There is no road that returns us to what may never have been, but there are ways forward.

1

CAN WE TALK ABOUT AGRICULTURE ?

We need to talk about agriculture.

We have problems in talking about the subject of agriculture, about the reality of producing food for millions and billions, about ecology, sociology, and economics. The tensions involved in such conversations started as early as when Neolithic humans began to settle in larger concentrations, separated from the land and the traditions of rural life. The story of Eden is one such threnody.

Conversations that I have had about agriculture with friends, students, academic colleagues, people sitting next to me on airplanes, and interviewers usually end up with us deciding between talking about the complexity of agriculture or about the happiness of the pig. I know at the outset that I do not stand a chance in the face of Wilbur in *Charlotte's Web*, who convinced America's children of the 1950s of the innocent virtue of pigs, of the sheepherding pig in *Babe*, and even of poor Snowball in *Animal Farm*. Next came *Chicken Run* and the revolt of anthropomorphic poultry. With this proliferation of talking animals, talking about the reality of agriculture has become even more difficult.

In my introduction, I pledged to constrain my own perspective and recommendations within the goals of affordability, safety, and equity. But in talking about affordability, the discussion often turns to, "What do you mean by 'affordable'?"

"Generally," I say, "food that people can afford to buy."

"No," my partner in these dialogues says, "it depends what you mean by 'affordable.' The way we produce food now really makes it unaffordable for all of us because of all the costs to the environment and our health. You pay now or you pay later."

"But when you go to the store, you have to pay now," I object.

"Well," she says, "we want to change all of the policies that have produced food that is inexpensive to the consumer but costly to the environment, that have encouraged high meat consumption as well as subsidized corn and soybean production for animal feeds."

"Yes," another says, "if we could only increase folks' understanding of the health, environmental, and ecological costs associated with what we produce and choose to eat, then diets would change."

"Look at the growth of farmers' markets and community-supported agriculture," she says. "There is now an ever-expanding market for the kinds of sustainably produced foods that we want to see more of."

"But who can afford to buy these foods, and who can really afford to produce them?" I ask.

"There's more to agriculture than profits," they say. "That's the agribusiness perspective."

"Farmers must be paid, too," I say. "And how many people do you think you can feed with community-supported agriculture and farmers' markets?"

"We can feed the world and feed it better," she asserts.

"I'd like to be optimistic about that," I limit myself to saying.

"It won't happen unless we work to make it happen," she says. "We have to support family farmers because they are 'stewards of biodiversity,' protectors of the climate, and the core of rural communities."

I protest: "Where's the evidence that small farmers can feed the world? Even a medium-sized city? At prices that most of the people—even in our relatively affluent country—can afford?"

"This is not about evidence," they all say. "This is about which side of the future you are on."

"This is about aspiration," another one says. "Think of what Bobby Kennedy said: 'There are those who look at things the way they are, and ask why . . . I dream of things that never were, and ask why not.'"

"I can agree with the first part," I say, "but I'm a bit worried about the second."

The conversation inevitably leaves the issue of food affordability and turns to the ethical values of the happy pig in his sty open to the woods, inner-city children learning how to grow vegetables in neighborhoods devastated by urban renewal and the loss of jobs, earnest college students sorting kale and chard for community-supported agriculture (CSA), locally grown foodie cuisine crafted at restaurants in repurposed industrial buildings, busy farmers' markets occupying parking lots and other spaces throughout the city, and aquaponics—a combination of hydroponics and aquaculture—tanks in a city park.

Resisting the endorsement of such projects becomes tiring and difficult because they are freighted with far more than producing food. Some consider it downright "grinchy," an act of *trahison des clercs*, that is, a betrayal of intellectual, artistic, and moral standards by those academics (like me) who should know better than to protest against such seemingly worthwhile endeavors. But I am with Chang-rae Lee, whose novel *On Such a Full Sea* tweaks these idyllic images in his sci-fi dystopia of my city of Baltimore turned into "B-Mor," a community of serfs who labor in aquaponic-like farms supplying food to the elite beyond their walls.

We have problems in talking about the totality of agriculture for many reasons. One is that fewer and fewer Americans have any direct experience of agriculture. Most of us are at least a generation removed from farming as it used to be before industrialization swept away traditional farms and farm communities. In writing this book, I did not expect to call upon a personal archive of memory, which has only slowly emerged, like repressed memories brought forth through the aid of others. In this case, one of my editors prodded me to revisit them from the long distance between a little girl born just before midcentury, who fed chickens and helped lead cows home from pasture, to a thoroughly (but not completely) urbanized American coming to these topics through the lens of academic science.

I am part of the demographic deluge of the Baby Boom, which brought to an end a long process of migration and change that finally severed the connections between most Americans and the experience of traditional rural life. This generational change was only a vast speeding up of a slower erosion of rural life that occurred over millennia in the bumpy but continuous movement of country folk to cities. My mother, who in her lifetime left the farm and saw the end of her family's centuries of connection to the land and farming, knew there was something important in giving her children, born in the city, a glimpse of what had been abandoned. From my birth through the age of six, she annually packed me and my siblings into the car (first a Crossley, which she would drive up on the sidewalk to get around city traffic, and then a lumbering brown Plymouth station wagon) and drove us from Washington, DC, to Marlboro, Massachusetts, to spend a month at her parents' farm. She convinced my father to accept a job in New Hampshire, where her mother was born and several uncles and great uncles still farmed. There we had much more intensive contact with farming—real farming—at my uncles' and with what I now recognize as the vanguard of the postwar version of a repeated trope in American history: returning to the land.

Fifty years later, there are few city families with connections to relatives still on the farm. Yet many of my friends and colleagues in Baltimore, often those who are African American, share my mother's determination to immerse their children, at least for a while, in the rural world through still vivid connections with family living in small towns in the South.

These recently recovered memories give me no special expertise about most of the topics in this book, especially about agricultural technology and economics, but they do give me access to some notion of what it was really like to farm before the modern era of industrialization. I find it hard to have meaningful discussions about agriculture with those who have no direct understanding of traditional farming. A fog of romanticism gets in the way of talking about the reality of agriculture.

Possibly the greatest impediment to talking about agriculture is its importance—anything as important as agriculture can be expected to be hotly debated. I quickly learned that talking about agriculture is contentious, but I did not expect the many ways in which contention arises. From industry and the US Department of Agriculture (USDA), I expected controversy, and I encountered rough seas in my first dealings with the poultry industry on the Delaware, Maryland, and Virginia peninsula, known locally as "Delmarva."

I expected pushback from industry and the USDA, but I was often surprised by its brazenness. The Pennsylvania secretary of agriculture informed me, as we sat down together at a table in the hearing room of the state legislature, "I'm in favor of agriculture." When I attempted to assert my agreement, he interrupted, "The bigger the better." An official from the Perdue Company, founded by the originator of industrial poultry production, while attending one of our community meetings (which are always open to all) disingenuously informed me that the reason we found so much *Campylobacter jejuni* (the main cause of gastroenteritis worldwide) in chickens was because of the presence of cats in poultry houses. Why would any chicken farmer allow a cat inside the henhouse? I was so preoccupied by this irrational response that I could not explain to him that *Campylobacter* is predominantly carried by birds, including poultry, not by cats. That was early in my introduction to the world of intensive broiler production, and I was too astounded to ask questions.

I was similarly caught by surprise by those veterinarians who in 2004 attended meetings where I gave my first national talks on our research in Delmarva poultry farms, one convened by the Environmental Protection Agency (EPA), and the other at the American Public Health Association (APHA). At the EPA meeting, I arrived at the meeting room five minutes before my talk to hear a veterinarian opining that he was not sure there was such a big problem with antimicrobial resistance. I quickly scrapped my planned introduction to begin, "There is no question about whether antimicrobial resistance is a huge public health threat; the only question is, how much of it are you responsible for?" At the APHA, my talk was interrupted by Dr. Liz Wagstrom, then scientific director for the National Pork Council, who announced that she could not possibly accept my characterization of swine houses as being "crowded and unsanitary." But by then I knew to come prepared and to push back hard. I showed my next slide, which was a USDA photograph of the interior of a swine house. I replied, "Dr. Wagstrom, if you don't think this is crowded and unsanitary, then I suggest that the next time you go into a hospital you ask to sleep in a bedpan."

In the hallway after that exchange, I was quickly informed by two of my students, both veterinarians, that much of the profession was captive to agribusiness in much the same way that "Big Pharma" had for decades toyed with US medical schools and their students before that profession repudiated their gifts of books, meals, doctor's bags, and stethoscopes, a decision that was greatly hastened by public revelations of the extent of industry influence. Other forces have stripped this critical profession of its independence, including an oversupply of veterinarians that exerts economic pressures to reduce practitioners' incomes. According to my students, animal production agriculture offers some of the more lucrative positions, and it funds much of the research at schools of veterinary medicine. This problem is reinforced by the politics of agricultural research more generally—schools of veterinary medicine and colleges of agriculture tend to be located at land-grant universities and often in states with major agriculture economies. Both of these types of academic institutions receive more support from pharmaceutical and agribusiness than from the government, and they are vulnerable to both local and national political and industry pressures.

The antiscientific nature of some of the pushback also surprised me, although I, along with most of the country, am no longer surprised about the shameless denial of fact that pollutes much of our political discourse. Over and over, with strikingly similar language, industry and government have asserted that there is a critical lack of research on key questions, such as whether feeding arsenic to chickens increases levels of arsenic in poultry products. As late as 2013, the National Poultry Council continued to assert that arsenic in poultry feeds does not increase arsenic in chicken meat, less than a week before the Food and Drug Administration (FDA) finally banned the use of arsenicals in poultry feeds, finally acknowledging the evidence we had generated of their health risks. These denials by industry and government of the knowledge we have about the health impacts of drug use in animal feeds are particularly striking given the extensive research performed in Europe. I had carefully read these papers before we started our own studies on the health risks of industrial food animal production, the first to look beyond the grocery store, to aim for the heart and not just the stomach. In Scandinavia, for instance, science had stimulated public concerns, and for years the public had driven governmental response.

Staff scientists at the FDA assured me in 2005 that the idea that bacteria could shuttle antibiotic-resistant genes back and forth within microbial communities had never been demonstrated outside the lab. Dr. Joshua Lederberg won a Nobel Prize for this finding in 1958, and the first clinical report of horizontal gene exchange among human pathogens was reported less than ten years later.

But it is not just from industry and government that I have experienced this kind of resistance. As the writing of this book has progressed, I have tested my own assumptions and I have changed many of my prior opinions, which—as I was taught—is the way that science moves forward. But, as a result, I have realized that more than a few friends and colleagues will no longer speak to me. I have found myself the target of quite personalized disagreement, particularly from those who consider that I have "betrayed" the values of those who oppose the industrial model.

And I am not the only such target. As reported by John Vidal in *The Guardian*, the Bill and Melinda Gates Foundation has been castigated online as being part of a vast conspiracy that includes the Monsanto Company and eugenicists because of its measured endorsement of biotechnology as one tool for improving agricultural productivity in Africa.

Two other impediments to change are that conversations about agriculture are complicated by lack of contact among officials in public health, ecology, and agriculture, and by the large impact of money and political influence on government and science. That is not surprising. Almost all colleges of agriculture and veterinary medicine are located at universities without schools of public health, so opportunities for discourse are limited by distance. All of these factors impede communication. Sometimes we use the same words with different implicit and explicit meanings, such as *sustainability*, *equity*, and *development*. Sometimes we do not even use the same language when we intend to refer to the same concepts, such as when we confuse sustainability with efficiency. More deeply, when we talk about agriculture, we are not always talking about *agriculture*. We are often talking about our visions of society, our hopes for personal happiness and for the future of our children, our loyalties to place and culture, our images of the past and future, our politics both local and global, our concerns about health, and our sense of uncertainty in a disrupted world at all levels and definitions. As a result, discourse on agriculture is increasingly fractured by perspective as much as by disputed facts or economic interests.

This book respects the importance and relevance of all these perspectives, but we have to find a way to a shared or at least an accepted base of knowledge and facts in order to separately and together reach the more difficult conversations about values. I am not sure how to achieve this goal, but I have hope. Many years ago, I was able to break through a similar fog during a radio debate with a representative of the lead industry. He scoffed at the campaign, which I was defending, to ban *all* uses of lead, which he considered to be unfocused and silly because it opposed uses of lead that he considered to be of minuscule risk. As an example, he cited making model soldiers out of lead and mockingly asked if I wanted his collection removed from his shelves. Before I could answer, he went on to recount the joys of teaching his grandson how to pour molten lead into the old molds he had inherited from his own grandfather. The distance between us shrank to the space of a personal conversation. I asked him if he had thought to have his grandson's blood lead levels checked. "Do you think I should?" he asked, in the voice of a loving grandparent, dropping the stance he had been asked to assume. "I do," I replied in the voice of a parent, not the advocate I had assumed. Will we be able to find that common ground in the conversation about agriculture? I once ate fried chicken with Bill Satterfield, the director of the Delmarva Poultry Industry Association, to assure him that my concerns were not driven by vegan or vegetarian politics.

The problem of communication begins with underlying disagreements on how to value agriculture, by which I deliberately mean to include a range of meanings of *value*, from ethics to the moral and political economics of the classical British economists David Ricardo and John Stuart Mill. A deep and powerful literature grounds the discussion of agriculture and the critique of its industrialized methodologies in ethical, social, and moral values. This perspective directs its comments not only to the particular impacts of industrial agriculture, such as its disruptions of natural systems, but also to the very notion of industrializing agriculture. It claims that agricultural production is fundamentally different from other productive activities of humans and is therefore off-limits to industrialization. "Agriculture has certain features that differ from all other industries," asserts Michael Tauger, writing his recent history of agriculture, because "food takes precedence over all other products [and] life forms are much more complex and less fully understood than most raw materials used in industrial production." The moral objection to the intrusion of technology into agriculture is vivid in the phrase *The Machine in the Garden*, the title of a book by Leo Marx.

This view of agriculture, as being separate and distinct from industrialization, makes little sense. Although food is a necessity, so are other products of human activity (for example, housing, heating, water supply, medicines), and it is debatable whether life forms are less fully understood or understandable than the inanimate materials involved in manufacture by humans. Our new technology to edit the genome suggests not. The technological transformation of agriculture from the garden into a machine of production is no recent event. Beginning in the Neolithic Age, the first humans took up sticks and broke the ground to plant seeds and laid stones to direct the flow of streams to water plants as they grew. Not that everything of importance that humans make can be easily industrialized, but privileging agriculture apart from industrialization and technology creates an obstacle to conversations about agriculture as it is.

Nevertheless, these statements oblige respectful acknowledgment insofar as they reflect the experienced or perceived tragedies of earlier industrializations. *The World We Have Lost* is the evocative title of Peter Laslett's book on the disappearance of rural life in England during the age of industrialization. We have lost many past worlds and societies over the centuries of modern and postmodern events. Karl Marx imbues *Das Kapital* with the mournful evocation of everything solid melting into air, which reminds us to respect, but keep our eyes open to, the smaller tragedies of preindustrial society. *The Machine in the Garden* expresses a memorable concept: the conflict between the pastoral ideal of Arcadia and industrialization in the nineteenth century. I remember reading and heavily underlining this text as a student in the late 1960s before I went on to get a degree in engineering.

"Wets and dries"—Margaret Thatcher said it best with her succinct taxonomy of the debate over values in social policy as one between the "wets" and the "dries." For the Iron Lady, the wets were those moderates in the Conservative Party spectrum who were soft on social issues and opposed to a strict monetarist policy on the ethical grounds of its heavy burdens on the poor. The dries were hardliners who were opposed to the welfare state on equally ethical grounds of weakening individual responsibility and resolve. To clarify references to the discourse on agriculture, I have adopted Thatcher's terminology without prejudice. I apply the term *dry* to agricultural technology and industrial food production (bearing in mind that this is not a pejorative term; rather, it is consistent with the goals of productivity, economic efficiency, and reducing risk). I apply the term *wet* to a set of alternatives to industrial systems that place value on social and biological ecology in terms of perspectives, goals, and methods. Agroecology is an important, but not the only, position within the wet perspective, and it has many definitions, including "the application of ecology to the design and management of sustainable agroecosystems; a whole-systems approach to agriculture and food systems development based on traditional knowledge, alternative agriculture, and local food system experiences; and linking ecology, culture, economics, and society to sustain agricultural production, healthy environments, and viable food and farming communities." I draw upon the voluminous literature in agroecology. Major universities have instituted courses and centers in agroecology, including in the United States as well as in Denmark, Mexico, the Netherlands, Norway, and Spain. But agroecology is not the exclusive perspective in this debate. Likewise, the "dries" are not simply everyone else, but they do share an appreciation for the importance of technological approaches to food production.

On the face of it, the wet perspective occupies much of the attractive high ground in many debates about agriculture. The cultural depth of references in the wet perspective—drawing upon religion, poetry, and folklore in many cultures—creates a difficult challenge in discourse. This perspective draws upon Arcadian nostalgia and leverages connections among animals, humans, and ecosystems within the natural world.

This perspective embraces a broader agenda that includes resistance to private profit, market-based economies, economic concentration, dominance of urbanization, and globalization. In this mixture of values and allegiances, there are similarities among those who participate in "alternative" agricultures, such as organic farming and CSA, and religious communities in terms of the importance of shared beliefs and participation in communal activities. The religious implications may not be exaggerated, given the role of gardens as religious and moral symbols in many cultures, as well as the persistent cultural memories of traditional family farms, as discussed in the introduction of this book.

The dries can also invoke religion, tracing the moment of technological intrusion into nature in the Judeo-Christian-Islamic tradition back to the expulsion of humans from the Garden of Eden. This act has powerful reference to the first technologies of agriculture, as shown in a lovely Romanesque sculptured capital from the Cathedral of Parma depicting Adam and Eve after their expulsion, forced to take up the first technologies in order to survive, a shovel and a stick for Adam to dig the earth and a spindle and a wheel for Eve to make cloth. No wonder agricultural technology is associated with sin. No wonder the notion of a "golden age" of pretechnological agriculture has been conflated with the prelapsarian condition and extended to claim a universally privileged moral position for preindustrial agrarian life.

Against this powerful imagery, it is hard to advance the position that agriculture is technology in the fundamental sense of human engineering for human good. It is considerably less poetic than Hesiod or the Book of Genesis to assert that agricultural history is embedded in the history of technology and that the "special status" claimed for agriculture as apart from industry and technology has never been the case. Agriculture is not a romance of life close to the earth; that was Eden. Agriculture was never a part of the human condition in paradise.

But the technological, or dry, perspective is not devoid of deep values. Claiming agriculture as technology is strongly linked to an ethical compact, an agreement made over and over again within human societies, to ensure that we would continue to be fed as our numbers grew and we lived together in larger and larger groups. This promise began in the earliest Neolithic societies and continues to the present. But advocates of the technological perspective are not always the best communicators of moral values, stuck as they are with a less poetical and denser style of writing. As a consequence, the moral values of technology are less frequently heard, and, in the dry language of technology, it is not hard to ascribe a heartlessness to the technological perspective.

Now for some examples of wet and dry. Wendell Berry is an eloquent and self-described proponent of the perspective that rejects industrial technology and organization in agriculture on the grounds of fundamental moral validity. His writings about agriculture are explicitly embedded in ethical, social, and moral definitions of "value," dividing the "sides" in the debate on moral grounds. In Berry's words, proponents of the technological (dry) side are behind the transformation of agriculture because

they believe that a farm or a forest is or ought to be the same as a factory; that care is only minimally involved in the use of the land; that affection is not involved at all; that for all practical purposes a machine is as good as a human; that the industrial standards of production, efficiency, and profitability are the only standards that are necessary; that the topsoil is lifeless and inert; that soil biology is safely replaceable by soil chemistry; that the nature or ecology of any given place is irrelevant to the use of it; that there is no value in human community or neighborhood; and that technological innovation will produce benign results apart from any culturally prescribed concern for nature or human society.

Berry claims his perspective is representative of those

who want to preserve the precious things of nature and of human culture and pass them on to their children. They want the world's fields and forests to be productive; they do not want them to be destroyed for the sake of production. They know you cannot be a democrat (small "d") or a conservationist and at the same time a proponent of the supranational corporate economy. They believe—they know from their experience—that the neighborhood, the local community, is the proper place and reference of responsible work. They see that no commonwealth or community of interest can be defined by greed. They know that things connect: that farming, for example, is connected to nature, and food to farming, and health to food—and they want to preserve those connections. They know that a healthy local community cannot be replaced by a market or an entertainment industry or an information highway. They know that, contrary to all the unmeaning and unmeant talk about "job creation," work ought not to be merely a bone thrown to the otherwise unemployed. They know that work ought to be necessary; it ought to be good; it ought to be satisfying and dignifying to the people who do it, and genuinely useful and pleasing to the people for whom it is done.

Note the words "neighborhood," "community," "connections," "good," "dignifying," and "pleasing." Note the explicit denial of "care," "affection," "community," and even life itself on the part of his opponents.

This is beautiful, persuasive, and highly divisive language. Nothing in the language of agricultural technology approaches its eloquence. But Berry is hardly accurate in describing the dries' perspectives or motivations, and as such this language does not encourage conversation; in fact, it equates any acknowledgment of another view with a dialogue with the devil.

The technologists do not compare in terms of rhetoric, and some of their language conveys an equal lack of respect combined with an assumption of omniscience. Here is one of the driest examples, from the economist Jeffrey

Sachs in a book about development (the sheer length of this quote speaks to the problems in equivalent communication; dries tend to details):

> The real story of development over the past two centuries would go something like this: The Industrial Revolution gained steam first in Great Britain, in part thanks to the country's aggressive policies to overtake Indian textile manufacturing, and for many other reasons as well (including accessible coal deposits). By the early nineteenth century, the technologies that were first developed in Great Britain began to spread globally. The pattern of diffusion was determined by a complex combination of politics, history, and geography. In Europe, technology generally moved eastward and southward to the rest of Europe and northward to Scandinavia . . . Outside Europe, in the nineteenth century, industrialization spread most successfully to places with good geography: countries that happened to have local coal deposits or other low-cost energy sources, industrial inputs such as iron ore or cotton, or easy access to international transport and world markets. It tended to avoid places that were disease-ridden, far from ports, mountainous, or inhospitable to farming. Imperialism mattered, too . . . The advent of high-yield crops in the 1950s and 1960s (the "green revolution") spurred rapid agricultural development mainly in places that enjoyed reliable rainfall or were suitable for irrigation. Sub-Saharan Africa tended to lose out . . . Today, however, Africa is overcoming these problems one by one, thanks to new energy discoveries, long-awaited agricultural advances, breakthroughs in public health, better infrastructure, and greatly improved information, communications, and transportation technologies. Africa may finally be at the tipping point of rapid and self-sustaining growth.

Here the value words include "technology," "diffusion," "industrial inputs," "agricultural advances," "breakthroughs," "infrastructure," and "transportation." The words "nature" and "community" are absent.

These contrasting vocabularies signify an almost complete failure of communication. Wes Jackson, another wet, has characterized this debate as a "cultural battle" between "the human cleverness people" and "the nature's wisdom people." More pithily, Earl Butz (secretary of agriculture in the Eisenhower administration and often considered the leading proponent of industrialized agriculture in the 1950s), in anticipation of a debate with Wendell Berry, reportedly remarked, "I have a feeling that Dr. Berry and I haven't met tonight. Perhaps we won't." Such opposing commentary speaks to what Jackson has referred to as the "moral economies of food."

It will be unpopular, but in this book I suggest a need for both types of people to transcend these comments in order to find common ground in talking about agriculture. Finally, scrutiny needs to be applied to the moral issue of whether agroecology and alternative methods can feasibly support populations in the whole world or any segment of it—a major topic in this book.

There are those who argue that because we in the advantaged, developed world can feed ourselves, we should therefore lead the way in developing reforms that support new paths in agriculture. Keeping in mind that one of the important factors in the rise of industrial food animal production was to provide meat to American cities, it is important to examine the extent to which alternative paths have been able to meet our domestic demands for safe, nutritious, and accessible food. We can reduce some of the controversy by asking whether alternative agriculture is viable within developed countries. In answering this question, we need to think seriously about satisfying not only consumers but also the farmers and other workers in food production. To what extent are alternative methods capable of providing a livelihood for those who participate in these systems?

We have to ask about the sustainability of agroecological methods. Sustainability includes both the ecological and economic viability of farming in the United States. Of course, these concerns are not absent from industrialized food animal production, where, in comparison to the agricultural industrialists or producers, the livelihoods for growers and workers in farming and food animal processing are relatively modest. Nonetheless, these occupations are often the highest-paying jobs in the regions in which the industry is concentrated, as I was forcefully told by chicken growers in Maryland, swine farmers in North Carolina, and slaughterhouse workers in South Carolina.

Facts are scarce on this subject because many of these operations fall below the level of production at which the USDA or state agencies collect economic data. The USDA has generated some information on the overall economics of organic production, but only at the aggregate level. In the 2007 Census of Agriculture, organic farms had high production expenses ($172,000) compared to the average for all other farms ($109,000). Moreover, organic producers did not contribute to regional or national food systems, selling most of their products locally, defined as within one hundred miles. There are studies on CSAs, or microsystems that link farmers and consumers at the local level. In principle, operating locally should encourage profitability, because with only one step between producers and consumers the pass-through of costs should be relatively direct and simple. As admitted in many popular books advocating adoption of the old traditions of agriculture, however, such as Michael Pollan's *The Omnivore's Dilemma*, and as anyone who has tried knows, the agroecology movement restores many of the more challenging aspects of preindustrial modes of production. Considerable contributions of human labor, often off the farm, are required to support the relatively small levels of production of these farms. Some agroecologists, including Prince Charles and Wendell Berry, would say that such increased labor is outweighed by the moral values of returning to the land and participating in making one's food. Similar opinions were expressed by early Zionists in Israel as well as the Red Guards in China on the moral rationale for resetting urbanites and intellectuals to the fields. But pipers must be paid, and resources must be found in all food systems to compensate human labor. Consumers who participate in harvesting and defraying transportation costs contribute some of this labor. As found in a survey conducted in Northern California, which has a highly active local agricultural sector, members of CSAs significantly subsidized transportation costs by traveling to the farms or markets at personal expense. Such activity can be a matter of personal choice, but when it is necessary for the economic survival of alternative farming, it indicates some basic lack of sustainability in the model. Laura DeLind, an academic who undertook CSA farming as a commitment to the larger package of alternative economies and communitarian relationships, has written a poignant, cautionary tale of her experience. Her story is reminiscent of *Cold Comfort Farm*, the satirical saga of the Starkadder family and the vicissitudes and viciousness of traditional rural life. Eventually the commitment wears thin, and other demands on farmers' and consumers' time and resources compete to erode participants' allegiance to the concept of communal agriculture.

I know something about that tension between the agrarian ideal and its reality. I grew up in a mixture of agrarian experiences, including doses of reality from my maternal grandparents, who farmed to make a living in a manner closer to the preindustrialized era in scale and technology. When I was seven, my family moved close to a communitarian experiment in farming near Canterbury, New Hampshire, where a group of exiled liberals adopted various productive roles of the preindustrial world (such as weaving, furniture making, and pottery) along with farming by non-farmers. Even as a young child, I could see that the farming part did not make much sense, as none of those doing the farm work made a living at it and most of them seemed largely unhappy—especially the women and children. My mother was attracted to the ideals of this community and for several years sought to buy an abandoned farm in order to raise goats and make cheese (this was well before more than a few Americans even knew that goat milk could be made into cheese). My very urban father endured without protest visits to a series of rather nightmarish ruined farms in rural New Hampshire and Maine—houses with gaping holes in the roof, windows with ill-fitting casements, ladders for staircases. Fortunately for us children (in retrospect), no property ever seemed exactly right to my mother's vision. So I look upon this present movement through something of a lens of a personal past.

Beyond participating in food production as in the CSA sector, the main economic support for alternative methods is the willingness of some consumers in affluent societies—a relatively small number—to pay considerably higher costs as compared to products raised by conventional methods and sold by large corporations. These costs can be very high, for example, as much as a sixfold difference in the price of conventionally produced chicken compared to those sold at farmers' markets (based on personal observation). This extraordinary cost is rooted in the inefficiencies of traditional agriculture (which has been the main driver of technological change in farming throughout history). It is also the reason why these sectors are unlikely to displace the industrial food systems in the national food basket or to penetrate the markets in other countries. If we look at consumption of meat and poultry products in most developed countries, it is clear that industrial agriculture is the main source of consumer food.

It will take major changes in these alternative systems to displace industrial methods. As noted by World Watch, 67 percent of all poultry products and 42 percent of all pork products globally are produced by factory farms. Industrial methods of food animal production dominate in the developed world and are continuing to expand in the developing world, notably Brazil and China.

I insist that there is an ethical dimension to this reality. The higher price of food produced by alternative methods, including CSA products, excludes most consumers from participation, even in affluent countries. Although Prince Charles responded to the observation that such production is much more expensive with the comment "Well, so be it," this position is not likely to find wide support. Queens and princesses in damask and lace playing shepherdesses as in the paintings of Fragonard are unlikely to have to know the true cost of raising lambs. And even royalty must eventually pay the piper: in 2013, Prince Charles's organic farm shop closed because of mounting debts, according to a report in *Time* magazine.

What is clear is that despite the claims of its protagonists, the wet path is not producing food at anywhere near the same level or comparable consumer price as industrial modes of production. Expansion of this sector will require major changes in order to generate the supply needed to meet demand within the income constraints of most of the world's population. This is unlikely to occur in a model that is detached from the usual drivers of producer profit and consumer economic choice.

Alternative agriculture is much like the traditional crafts sector in highly developed countries. Few craftspeople make their living from pottery or weaving or glass blowing; for most, these activities are hobbies undertaken for personal interests rather than economic reasons, made possible because most practitioners have access to other financial resources. The same is true for many agroecological farmers, few of whom report coming from farm families but are more likely to self-describe as recent adopters of a chosen way of life that is not dependent upon financial returns. None of this is to deny the right of those who can enjoy a lifestyle they choose, who are able to purchase hand-loomed rugs rather than shop at IKEA. But we must acknowledge that it is largely irrelevant to the serious questions of present-day agriculture.

So what is the point of alternative agriculture in the developed world? Who is purchasing the expensive products of this agriculture? Surveys in the United States indicate that purchasers of alternatively produced food products (crops, fruit, meat, and poultry) themselves tend to be relatively affluent, well educated, and committed to a range of social ideals. For this group, environmental concerns and supporting local production take precedent over price (90 percent versus 30 percent) in terms of personal priorities in making choices about food purchases. This is, of course, quite different from most consumers in the United States, for whom convenience and price are ranked as the top concerns in choosing food products.

CSA farmers are also distinct from other farmers. In a survey of CSA farmers in California, most were not from farm families and in fact had little experience in farming prior to setting up relatively small operations within CSA networks. Some advocates of alternative farming seem to have a remarkable insulation from reality; in fact, one of my colleagues from the conversation that opened this chapter claimed that one admirable characteristic of CSA farming is that it "frees the farmer from having to seek profits." Certainly, if my grandfather heard such a statement, he would be astounded. "How," he might ask, "am I to buy my daughter shoes? Or medicines for my wife?"

To be fair, some of my comments are often appropriately rebutted in part by critics of industrialized agriculture with equally challenging questions. Does industrial agricultural "pay its own way," or is its economic efficiency a mirage created by subsidies and giveaways in terms of system-wide decisions not to include externalized costs as well as subsidies? What about its high costs to environment, health, and society? This position is strongly advanced by those who argue compellingly that industrial agriculture floats on a support system that excludes both unvalued and undervalued costs, including impacts on health (and concomitant burdens on healthcare systems) from foodborne and zoonotic diseases; workplace health concerns; environmental impacts on terrestrial and aquatic ecosystems, including ecological services (the assistance that intact environments provide to our life support of clean water and aquatic food); reductions in biodiversity; terrible impacts on animal welfare; undervalued costs of soil erosion and loss of arability; wasteful uses of water; greenhouse gas emissions; and reliance on fossil fuels for energy. In addition to explicitly not counting these costs, there is a "vast series of implicit subsidies to cheap industrial food" that bolster economic support for industrialized agriculture in most developed countries. These supports have ethical and economic impacts beyond national markets by increasing global food insecurity and continuing the dependence of many of the world's poorest nations on food supports from rich economies.

Subsidies is also a contested term. Both subsidies and externalities are ways of hiding or shifting costs away from the particular enterprise to society at large. Much of the policy debate on agriculture in the United States focuses on subsidies in national policy, in which the antisubsidy group includes surprising allies, some (usually fiscal conservatives) claiming that these policies increase the price of food to consumers, and others (usually proponents of alternative / local / organic farming) claiming that they decrease food prices for conventionally produced food. The language of this debate, like other topics in agriculture, interchangeably uses the word "subsidy" with words and phrases like "support," "assistance," and "aid to producers." The Organisation for Economic Co-operation and Development (OECD) recommends using the term "producer support estimates" to cover all policies that governments provide to farmers, regardless of category (direct payments, price supports, and other assistance). This rather stiff terminology helps us to compare the difference between actual prices and receipts to what these values would be without the whole range of supports.

Over the past decade, there have been overall reductions in total support to producers in OECD countries, and, at present, the extent of producer supports within those countries is uneven. In the European Union (EU), total supports constituted 20 percent of the receipts to farmers in 2010, whereas for the United States, total supports were 7 percent of total receipts, among the lowest in the OECD. Generally, this analysis also indicates that agricultural supports contribute relatively little to the difference between the cost of food and its "real cost." The externalizing of the broader impacts of industrial methods deserves more attention in terms of distorting national and international markets for food.

The food market is also distorted by the fact that many countries have used several means to protect traditional agriculture and methods that are valued "non-economically" (such as social and ethical goals), including tariffs and trademarks, which are economic barriers to trade, to raise the bar for entry of goods into protected domestic markets. This is such an embedded strategy that reducing tariff barriers to agricultural trade has stymied the international community for decades. Usually not mentioned by alternative advocates but prominently considered in the economics literature, however, is the fact that the adverse impacts of these tariff policies take a greater toll on consumers and farmers in lesser developed countries as compared to those in affluent countries. Because agricultural supports generally produce commodities at lower prices for importing countries, subsidies and tariffs imposed in developing countries additionally increase the costs of producing food in these countries, as evidenced in the case of India's protection of its domestic poultry production sector.

But the argument is often recast: if we are to have subsidies, why should alternative methods not receive support as well? The answer is that they do, because national agricultural policies are not limited to economic goals, even in market-based approaches to agriculture. In a survey of policymakers' rationales for agricultural policies that include price supports and subsidies, a number of non-economic objectives or moral economies were expressed, including supporting farmers and farming communities as well as preserving small (family) farms, in addition to the national economic objectives of income and price stabilization, regional development, environmental protection, agricultural efficiency, and competitiveness.

A major objective among OECD countries (particularly in the EU) is what is called *food sovereignty*, or protection for special products, usually identified as foods that are culturally important rather than essential to national food independence. These values are remarkably similar to those held by US supporters of CSA farming.

Government mechanisms for the purpose of supporting alternative agriculture have been implemented in only a few countries, such as Sweden, where conversion to organic methods by small farmers has been subsidized by direct payments to farmers and by negative subsidies through increased taxes on chemical fertilizers. Since 2008, US farm policy has adopted subsidies that benefit alternative methods by supporting conservation and environmental protection, urban farming, and organic food production. These policies are certainly within the purview of national politics, but it should be clear that much larger producer supports would be needed in order for alternative producers to achieve economic returns sufficient for an independent livelihood and to make the price of alternatively produced food closer to or actually competitive with that of industrial production. It is likely to be politically difficult to argue the case for supporting alternative methods of food production until consumer demand reaches a level that moves these products from a "niche" item for a small segment of society. Moreover, the costs of agroecological methods of food production are being challenged under conditions in which food insecurity is increasing, as is the case in the United States and in many countries hard hit by the recent economic crisis.

Critics of the US farm bills and programs rightly point to the fact that most recipients of support are large enterprises. But these agribusinesses are not the only beneficiaries. Moreover, there is a practical reason for directing support to large producers. Much of the farm supports in the United States are more food support policies than producer support policies. They fund supplemental nutritional aid programs through purchases of food for domestic aid (what used to be called the "food stamp program"). Approximately 46 million Americans were supported for a total of $75 billion in 2014, including over $15 billion for children's nutrition programs such as school lunch, and $2.4 billion was allocated in 2014 for international aid through the US Agency for International Development's Office of Food for Peace programs. A good part of this international aid has gone to countries in Sub-Saharan Africa and southern Asia. There is abundant criticism that these programs benefit the largest corporations in agriculture and can introduce price distortions, but the largest producers tend to be able to guarantee a reliable source of large surpluses available for purchase by these aid programs. My conversation with the agroecologists above raised the issue of the contradictions in these programs in terms of health goals, such as obesity prevention. Parts of this argument are not well founded. On the radio program of the perennial *Freakonomics* gadfly Stephen Dubner, economist Daniel Summer responded to questions about agricultural "subsidies" and obesity in 2008. Summer pointed out that supports have relatively small effects on retail prices and thus little influence on consumer selection of so-called bad foods, like high fructose corn syrup.

Ending these support programs as part of a goal to reduce or end support for large agricultural enterprises would clearly have major impacts on both domestic and international welfare and development programs. To argue for the inclusion of products from smaller producers in this system would require that this sector generate reliable surpluses, which would necessitate much greater levels of productivity. Moreover, the costs would presumably be greater for government programs to purchase products from these sources. Finally, such inclusion would challenge the importance of local production and community connections as one of the moral objectives of agroecology.

These topics are worthy areas for fruitful discussion. There is an important need to acknowledge the role of multiple policy goals in current farm policies and for a thorough economic analysis of industrial food animal production (including policies that authorize externalizing major costs) and the extent to which policies support low consumer costs versus the amount of support required by alternative producers in order for farmers to make a living and for their products to compete in the market. Like the rest of talking about agriculture, however, we need to air our assumptions and definitions, commit to a consideration of the evidence, and identify those concerns of mutually accepted importance in which improving the conversation may make a real difference.

2

CONFINEMENT, CONCENTRATION, AND INTEGRATION

What Is Industrial Agriculture?

Industrialization is not in itself a bad word, so how has it acquired so much negative baggage in the context of agriculture? Is this baggage all deserved? How much of it is inseparable from the way in which industrialization has been implemented and permitted to operate, with inadequate social and economic controls?

Many things in our lives today are "industrial." Much of what we use, the work we do, where we live, and how our societies are organized economically and socially is industrialized. All these aspects of our individual and social lives reflect changes that started nearly three hundred years ago in a period generally known as the Industrial Revolution. For the purposes of this book, in a great oversimplification of economic and social history, I use *industrial revolution* to refer to those technological and organizational innovations adopted to increase the production of goods and lower costs, with resulting changes in both society at large and the relationship of individuals to society, or, as economists say, of work to capital. Even cloistered monks at Solesmes now make and sell compact discs of Gregorian chant, and the Old Order Amish market their traditionally produced goods to modern society.

Modern food animal production deserves the nomenclature of industrialization because it involves modes of production characteristic of industry.

Work in agriculture now involves performance of specific and relatively limited tasks in production, the replacement of human labor by mechanical energy, and an assembly line to unify separate operations into the production of consumer goods like food animal products. Finally, modern food animal production is industrial in terms of its economic and structural organization, with one economic unit that directly or indirectly controls the central processes of production, from inputs of raw materials to retail products.

The main social impact of industrialization in agriculture is similar to that experienced in other areas of production, that is, replacing the older economic model of a series of linked or dispersed but economically independent farmers, who bred and raised animals, fed them to maturity, and took them to traditional local markets in nearby cities and towns. This traditional organization of agriculture has largely disappeared in many countries, with considerable impacts on rural communities. Whether or not we are entering a postindustrial period in which the almost-vanished world of traditional agriculture as a craft is being revived is a matter of great debate.

The last great agricultural revolution of the twentieth century, industrialization has been remarkably neglected by historians of agriculture. Marcel Mazoyer and Laurence Roudart, historians of the long perspective of human agriculture starting with the Neolithic Age, refer to the "immense and contradictory transformations" that changed agriculture in the twentieth century, but they limit these transformations to what they call mechanization, chemicalization, and motorization. By these clumsily translated terms, they mean the invention and use of increasingly powerful mechanized equipment to handle most of the tasks formerly done by human labor in crop production, the use of synthetic chemicals to support crop growth and to control weeds and pests, and the facilitation of trade and markets in agricultural products through systems of motorized transport. Nowhere is there even a mention of industrialization or the transformation of food animal production, except to connect increased yields of feed crops with increases in domesticated animals. They never mention the subject of this book: the social, agronomic, and economic transformation of agriculture from its traditional grounding in rural societies, pasturage, and smallholder enterprises into the integrated model of confinement, concentration, and integration, with long market chains that extend from breeding animals to selling products to consumers. And their being European does not excuse this omission. Since 1970, most of Europe's chicken and pork has been produced in the industrial model, and the several Common Agricultural Policies of the European Union and its predecessor the European Economic Community have been built around furthering and supporting this model.

The invisibility of this topic is the reason I wrote this book. Because there is currently no comprehensive historical treatment of this transformation on the scale of their great work, I include some of this missing history.

Agriculture was one of the last major sectors of human productivity to be fully industrialized in terms of a complete reorganization of the structure of agricultural work. Some historians have argued that agriculture could and would never be industrialized. Sigfried Giedion, for example, a historian of technology and architecture, contended that production involving the growth of organisms was inherently different from other productive enterprises and that the "resistance of the organic" would prevent agriculture from full industrialization, although he recognized that automation could transform slaughter and processing. Immanuel Wallerstein, historian of world systems including agriculture, also argued for an exemption of agriculture from the industrial model, although he includes agriculture in the capitalist transformation of European society starting in the sixteenth century. This position continues to be asserted to this day.

From our stance in the twenty-first century, surrounded by most aspects of our life as consumers, including being fed by a fully industrialized model of agriculture, we would have to deliberately blind ourselves in order to hold to the view that agriculture has any privileged position in terms of insulation from industrialization. But this perspective is still endorsed, more as a matter of "should" than "could," by agroecologists like Wendell Berry and Wes Jackson. Agroecologists follow in the steps of a long tradition of regret—sometimes expressed violently—for the loss of preindustrial societies. Friedrich Engels and Karl Marx, writing in *The Communist Manifesto*, eloquently reflected on the condition of despair of industrial workers, which was linked to the loss of the sustaining power of old social institutions. But unlike Berry and Jackson, Engels and Marx looked with equally clear eyes at the lot of preindustrial workers. They were not among those urging a return to older traditions as the resolution of the disquiets of industrialization and modernity. The historical record is inexorable. Nothing that has been industrialized has ever been returned to an earlier technology or social organization without withdrawing from society or through considerable force, as in Cambodia, where the population was forced back into rural penury by diktat. No adult has ever become a child again, except through the ravages of dreaded diseases that literally unravel the brain. Leaving aside the biological analogy, Marx and his leading postwar interpreter David Harvey are the best resources for explaining this phenomenon, not in the terms of happy utopianism, as satirized by Voltaire, but in recognition of the philosophy of Plato, in *Cratylus*: once we step in the river of change, both we and the river itself are changed irrevocably.

The delay in agricultural industrialization, almost two centuries after the first events of the Industrial Revolution in England, is strongly related to its historically inflexible conditions. Over the millennia, agriculturists have repeatedly invented and adopted technological changes in pursuit of increased productivity. Prior to the twentieth century, however, preindustrialized inventiveness in agriculture was limited by the fact that it is not easy to relocate agricultural production or to find substitutes for the basic inputs of climate, arable soils, and water. By contrast, the textile industry—the first to be completely industrialized—was based on innovations that increased its flexibility in terms of location. Textile mills can be and have been built far from raw materials of wool or cotton, and the work of humans can be and has been substituted with cheaper labor as well as by mechanical energy. Textile mills were originally constrained by proximity and access to sources of running water for energy to drive machinery or generate steam, but coal made it possible to generate steam and operate without environmental constraints. The availability of human energy was inverted, too: workers, like my great-grandmother in New Hampshire, were willing to move from the country to work in the textile mills of urban areas, meaning that mills no longer had to be located near existing surplus labor. Work in textile production was broken down into simple parts defined by the technology required for specific tasks. Some of these tasks, such as loading bobbins, were simple enough for children to perform. As a consequence, the history of textile manufacture is a series of geographic and social displacements, beginning with the movement of skilled weavers from countries throughout Europe to England (including some 25,000 Huguenot weavers from France in the wake of religious and political upheavals in the eighteenth century).

Supported by a remarkable record of technological innovations and harnessing new sources of energy from water flow and steam power, England's textile industry grew almost as fast as the broiler industry was to grow in its early years in the United States, with over a hundredfold increase in the number of looms in less than fifty years. But the English hegemony in textile production was short-lived: enabled by pirated technology, lower labor costs, and equally abundant sources of energy (coal and water power), the center of the textile industry moved to the United States in the mid-nineteenth century. Here, the industry first flourished in the Northeast, but within sixty years, the Southern states succeeded in attracting the mills with the same advantages along with the additional draw of freedom for the owners from the demands of an increasingly unionized workforce. Within the last quarter of the twentieth century, textile production moved again, this time to Asia, where the continuing movement from country to country has reflected the search for lower costs (mostly related to labor) with little loss of profit normally associated with translocations. Such movement, too, is similar to current global trends in food animal production.

Unlike textiles, agriculture—throughout its early modern revolutions in productivity throughout the sixteenth and seventeenth centuries in Europe—remained inflexibly rooted in geography, tied to the natural world through its necessary inputs of arable soils, available water, and favorable climate. Mazoyer and Roudart write as if these geographical constraints are still at work, with some loosening of the boundaries for crop production accomplished by chemical inputs that can improve soil fertility and constrain the onslaught of pests.

In the case of agriculture, unlike the hard goods of textile manufacture, the perishability of agricultural products in the era before refrigeration also imposed limits on location of production in order to be close to markets. Until these traditional linkages could be severed, the full industrial model could not be implemented. The delay in agricultural industrialization is therefore understandable, as technological advances were needed in multiple areas to free agriculture from the constraints of location.

The first of these links to be dissolved was the obligation to Adam Smith's concept of the market with the revolution in transport, accomplished first by steam power (trains and ships) and then automotive transport and, most importantly, by refrigeration. But the full achievement of flexibility was realized through the invention of chemically assisted crop production, bio-technology, and confinement as a means of raising animals. Chemical assistance in the form of fertilizers and pesticides improved arability, which is the ability of land to support growth of crops for consumption and forage. Biotechnology broke the environmental requirements of certain plants, most notably in Brazil. And the first defining aspect of industrial food animal production is confinement of animals, which eradicated the need for pasturage and arable land and water to grow crops in the same location where the animals were farmed.

After confinement came concentration, the production of large numbers of animals within a small area. This concentration was economically critical because it supported the investments in larger-scale growing operations while keeping prices low for consumers. Concentration of food animal production then drove concentration of crop agriculture to produce feeds for confined flocks and herds.

Industrialization required a further step, nothing less than the reorganization of agriculture in terms of labor and capital. Similar reorganizations had already occurred several times throughout the history of agricultural development in the post-medieval world. In the twentieth century, however, the reorganization of work and economic relationships in agriculture was far more transformative. The industrial model required a new, highly integrated organizational structure, beyond technical changes, to achieve its full potential to increase the efficiency of production.

As a consequence of confinement, concentration, and integration, the industrialization of food animal production has changed the landscape, social order, and economic structure of agriculture.

Although late in coming, agriculture responded to the same set of circular drivers of demand and supply that operated in other areas of industrialization. That is, changes in production methods were necessary to respond to increased demand, which is largely driven by social and demographic changes. Increased supply, in the case of agriculture, supports increases in population, particularly where concentrated in cities, which then supports further population growth and urbanization, which in turn generates further increases in demand to be met by further increases in production. This cycle has been constant in the history of agriculture since the beginning. As Mazoyer and Roudart explain, the earliest changes in agriculture, such as the end of the fallowing system, followed on and then drove major social changes in the organization of work, namely, the rise of a defined farming class, which served and supported the increasing size of human settlements.

Outside forces have also been important in reshaping agriculture. Demographic shifts from country to city involved and responded to the end of a labor system that tied rural agricultural workers to the land as well as an immovable supply of workers in cities created by the apprenticeship system of the guilds. Improvements in agricultural production in the seventeenth century created a large surplus of the agricultural workforce, which sped the movement of populations to cities with increased opportunities for work without the burdensome control of the medieval system that tied workers to the land and landowners.

To the economic historian, this same process is seen somewhat differently, in terms of the requirement of an economic revolution to set the stage for the revolution in production. The availability of capital supported increased investment in agricultural technologies in northern Europe, which in turn supported tremendous increases in productivity along with significant reductions in the amount of human labor required to produce crops and animals. The excess labor supply in rural areas contributed to the growth of cities through internal migration of people in search of work, and the growth of cities increased the demand for food that further encouraged the reorganization of agricultural production. This revolution is seen clearly in the differing trajectories of urban and rural populations, decreases in the agricultural workforce, and increases in agricultural production evident in England and the Netherlands—but not in Italy or Spain—over the period from 1650 to 1700. After this transition (a revolution 150 years in the making), the size of the agricultural workforce and the size of farms in England and the Netherlands remained relatively unchanged from 1700 to 1830, while productivity continued to meet the demands of growing cities. After that point, technological changes and the relaxation of national trade barriers sustained growth and change in agricultural systems in these two countries, with much less of an effect on the Ancién Regime of France and Spain, where national wealth was controlled by the monarchy and was not available to private investments. Gilding churches and building Versailles led these kingdoms to an economic dead end, whereas building canals and railroads empowered and underwrote social and political evolution and revolution in many areas of production in the northern tier of Europe.

The old system of landowner-managed agriculture, known as *latifundia* in Latin, with its inability of workers to own land and the intensive burdens on human labor, dominated European agriculture from Roman times to the present in southern Italy and Spain and Portugal, as documented by José Saramago and Carlo Levi, among others. Elements of this old system, including dependence on slave and indentured labor, were transferred by the Iberian colonizing powers to the Americas for tobacco and sugar cane production, along with mining. Overall, the agricultural revolutions in England and France, preceded and followed (respectively) by the industrial revolutions in these countries, eventually set the colonies of North America on a different social and economic trajectory. But, in many ways, industrial food animal production (especially in the American South) has retained some of the worst aspects of the *latifundia* system.

One of the striking differences in agricultural transformations before the twentieth century is the speed with which they took place. Prior to this last revolution, no sharp demarcations in the development of agriculture had occurred since the fifteenth century, but rather a series of punctuated changes in society along with technological innovations in agricultural production unfolded over time. It was mostly completed first in Britain by the seventeenth century. In contrast, the events of the twentieth century that resulted in industrial food animal production were considerably more rapid. Reading Mazoyer and Roudart is to be gently rocked over a calm sea of the millennia from 10,000 BCE to the present, during which the first agricultural revolution was followed by the second after some five thousand years, and then by the third after two thousand years, and then by the fourth after one thousand years (or first modern revolution in their terms). Put in more concrete terms, wheat yields in England increased fourfold, from half a metric tonne before the year 1000 to two tonnes in 2000. Then things really sped up. Both crop and animal production increased over the first seventy-five years of the twentieth century by 300 percent for wheat and 650 percent for poultry. It took only forty years for the industrial model to emerge from broiler chicken production in a few states in the United States to replacing traditional agriculture, first from broiler production and then swine production nationwide, and then less than twenty years more for agriculture in much of the developed world to be similarly transformed. The speed of change is even quicker in developing countries.

On its own terms, industrialized food animal production has exceeded the local, regional, and even national demands for increased food. In the words of the OECD, "It would have been impossible to achieve this with the old ways of doing things, where to increase production you have to increase the area under cultivation and pasture, either by expanding onto second-choice land or by conquering new territories. The answer was intensification—producing much more from a given area or number of animals."

As defined by the numbers of animals produced by a nation, or within a region, or by one enterprise, the scale of food animal production is much greater than that of any previous mode of production. Industrialization has also shrunk aspects of agriculture. The numbers of farms and the size of the farm workforce are smaller in total and in terms of productivity. In 2012, a poultry company in Thailand announced the development of systems that can produce one million birds at one time. Maryland, a small state that is increasingly less rural, produces between 600 and 800 million broiler chickens a year within in a very small region of a small state.

Of course, nothing happens by itself. Much of the groundwork for this transformation was laid in the United States prior to the first stages in large-scale production of broiler poultry through central investments in research and training in agronomy and the application of this research to farming. The collapse of regional agricultural systems, particularly in the South, and shifts in consumer demand also contributed to the speed with which new methods were adopted. The economic shock of the Great Depression was also important because, among other impacts, it shattered much of the traditional organization of smallholder crop and animal production. The rural workforce was either displaced to the west or to the north, or suffered in place. This underemployed workforce became the fertile field for contract agriculture.

The industrial revolution in agriculture differs from earlier history by its broad and far-reaching effects, including the shock of rapid change, one of industrialization's distinct characteristics. All forms of industrialization—or modernity—impose disruptions on traditional societies, including work and life. In the extraordinary words of Marx and Engels, writing in *The*

Communist Manifesto what they hoped was the elegy for capitalism and the Industrial Revolution, "All that is solid melts into air, all that is holy is profaned, and man is at last compelled to face with sober senses, his real conditions of life, and his relations with his kind." Industrialized agriculture is different from traditional methods and organization, just as the industrial production of cloth is unlike that of smallholder weavers, but it is more extensive in its differences with its past. Although many social critics and writers confronting the Industrial Revolution in manufacturing, particularly in Britain, lamented the disjuncture caused by industrialization between nature and society, this break was not imposed on all elements of the work itself. Weaving was still weaving, if done by machines or by hand, and coal mining was still coal mining, whether done with or without mechanized transport and tools.

But in the case of agriculture, industrialization has had impacts beyond human society, changing the relationships between humans and animals that had developed over millennia and, even more deeply, our relations to the natural world. On a community basis, industrialization has severed individual, local, and regional histories of food animal production as well as the connections between farmers and consumers that were also largely local and personal. This sense of loss, of difference, is the source of much disquiet about industrial food animal production and drives an influential community of writers on the imperative of reforming agriculture by supporting traditional methods without acknowledging the challenges to sustaining productivity.

We can now consider the key aspects of industrial food animal production—confinement, concentration, and integration—in more detail. Confinement and concentration are the key aspects of *intensive* food animal production. Integration is the key aspect of *industrial* food animal production. They arose roughly in that order but quickly joined in a powerful feedback loop to drive the replacement of traditional agriculture. For that reason, the words *industrial* and *intensive* are not synonymous in this book. By speaking carefully, we can dispel some of the baggage attached to these words. The words *intensive food animal production* accurately describe the scale of modern food animal production, whereas *industrial food animal production* describes its organization. This book intends no criticism or moral stance by designating modern agriculture as intensive or industrial.

Confinement refers to modern management practices in raising animals for food by keeping them in buildings for the purposes of efficient management and enhanced productivity, separating animal production from the constraints of time and space. Confinement also separates animals from the natural world and constrains their natural movement and behaviors to a small and highly controlled space. Confinement was an early innovation adopted in broiler poultry production, possibly done first, at least in part, by Mrs. Cecile Steele in Ocean View, Delaware, in 1923. But whatever she did was limited in application, as the birds in Delmarva chicken houses at the time were still free to leave their houses and forage in the yards. Full, lifetime confinement was an innovation more properly attributed to Arthur Perdue and some others such as John Tyson, who, unlike Mrs. Steele, were not extending traditional methods but were rather non-farmers and businessmen looking from the outside to devise more profitable modes of production.

Confinement broke the environmental limits inherent to traditional agriculture. By separating animals from the outdoors and providing manufactured feed, animal husbandry was freed from natural variations that tied it to crop production. It is no longer necessary to raise animals only in regions where feed grains and grasses are also grown. With confined operations, animal numbers are no longer limited by the supply of natural resources or the overall carrying capacity of a region. Carrying capacity is an ecological concept that refers to the maximum number of organisms of a particular species that can be supported indefinitely in a given environment through food, water, or the services of an ecosystem (such as resource recycling or decontamination of natural effluvia). Because of innovations in transport (with which both Arthur Perdue and John Tyson were acquainted prior to getting into the business of raising chickens), it was no longer necessary to raise animals for human consumption close to populations of human consumers. Agriculture became free to adopt all the advantages of flexibility that favored the growth of textile production in locations far from natural resources of inputs and consumers. Without confinement, there would be no industrial food animal production.

With this freedom, an ancient solidity has melted into air, to borrow the language of Marx and Engels. A real and symbolic distance now exists between most of us and the farmers and animals that source the meat and poultry of our diets. This distance contributes to our lack of engagement with the difficult issues of modern food animal production. This failure to fully understand the broader impacts of industrialization is not unique to agriculture, but it is intrinsic to agriculture. By decoupling agriculture from the natural world through new types of organization and technology, the industrial model has succeeded in decoupling us as well. This disjuncture is a major source of the frustration voiced by Berry and others in the agroecological movement. No longer is the relationship between humans and the animals we raise as close and personal as in the past, with signs of respect as simple as giving animals individual names. It is impossible to name or identify individual animals in flocks of 30,000 to 100,000 chickens or in herds of 2,000 to 7,000 pigs. Even when we used to give our animals utilitarian names, like the children of my friend Gretchen Vannote, who named their pig Din-Din, a personal encounter is lost when animals become an undifferentiable mass. Our feelings for them as individual organisms diminish. Few growers speak with affection for these large collections of animals. On country drives, we do not see the animals on intensive farms, as they are never outside.

Our behavior changes with respect to animals in industrialized agriculture. Likewise, separated from us and the natural world, the behaviors of animals are also affected. We have "petting farms" just like we have "petting zoos," a semiotic signification of the rarity of being close to both domestic and exotic animals. While public health officials worry about this activity, the public loves it as a vestige of a former relationship.

Animal houses are now kept completely separate from human domiciles. Few children enter the confinement houses; these are not the animals treasured by 4-H Club members and groomed lovingly for special shows. I remember as a child treasuring the body warmth and smells of my grandfather's dairy cows. The house was connected to the cow barn by a series of tool sheds redolent of their own smells of leather and oil, and we were aware of the reassuring presence of the cows. On especially cold nights, we were allowed to sleep in the hayloft above the stalls to share the warmth they generated. As animals alike, we all watched the fireflies through the cracks in the wooden walls that housed us. We were not overly sentimental about these animals; we knew that one of the chickens we fed in the morning might end up feeding us at the dinner table, and we were taught how to catch and kill them for that purpose. One night, my older brother and I were given feathers saved from the old cock in the stewpot to wear in our hair. Familiarity can breed respect (not always contempt), but this possibility is lost in the commodification of animal production.

Our regret over the loss of this respect should be tempered by the realization that the history of animal domestication by humans has been a story of progressive confinement, from the unfenced domains of herder agriculture still existing in Mongolia, to the expansive cattle ranches and *estancias* in the Americas, to the smaller enclosed meadows for dairy cattle, to the pens for chickens and hogs, and finally to the confinement housing of today's food animal production systems. But earlier forms of confinement consisted of defined spaces that were still within natural settings, such as fenced fields, whereas the modern concept of confinement in agriculture has the dual implication of a physical structure and psychosocial separation. Michel Foucault has written powerfully on the concept of physical and psychological confinement in such centers of production as schools and prisons; in his view, these are like the "dark satanic mills" of William Blake, places of confinement and separation. Confinement is also an apt description of the conditions of many workers in agriculture, especially in the slaughter and processing of food animals. Sometimes these workers can be transferred from one state of confinement to another. Under the Prison Industries Enhancement Act, prisoners are hired out to chicken processing plants in many states, including Maryland. These operations rigorously constrain workers' freedom of movement—for example, to use restrooms—within facilities as well as in and out of facilities. In North Carolina in 1999, twenty-five workers who were locked into a work area of a poultry processing plant died in a fire.

For both animals and the workers who slaughter them, confinement serves the additional purpose of hiding aspects of production from public gaze. These physical barriers have been augmented in some regions of the United States by legal restrictions on public access behind the doors of confinement houses and processing plants. Several states have passed legislation, called "ag-gag" laws, that criminalizes revelations of conditions in intensive agriculture and slaughterhouses. After passage of the Clean Air Act in 1971, the US chemical industry invoked a similar strategy in an attempt to prevent the EPA from even flying over their factories to sample air. The courts overruled this tactic, but no constraints on ag-gag laws have yet been imposed. Part of the moral economy of modern agriculture depends upon forgetting, that is, forgetting the traditional images of something closer to a partnership or at least a compact between humans and animals. Forgetting is easy when our ability to see new realities is blocked.

Confinement is also unmistakable to the animals themselves, as they are confined by limiting their ability to move within confined spaces—most dramatically evident in the farrowing crates where nursing sows are kept, which are so small the animals cannot move—as well as by preventing their access to natural environments that support animal behaviors such as chickens dusting or hogs wallowing. Any view of a poultry house—with as many as 100,000 birds—or a swine house—with as many as 8,000 pigs—or a salmon farm—bristling with the dorsal fins of thousands of fish—imprints itself on the mind of the human observer like the image of Africans packed into ships to sail the Middle Passage into slavery in the New World. To investigate how the animals react would take more than the empathy of Temple Grandin, who has demanded our consideration of animals as fellow creatures, and the science of E. O. Wilson, who has studied animal behavior under anthropogenic stress.

Concentration was the next step in industrialization, referring to the density of animals produced not only at a given location but also within a region. Concentration at any level is an important aspect of increasing the efficiency of production. In food animal production, concentration is central to making large profits on small margins. Geographic concentration also serves the needs of the central focus of animal slaughter and processing by reducing the costs of transporting animals to and consumer product distribution from the slaughterhouse. Even in an era when elements of meat and poultry processing are outsourced globally (as in new arrangements between the United States and Chinese poultry industries), there remains a compelling economic argument for regional density of animal production to support the first steps from the farm to our forks.

Confinement enabled concentration. There are likely to be some limits on concentration and on productivity, but these limitations can be stretched considerably by a number of strategies, such as constructing multilevel buildings, as in the Netherlands for pigs; importing feeds from other regions and even internationally; and exporting wastes. The annual production of poultry in even one county in the states of either Delaware, Maryland, or

Virginia can be as high as 200,000,000 birds. The number of hogs processed each day in Tar Heel, North Carolina, is almost 35,000. These figures reflect an enormous concentration of production. Under traditional methods, this volume of production would be impossible for the generation of poultry, throughput in processing, or the handling of wastes in the traditional manner of recycling to improve the arability of land. Confinement solved the first challenge; outsourcing addressed the second.

Integration is the last step in the revolution of food animal production, the step that moves this human activity fully into an industrialized model. Confinement and concentration increased the productivity of food animal production. But the capstone of agricultural industrialization was the adoption of a centralized organizational structure of ownership and profit. Integration is the least commonly understood term in industrial food animal production, but it is arguably the most important characteristic of the modern model. Integration dictates much of the way in which intensive—or now we may call it industrial—food animal production operates. Integration refers to an organizational structure in which the overall control of production is centered in one economic entity (the integrator), and all activities related to production are carried out either through direct control by or contractual arrangements with the integrator. Integration industrialized food animal production most clearly in economic terms, and it has largely supported the industry's remarkably rapid growth and expansion worldwide. Because integration separates modern food animal production from traditional agriculture, it has had the most profound social effects of the industrial revolution in agriculture.

Integration is not the same as a monopoly, but it has arguably many of the same impacts in terms of restraining trade and reducing the economic power of workers in the production chain. A monopoly is a form of *horizontal* integration, in which one or few enterprises dominate an industry; *vertical* integration, which is the model of industrial food animal production, occurs when one enterprise controls all the economic sectors that relate to its product. Although, in the beginning, the US government brought lawsuits against the new model of integration on the grounds of excessive economic concentration, these cases were unsuccessful in breaking the hold of integration on food animal production. Courts have repeatedly determined that integration does not constitute a monopoly.

Integration of the industry was dependent upon concentration, which in turn was dependent upon confinement. There are many events in the rise of broiler poultry production, but its extraordinary economic successes (in both reducing the costs of food and increasing the profits of producing) are a result of integration. And the key to the success of integration is determining what part of the production sequence is the most critical to control and constructing the enterprise around that critical node. It was not the ability to raise more than a few chickens at a time, like Mrs. Steele and other early broiler producers did on the Delmarva peninsula. It was not even the control of the supply of animal feeds, which was a mechanism adopted first in Georgia. It was the genius of two early entrepreneurs, Arthur W. Perdue and John Tyson, who recognized the centrality of the processing plant in broiler production and on that basis constructed the road to industrial food animal production.

Similar innovations in structure had been achieved in the first years of the automotive industry, which was itself a highly integrated structure, but integration in the poultry industry occurred in the reverse order of what historians and sociologists call "Fordism." Henry Ford began by trying to own everything related to automobile production, but he later adopted the model of so-called "flexible accumulation" through outsourcing and contracting many of these elements. In the poultry industry, integration began with Arthur Perdue when he began to buy hatcheries and then feed mills and slaughterhouses.

By occupying these nodes in the production system, integration permits industry to control both costs and prices. Integration can also increase profitability for the enterprise by excluding, or in economic terms externalizing, higher risks and cost centers from the enterprise. In the textile industry in England and New England in the eighteenth and nineteenth centuries, for example, mill owners did not own or produce the cotton itself, which was subject to the vicissitudes of weather and pests; cotton production was economically separated from the enterprise. Also, the early mills did not produce consumer goods like clothing; this was also separated out to others to bear the risks of fluctuating price and consumer demand. Both of these cost centers are the most volatile, so it is advantageous for a business to separate these risky and uncontrollable activities from its integrated structure and, in agriculture, to shift to others the fluctuations and risks of natural resource availability, energy costs, and consumer economics.

It is little noted that the concept of integration preceded many of the technological innovations that enhanced poultry production, distinguishing it from the history of other industries. With the realization by Perdue and Tyson that controlling the slaughterhouse was the key economic nexus between raising and eating animals, the growth of integrated industrial food animal production started, and the traditional temporal sequence of farmers raising animals to the point of selling animal products, stretching back to Neolithic culture, was abandoned.

But the integrated model is not a complete innovation in agriculture. Some of its roots may be discerned in sharecropping or land rents, well known in the geography and sociology of the rural American South, where industrial poultry production began and is still largely centered. Some have argued that *latifundia* agriculture—characterized by large farms under one owner—also presaged elements of integration. This is not a useful comparison, as the *latifundium* was more of a continuation of slave-based agriculture or serfdom than an innovation transforming the economy of smallholder entrepreneurial agricultural production. Moreover, in industrial food animal production, integration extends far beyond the scope of a large farm raising inputs, such as sugar cane, and producing products, such as rum (an industry that is sometimes claimed to be the progenitor of agricultural integration).

In the fully integrated model, the "integrator" is the economic entity in food animal production that controls the generation of young stock—chicks or piglets, and now spat and fry for oyster and fish farms—through hatcheries, the formulation of feeds, and the processing of live animals into consumer food products. But the integrated model succeeds as much by what it does not control as by what it does control. Notably absent from the direct chain of integration is the actual raising of animals, which is where the hardest and highest-risk work resides, as small farmers have always known, and management of wastes, which incurs the greatest expense and is where the least profit is likely to be made. As agriculture continues to be exempted from regulations in many domains, particularly of its waste streams, integrators continue to be able to omit these activities from the costs of doing business.

Integration is most important when, as in food animal production, the industry needs to control its inputs. In the case of agriculture, controlling animal raising in order to assure a predictable flow of animals into slaughter and processing plants is where integration matters most. Integrators maintain this level of control in food production through binding contracts with the farmers who "grow out" the animals from chicks or shoats to market weight. Through these contracts, the integrator also controls all the conditions under which animals are grown, including animal feeds and veterinary oversight. Under the contract system, the integrator is able to assign costs and risks to contracting farmers or growers, which usually include the costs of constructing, modernizing, and operating the confinement buildings in which the chickens or pigs are raised and supplying water and energy for the houses, including ventilation. The farmer supplies the relatively minimal labor needed to manage the growing process, carry out repairs as needed, and intermittent "cleanout" of the buildings.

The genius of integration in agricultural industrialization was to recognize these key nodes of production and to control both costs and prices by occupying the most profitable ones. Integration excludes higher cost centers from the enterprise—such as with cotton production in England and New England in the eighteenth and nineteenth centuries. Like mill owners and automobile manufacturers, they separated the risks of fluctuating price and consumer economics.

The integrated model is not without benefit to farmers, as it reduces the risk of economic loss even as they must sign away much of their traditional autonomy. The highest risks to farmers have traditionally been the unpredictable and catastrophic events that can take place between investing in seeds and fertilizers or in young animals and their feeds and realizing the gains of selling produce and animals at maturity. Some of these risks are associated with natural events (invasive pests or diseases, droughts, rains, and early frosts), and some are related to fluctuations in the market for raw materials (fertilizers for crops and feeds for animals) and the eventual price paid for the products. There are what the economists call *perverse incentives* in terms of productivity in agriculture. Not enough production and the market fails; too much production and the prices fall. Because the farmers' initial outlays for future production are determined much earlier in the process, it is difficult in the traditional smallholder system for the individual farmer to increase or decrease any output in response to fluctuations in costs and income. Holding back crops or animals from the markets to "game" prices is not feasible, as crops rot and animals die. Under the contract model, the integrator sets a price for the product at the outset, reducing risks to the farmer; for many farmers with long experience of busted seasons, this is reason enough to sign a contract.

Even with the buffering of contracts, externally driven changes in commodity prices (for corn and soybeans, the staples of food animal diets) can have drastic impacts on the economics of food animal production, with effects on integrators as well as farmers. The US "experiment" to divert corn from animal feeds into feedstock for biofuels drove up prices and caused large increases in production costs for poultry and swine in the United States and globally. From 2001 to 2008, the production costs of broiler poultry almost doubled, largely driven by increases in the price of corn, which constitutes approximately 60 percent of poultry feed. The actual costs for integrators more than doubled in two years. The increased demand for corn for the fuels market also affected the price of phosphorus, an essential constituent of fertilizers, which in turn increased the cost of producing many other food and feed crops worldwide. Some of these costs were transferred to consumers, as usual, but there is considerable price inelasticity or inflexibility in food as a commodity that is related to consumer behavior. In addition, food is a perishable commodity, so it is not possible for either producers or consumers to hoard food to keep it off the market until prices or costs change.

The impacts of these market changes were felt outside the United States, and beyond the integrated industry they were even more dramatic, so much so that in 2012 the head of the Food and Agriculture Organization of the United Nations (FAO) formally asked the US government to relax its regulatory quota on the amount of corn that by law had to be diverted to biofuel production in order to protect the supply for smallholders in developing countries. Much like the energy market, no one is really immune to the integrated system of food production and to its global reach.

Another aspect of the current state of industrialization in food animal production is outsourcing. It was only a matter of time before integrators discovered the economic advantages that this strategy offered by labor costs. With increasing reductions in the costs of transportation, the industry has realized savings by dividing up the work of animal slaughter and processing. Slaughter remains in the United States, but some corporations are now sending chicken carcasses for further processing in Mexico and China, a practice known as "added value production." This trend accelerated with the shrinking margin of profitability of food animal production as well as with the industry's growth in other countries. The value of this practice is such that the industry has successfully lobbied the USDA to approve the re-importation of poultry products processed in China from chicken carcasses exported from US integrators. Because the chickens originated in the United States, no country-of-origin labeling is required.

Everything that is solid eventually melts away. The integrated system of agricultural production is associated with a melting away of much that is valued by traditional societies. Integration undermines both social and economic autonomy by completing the trends toward the advantages of capital as opposed to labor (not that agricultural labor ever had much advantage in societies). It is purposefully designed for the advantage of the integrator in the allocation of costs and profits to the owner of the corporate entity that integrates production. Workers, including farmers—in the integrated system they are usually termed "growers," which is more in line with the newly limited delineation of the responsibilities and loss of autonomy—have little control over the profit stream and participate in a strictly limited part of the overall process of producing food from animals under terms set by contracts written by integrators. The integrator defines the conditions of growing, feeding, and managing the chicken house; for contractual arrangements, any deviation from the contract is grounds for the integrator to refuse to buy the birds at the end of the growing cycle. If a purchase is refused, the grower is left with the expenses of feed purchases, energy, water, and maintenance as well as labor. In most areas of intensive poultry production, dominated by integrators, it is difficult, if not impossible, for a farmer to sell a flock that has been refused by the contracting industry. Most states lack resources for direct marketing; certainly, no farmers' market could handle 50,000 to 75,000 broiler chickens—the population of one chicken house—at one time. Larger food outlets, both wholesale and retail, are themselves contractors with the integrators to purchase processed poultry; rarely do they purchase poultry directly from farmers. Even if they were to buy from farmers, there are few certified slaughter and processing houses outside the dominion of the integrators because of the costs involved. Smaller slaughter and processing operations can only produce a frozen product that meets USDA requirements.

The market for frozen poultry is not so large (as Arthur Perdue realized), and the market would have to be relatively local or at most regional, because growers lack the resources for long-distance transport.

Integration diminishes the power of workers in agriculture yet further. Human labor has never had much power in traditional agriculture. In the past, large landowners controlled the working and living conditions of peasants, peons, and serfs. In the Americas, slave labor supported the initial growth of agriculture-based economies, from tobacco in the north to cotton in the south, sugar cane in the West Indies and rubber production in Brazil. Today, many of the benefits that the industrial sector of agriculture receives from government have increased burdens on workers, for example, the exemptions granted from regulations in occupational health and safety as well as environmental regulations that increase risks to workers and communities. Employment practices that are illegal in other businesses, such as employing workers younger than age eighteen or undocumented persons, are exempted in law or practice (such as the bracero program for agricultural workers in the United States, by which undocumented immigrants were permitted to enter the country). Because of these irrationalities, agriculture continues practices that characterized earlier stages of industrialization, including working conditions that are no longer accepted in other industries and freedom from managing their operations from cradle to grave (as is defined in EPA regulations governing the safety of industrial products, releases from manufacture, and eventual product disposal). This very irrationality, in an industry characterized by advances in technology, production, and efficiency, points to the necessary path forward.

3

IT ALL STARTED IN DELMARVA

It was not, a poultry scientist at the University of Maryland in Princess Anne told me, Mrs. Cecile Steele and the mistaken delivery of five hundred chicks—instead of her usual fifty—that set in motion the transformation of animal husbandry. According to the story, Mrs. Steele hastily built a larger house and pen for her unexpected bonanza, worked mightily to feed and care for them, and with her success opened the door to the world of intensive food animal production.

The real story did take place in Delmarva, a peninsula made up of parts of Delaware, Maryland, and Virginia on the eastern side of the Chesapeake Bay. Mrs. Steele may have been among the first farmers there to raise chickens solely for meat, rather than using retired laying chickens for this purpose, and her success certainly illustrated the rapidity with which this industry expanded. Her own operations went from the legendary five hundred chickens in 1923 to ten thousand in 1925. Her broiler house is now at the University of Delaware Agricultural Experiment Station near Georgetown, Delaware, and it was listed on the US National Register of Historic Places on July 3, 1974.

Whether Mrs. Steele was the first to raise broiler chickens in an intensive manner is less clear. There is some claim by Arkansas for primacy in this endeavor, as the *Encyclopedia of Arkansas History and Culture* mentions that in 1916 John J. Glover of Cave Springs in Benton County purchased by mail several hundred high-quality White Wyandotte chickens. From this initial stock, Glover and his daughter, Edith Glover Bagby, started selling chickens for fast cooking, giving rise to the term "broiler." But this early foray into industrialization did not serve more than a local market, largely owing to the lack of transportation links between northern Arkansas and any metropolis. Mrs. Steele and those who came after her were able to get their chickens to the cities of the Mid-Atlantic over rail routes built in 1913 that connected Delmarva to the city markets of Baltimore and Philadelphia.

Broiler production usually dates to the early 1930s and was driven by many factors, among the first of which was the collapse of cotton as the mainstay agricultural crop of the South. Thereafter, bolstered by improvements in regional transportation, the industry grew rapidly, notably in Delmarva. By the mid-1930s, broiler production in the United States had increased to 34 million birds annually. The region comprising four counties on Maryland's lower Eastern Shore, two southern counties of Delaware, and Virginia's Accomack County accounted for about two-thirds of the total at that time.

A finger of sand lying like a beached whale atop a stony backbone, Delmarva accepted the eastward migration of American Indians in the fourteenth century and the westward thrust of English colonists in the seventeenth century. Topographically, it is almost flat, with easy entry to both seawater and freshwater, and it enjoys a relatively mild climate and long growing season. Delmarva seems endlessly flat, but it actually has a small geologic spine running north and south, resulting in a fortunate distribution of plentiful freshwater streams and rivers flowing from the middle of the peninsula to the Chesapeake Bay. The bay was a draw for migrating peoples, with its enormous riches of fish and crustacea as well as its sheltered harbors, culminating in the navigable shores of Baltimore fed by flowing rivers. Well into the twentieth century, steamers carrying tourists and the produce of land and sea traveled between the small town of Crisfield on the Eastern Shore of Maryland and the cities of Washington, Baltimore, and Norfolk.

This favorable location generated considerable wealth. First came logging and the production of tobacco in a slave-driven economy and independent watermen harvesting the fish and oysters of the Chesapeake Bay, and then small farms producing corn and vegetables for the growing cities to the north and south. Chicken production was an old activity of the colonists, according to Grace Brush, the paleoecologist of Delmarva. But until the twentieth century, it was still a relatively small economic enterprise. It is an experience to travel in Delmarva with Brush, who seems to know each bend of the river and each stand of white cedars as old friends. Together we have gone collecting sediments from the Pocomoke River to investigate the ecological footprint of the chicken industry over the past two hundred years.

In the history of Maryland, the Eastern Shore has launched a number of transformative citizens and events, including Frederick Douglass and Harriet Tubman, who was born in Cambridge (the town where the modern Black Power movement was literally sparked with Stokely Carmichael's famous call to "burn, baby, burn" this stubborn citadel of segregation). After them, Paul Sarbanes, Maryland's distinguished senator, was born in Princess Anne, and the artist Glenn Walker was born in Mardela Springs. The Eastern Shore has laureates in John Barth and James Michener.

Isolated settlements have persisted in the region for an extraordinary period of time, as on Tilghman Island, with its distinctive speech, as well as some of the first settlements of freed slaves before emancipation. It is still a place where one participant in our study of chicken house workers responded to a question about recent travel outside the county by asking, "You mean, outside Delmarva?" To some, the Eastern Shore remains an affront to the modernization of Maryland, sending a series of independently minded politicians to the state house, which once provoked a former governor, who was born and raised in Baltimore, to call it and its voters the "outhouse" of Maryland.

When I first moved to Baltimore in 1968, the city markets—Hollins Street, Lexington, Northeast, and Broadway—were surrounded by small shops where live birds were available for sale. Shoppers, like my mother, would stop there first to select their birds to be killed and cut up and then picked up after they purchased fresh fish and vegetables from stalls inside the market. These epimarkets no longer exist, and it is no longer possible to legally buy live chickens in Baltimore or in most large American cities. But Delmarva continues to supply a substantial portion of the chickens bought each year in Maryland and the rest of the United States.

Which brings us back to Mrs. Steele and what may or may not have happened with the five hundred chickens. She is the folkloric center to the narrative that Delmarva likes to tell about the history of poultry production on the Eastern Shore, and she is also representative of a way of agrarian life that no longer exists because of the real story. The real center of the story is quite different and embodies all the complexities of American economic development after the First World War, including the interplay of government and the private sector, as well as the large footprint of Henry Ford.

I will exercise some local chauvinism and claim that the real center of modern chicken production is Arthur W. Perdue, founder of the company that still bears his name and for many years held the position as the leading poultry producer in the world. John Tyson, who entered the business in Arkansas in 1935, was another early innovator in the industry. They are remarkably similar: neither of these two founding figures came from a background in farming and both worked in transport. With no connection to rural life, they looked to the market, not the barn. And that has made all the difference for the history of agriculture.

Arthur Perdue was a railroad clerk in Salisbury, Maryland, when he started his chicken business in 1917 with laying hens. He founded a poultry company in 1920, and in 1925, he opened a hatchery, selling White Rock chicks, the ancestor of today's broiler breed, to local farmers. By 1950, he owned hatcheries, slaughterhouses, and feed mills. He never owned a farm. His contribution was not in raising chickens but in establishing and expanding the first successful example of vertical integration in food animal production. Over the past ten years, Perdue Farms' global dominance has been displaced by emulators in the developing world, such as Star Poultry in Indonesia and JBS (Sadia) Brazil, but the company's primacy in innovation continues.

Arthur Perdue's impressive story is proudly displayed on the company's website, although the pivotal innovation that explains his success deserves a clearer presentation. When I teach my students about the Delmarva poultry industry, I ask them this question: "If you wanted to become the czar or czarina of broiler poultry production, what part of the industry would you want to control?"

Most of my students have little or no contact with agriculture. I often think mine may be one of the last generations in which a good deal of us had at least passing familial contact with farming and animal raising. In my case, it was my maternal grandfather, Alexander Gion, who farmed with great success in rural Marlboro, Massachusetts, doing well enough to send his only child, my mother, to Wellesley College in 1938 with a shiny Ford auto and a striking raccoon coat. I spent summers at his farm in Marlboro and learned to feed chickens and turkeys and to fear my pet goat, his gift to me (I was terrified of this animal, who delighted in entrapping small children within the radius of his chain so that he could run with amazing speed in a demonic circle and savagely trip them). During my childhood in New Hampshire, where most of my mother's family remained, I spent a great deal of time at my great uncle's dairy farm near Sunapee and worked (if it could be called that) during the summers with my friends at their parents' farms in Canterbury.

To get back to the impressively intelligent children of urban America, I asked them, "What do you want to own in order to control the poultry industry?" "The farms," they usually answer. Only someone with no experience of the exigencies and perils of smallholder farming would consider that a position of control. "The distribution of chicken products," some of the more economically savvy will suggest, confusing the final stage of production with economic centrality.

Arthur Perdue figured out the correct answer to this question. Control the processing plants. With this control, you sit at the nexus between raising animals on the farm—a messy, hardscrabble position—and the point of sale to wholesalers and retailers, a position subject to the unpredictability of consumers. As the processor, you can set the price paid to the farmer and the price paid by the retailer. Perdue took the raw material produced by others and turned it into products to be sold by others.

It was a fortuitous time, with at least four developments supporting expansion of poultry production and the centralization of chicken slaughter and processing: food sanitation, increasing consumer affluence, innovations in transport, and government policies.

Upton Sinclair played an important role with respect to sanitation. In 1905, he wrote *The Jungle*, first as a serial in a magazine called *An Appeal to Reason*. It was quickly republished as a book in 1906, and the public reaction to the nightmares of unsafe food that Sinclair described vividly was swift. *The Jungle* reached the White House, and, in the same year, President Theodore Roosevelt demanded and got new legislation to authorize federal inspection of food production in order to end the nightmares that Sinclair described so vividly. The nightmares related to unsafe food, that is. The degraded conditions of workers in the Chicago slaughterhouses did not provoke any comparable public reaction or presidential attention. Sinclair later said ruefully, "I aimed at the public's heart and by accident hit its stomach."

The new food sanitation laws and regulations favored the position of larger animal slaughter and processing because, from the perspective of government, these operations could be more readily identified and regulated. From the point of view of the industry, the larger plants were better able to absorb the costs of meeting the new standards. In this way, both reformers and capitalists found common ground, not for the first or last time in American economic history.

The growing urbanization and incomes of Americans drove increased demands for meat and poultry consumption just as has been the case in every other country since that time. It is no small thing that Herbert Hoover promised a chicken in every pot just before the crash of 1929. The New Deal fulfilled this promise. In 1942, Norman Rockwell's iconic picture of the fourth freedom—freedom from want—featured a plump bird on the Thanksgiving table (turkey production was industrialized in the late 1930s, shortly after broilers). This same image was echoed in the early advertisements I saw in Brazil in the 1980s that enticed the public into buying the new breed of chicken imported from the United States, complete with a blond-haired family gathered around a fat bird.

Technical innovations in transport made it possible for urban populations to be served by poultry producers far from metropolitan areas. Here, the similar backgrounds of Perdue in railroads and Tyson in trucking may have aided their rapid ascendancy, as they knew the importance of transportation networks to link hungry consumers in cities and unemployed and underemployed farmers in the country. Delmarva was the birthplace of two additional key innovations in transport relevant to the rise of industrialized broiler production: the invention that leveraged motorized transport above the railroads and the invention that made it possible for both rail and truck to deliver fresh poultry to the cities. Both inventions were the product of one man, Thomas Midgely, who worked on the northern side of the Delaware River at the Deepwater plant of the DuPont Chemical Company. (Midgely has the extraordinary distinction of discovering two of the most infamous chemicals of the twentieth century, tetraethyllead and chlorofluorocarbons, or CFCs.) The first invention made cars and trucks run reliably despite the relative inefficiency of the early internal combustion engine. The second invention powered refrigeration, which made it possible to ship chilled but unfrozen poultry products over long distances.

Regarding government policies, the expansion of poultry production continued after Hoover as part of the economic response to the Great Depression, which included the worst agricultural crash in US history during the Dust Bowl years, and through the huge economic mobilization of World War II. The poultry industry specifically benefited from massive expansion of federal support to and control of agriculture. As part of this support, the War Production Board of the US government exempted broiler chickens from domestic food rationing during the war. After the war, food became an instrument of US foreign policy, particularly useful in demonstrating the superiority of American capitalism as an engine of plenty in contrast to the repeated failures of collectivized agriculture practiced and exported by the Soviet Union. When Khrushchev visited the American Midwest in 1959, he did not visit a yeoman farmer, but Roswell Garst, a pioneer in seed hybridization and the founder of the Garst Seed Company, once one of the largest seed companies in the world and now owned by Syngenta, the world leader in crop biotechnology. Like Perdue, Garst was a man whose roots were not in the hard work of traditional agriculture. Instead, his success was enabled by federal agricultural policies and fueled by the close linkage between the growing food animal industry and the increasing demand for corn for animal feeds.

Back in Delmarva, Arthur Perdue realized by 1938 the need to reorganize the production of raw materials in order to support his integrated model of the industry. His slaughter and processing plants were Fordist in their use of automation and the assembly line in order to produce products cheap enough for mass purchase. Otherwise, the development of industrial poultry production ran on an opposite temporal track from automobile production. To run a factory and to produce a steady supply of consumer products, Perdue needed a dependable and orderly supply of chickens, his raw materials. The Ford Motor Company and General Motors formed strong partnerships with the oil industries to meet similar needs; for Perdue, no similar corporate model existed, and therefore there was no ready solution to the problem, aggravated by the fact that the primary production of chickens in 1920 was located within an unorganized sector of independent farmers.

Recognizing the advantages of controlling the flow of live chickens, Perdue and other early entrepreneurs—a class distinct from farmers—invested in the new broiler industry that constituted the raw material inputs into their plants. To partly accomplish this goal, many of them, like Perdue and Tyson, went into the business of supplying feeds and chicks. But the supply still did not meet the demands of processing, the central point in economic terms; they needed to establish an orderly connection between the supply of resources (chickens) with the distribution of output. To grow into a national industry, broiler chicken producers like Perdue needed a reliable supply of live chickens and they needed that supply to be carefully regulated, such that there was neither a glut nor a dearth of birds at any time. Confinement protected against seasonal fluctuations in poultry production, but confinement did not solve the question of synchronizing growing chickens with processing them. How did they achieve this synchronicity?

Perdue developed the integrated model of poultry production, one of the defining aspects of industrial food animal production. Integration represents both old and new strains of economic organization. Its goal is both economic and technical: to control costs and to ensure a dependable and organized supply of raw materials (birds) for the factory (the slaughter and processing house) so that production can be efficiently and dependably organized, reducing the risks of shortfalls. For consumers, this arrangement has a similar benefit of buffering them against the wider fluctuations in price of an unorganized industry, where acts of nature could suddenly increase the costs of smallholder production, and thus availability and food costs to the city residents. Herbert Hoover may have promised "a chicken in every pot," but it was Arthur Perdue who ensured that the chicken would cost more or less the same during both winter and summer, year after year. For farmers, the blessings of integration were mixed. What the broiler industry pioneered was nothing less than the end of independent poultry production. The integrators introduced the concept of contracts with farmers, one at a time, thereby turning what had traditionally been a group of independent farmers—sometimes linked in cooperatives, which is rare outside of dairy today—into an integrated supply chain from the farm to the consumer.

This transformation began in a specific region of the United States, what Steve Wing, an epidemiologist of industrial agriculture in rural communities in North Carolina, has called the Broiler Belt, which in his opinion may not be coincidentally colocated with the Bible Belt. The reasons for such colocation are not immediately obvious, as the Southern states—including those that comprise Delmarva—neither produced feed crops for chickens nor were they particularly close to major urban markets. The coincidence lies deeper in the Southern traditions of agriculture and their roots in slave labor in Delmarva as in the Deep South states of Arkansas and Georgia. With the collapse of the cotton market in the 1920s, the economic sustainability of much farming in the South also collapsed, leaving landowners and farmers with few options except to leave. But not all farmers left, resulting in a regional labor surplus that benefited the structure of the new agriculture. Farmers are more willing to sign contracts, workers are easier to find, and overall costs are lower in places with economic depression and lack of political power. The history of Tyson Foods in the *Encyclopedia of Arkansas History and Culture* admits that one of the advantages for growth of the industry in its present location of northern Arkansas was the hostility of state politicians toward unions as well as the availability of an economically depressed agricultural workforce in the wake of the fall of King Cotton in the 1920s. Unlike the slaughterhouses of the Midwest (the world of Upton Sinclair), the Broiler Belt is not fertile ground for organized labor.

The modern system of contract poultry growing owes a lot to the model of sharecropping developed in the South after the end of slave labor in agriculture; it is economically similar to crop liens in the days of cotton and tobacco, the main products in the states where intensive poultry production began. For Maryland, Virginia, and the Carolinas, crop liens for tobacco production were the immediate legal predecessors of contract poultry production. During Reconstruction, crop liens replaced slavery by debt peonage, this time an economic indenture but just as stringent, and they contain much the same language as a broiler contract.

In most broiler contracts, instead of renting land, the farmer essentially "rents" the birds from the integrator during the six to seven weeks it takes to grow a chick into a market-weight broiler chicken. Farmers must raise and then sell the product back to the integrator in accordance with all the terms of the contract, including using the integrator's feeds and operating and even modernizing the broiler house according to the integrator's requirements. The integrator usually supplies the workforce to catch the chickens, load them onto trucks, and deliver them to the processing plants.

In most states, this workforce is also contracted; in Maryland, however, a lawsuit against Perdue established the legal precedent that such workers were actually employees of Perdue, with the rights of salary and other protections afforded by Maryland law. The farmer, now designated by his new task as "grower," essentially "rents" the birds from the integrator and covers the costs of raising them through loans guaranteed by the lien. If sales are insufficient to cover the original loan (which can include costs of renovating poultry houses stipulated in contracts), the farmer goes into debt, sometimes for several harvest cycles, and sometimes into bankruptcy.

Farmers in the South and Southeast were conditioned by history to accept the dramatic changes in social and economic autonomy associated with contract poultry farming. In contrast, in the Northern states, where sharecropping was not a traditional mode of agricultural production, cooperatives have persisted in the dairy industry that is largely located in these states. Farmers in the Deep South knew sharecropping from cotton, and those in Delmarva knew sharecropping from tobacco, and they were not unaccustomed to contracts with buyers and the constraints that such an arrangement brought. As in the past, they had to surrender the entrepreneurial tradition of the market farmer, who can set his own price in a market where buyers deal directly with farmers—a model of the market frequently invoked by Adam Smith, the economist much loved by bankers. In turn, farmers gained the assurance that their product would have a guaranteed market through the integrator, such that they would assume the up-front debt involved in building chicken houses and paying for feeds, energy, and water.

The rise of the integrated model to dominance in poultry production was rapid but not without resistance. In the early days, farmers in Georgia and Arkansas recognized and publicly lamented their loss of autonomy, but, under the circumstances of a collapsed cotton-centered economy, they had few options to continue "free" or independent agriculture. Moreover, as integrators gained control of animals from before birth to slaughter and from the farm to fork, as the USDA likes to say, farmers had fewer alternatives to bring their animals to market, outside of integrator-controlled slaughter and processing operations. The US government, in the early days before its unwavering support for integration (typified by its provision of loans and subsidies to integrators rather than to farmers), intervened three times to object to the restrictive aspects of integration, but lost each case in court.

Over time, farmers had little choice but to cede more and more autonomy. As a result, the "yeoman farmer" of tradition has mostly disappeared, first in the South and then throughout the industry. In the fully integrated model, the integrator (in the early days Perdue or Tyson) controls the process from start to finish, beginning with generating the birds through breeding and in hatcheries, the formulation of feeds, and the slaughter and processing of live animals into consumer food products. The farmer, now designated by the USDA as "grower," is a discrete but limited link in this chain, supplying the relatively minimal labor needed to manage the growing process and the buildings in which the chickens are raised, along with water and energy for ventilation.

The integrated model, in addition to controlling the product chain, has enabled the industry (now often referred to as "producers," supplanting the traditional role of farms) to achieve the goal of outsourcing many of its cost centers, particularly those related to environmental impacts. The farmer—not the integrator—owns the wastes generated by poultry or swine as they grow. Waste represents one of the unprofitable parts of the industry, although, as uses are found for waste (such as consumer fertilizers or fuels for so-called waste-to-energy plants), the integrator takes ownership of that product as well.

Industrialized food animal production is no longer farming in the sense of a partnership among humans, animals, and the environment, in which careful stewardship permits humans to benefit from the favorable conditions of climate, arability, and water. The modern poultry house is an enclosed space, a building—often advertised as a turnkey operation—that can be situated anywhere. It is not necessary to build poultry houses in regions that can supply the feeds (corn and soybeans at base), because feeds are produced by corporations and shipped globally. Cargill, for example, now supplies the burgeoning food animal production industry in China from its Brazilian sources. The poultry industry does not have to be in close proximity to consumers. Access to transportation influenced the birth of industrial poultry production in the United States, and now, with international transportation networks, it is as detached from the location of its consumers as it is from the natural world. It does not even have to be located near its workforce. Animal carcasses can and are being shipped internationally during the stages of processing.

As a consequence of the changes in the economic structure of the industry, the spatial distribution of poultry production has been radically altered over the twentieth century. By 1979, the landscape of poultry production in the United States had shrunk, leaving entirely the Midwest and western states, and concentrated in the southeastern states of the Broiler Belt. Today, the broiler industry is regionally highly intensive and geographically highly constricted. In Delmarva, for example, nearly one billion broiler chickens are grown on a small ecological footprint in a small region of two small states, Delaware and Maryland, plus a fragment of Virginia. In many instances, the industry has grown most rapidly in highly fragile ecosystems, such as in the tidewater areas of Virginia, the hurricane zone of North Carolina, and above the permeable aquifers of Maryland and Arkansas, which has environmental implications for these regions.

Perdue's chickens conquered the United States with their high degree of standardization, reliable availability, promise of safety, and continuous improvements in production as well as innovation. If Americans wanted white meat, then the industry responded by breeding chickens with overdeveloped breasts and fragile legs, such that by the end of a growing season many animals can no longer stand. If Americans wanted a more pleasing skin, then some arsenic in the feed was of use, exploiting the cosmetic properties of arsenic first employed by the ancient Egyptians. If Americans preferred a less pale pink flesh, then Perdue added marigold extract to the feeds to make it yellower; marigolds have been used as a natural dye for centuries in China and Asia. Perdue also led the drive toward more efficient harvest of meat from chickens—the so-called takedown factor—which reached its apotheosis in the wholly deconstructed and reconstructed food item known as the McDonald's chicken McNugget.

Perdue's model conquered the industry. What started in broiler production became the model for the rest of the food animal industry—in fact, the USDA refers to the "chickenization" of swine production to describe the subsequent transformation of this industry into the integrated model with a handful of large corporations. Cattle ranchers likewise now refer to the ongoing transformation of their industry as chickenization.

The family tradition in agriculture persists in one manner. Food animal production corporations are among some of the largest corporations in the United States that are still family owned. Private ownership further insulates the industry, as does its careful separation of profit from cost centers. All in all, the industry is remarkably invisible to most Americans. The companies use persuasive imagery in their advertising and websites portraying themselves as small family farmers, with animals raised in natural landscapes illuminated by a kindly sun in pictures swathed in a glow of earthly perfection not seen outside of the paintings of Thomas Kinkade. The iconography of food animal production is seductive. Chickens and cows genially josh each other to promote consumption of the other in the "Eat Mor Chikin" campaign of Chick-Fil-A, for example.

In dozens of trips from Baltimore and Washington across the Eastern Shore to their prized Atlantic beaches, I never saw a chicken house before I started conducting studies of the poultry industry. When driving back and forth across the Chesapeake Bay Bridge and the necklace of Kent Island to conduct research, my team left the beach highway to loop down to Pocomoke City or up to Georgetown. At first, it was a game to spot the first chicken house after leaving Route 50. Now it is almost inconceivable to me that I could not have seen them earlier. Having alerted my friends and colleagues to the proliferation of chicken houses in this region, I learned from one of them about the unpleasantness of driving behind a chicken transport truck on the way back from the beach. That sighting stimulated an influential study, one that received attention from the press and inflamed reaction from the poultry industry. In this study, my research team followed chicken transport trucks over the last few miles to the slaughterhouse—the large Tyson facility in Accomack, Virginia—and collected air samples inside our chase cars. From those samples, we isolated the same pathogens that we had studied in chicken houses, workers, and chicken products. The industry responded by accusing us of unsafe driving in pursuit of their speeding transport.

Possibly the only economic force that can constrain the poultry industry in Maryland is competition for space between industrial agriculture and recreation. This will not, of course, end "big chicken" but merely displace it to other regions. It does not have far to go. The industry is currently growing strongly in Virginia outside of Delmarva, in North Carolina, in Pennsylvania, and in West Virginia. In West Virginia, poultry production tripled between 2001 and 2010, to a total of 90 million birds after the first large integrator, Pilgrim's Pride Corporation (now owned by the Brazilian integrator

JBS), bought into the local industry. In Virginia, both turkey and broiler production have grown rapidly over the same period, and the Shenandoah Valley now exceeds Accomack County in Delmarva as the leading area of production in the state. North Carolina, which used to specialize in breeding chicks for broiler production, has supplanted Georgia as the second-largest producer of broilers and has risen to third place in production of turkeys in the United States. Wilson, a wealthy city in North Carolina, was able to prevent a large development of poultry slaughter and growing houses from building in its county, but the integrator, Sanderson Farms, took its plans elsewhere, to a poorer county with a higher minority population. Sanderson constructed its new poultry complex in Robeson County, North Carolina, one of the persistently poorest counties in North Carolina.

These developments underscore how the flexibility of the industrial model detaches it from local pressures so long as there is an alternative location willing to accept the conditions inherent in its operations. This was a lesson learned by many of these same states in negotiating the transfer of textile production from the North to the South and from the United States to South Asia. Now we see this industry moving along a similar path, seeking the lowest level of oversight and regulation. This is why we have national agencies—like the EPA, the USDA, and the Occupational Safety and Health Administration—to prevent this race to the bottom, but over the past thirty years these agencies have been increasingly silent—and silenced—in the face of the power of agribusiness and the food production industry.

4

THE CHICKENIZATION OF THE WORLD

When I met him in Rome in 2012, Pierre Gerber worked for the FAO, one of the agencies of the United Nations (UN). This agency was assigned to Rome, where it occupies a building whose ordinary lack of distinction assumes real ugliness by its location on the Circus Maximus, among some of the greatest monuments of the Roman Empire. FAO's location provides the best view of Rome from the rooftop terrace—perhaps not as elegant as His Holiness's redoubt in the Vatican, but all in all a better view just off the Aventine Hill. Otherwise, it has a dismal exterior whose mediocrity is surpassed only by a maddening internal design that requires one to change elevators frequently from floor to floor owing to the discontinuity of its floor plans.

From Bologna, I had made an appointment to talk with Pierre Gerber, as yet sight unseen, on the strength of two maps he had published in 2006. They were maps of animal production in Asia, one for pigs and one for chickens (figs. 4.1, 4.2).

Pierre's maps of this accelerating trend were a cause of the urgency with which I took on a critical and productive analysis of the industrial model, and they inspired me to e-mail him in Rome while I was in Bologna. He was somewhat puzzled by my enthusiasm for his maps.

They made an enormous impression on me for two reasons. First, they provided me with the first visual evidence of the extraordinary magnitude and intensity of animal production in broad swaths of China and Indonesia, along with dense islands of productivity in Bangladesh, Indonesia, Malaysia, and Vietnam. Second, placed side by side, the two maps revealed the extent of spatial overlap between the densest areas of production of both species.

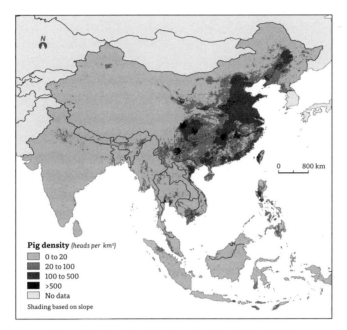

Figure 4.1. Density of pig farms in Asia. (Gerber 2006)

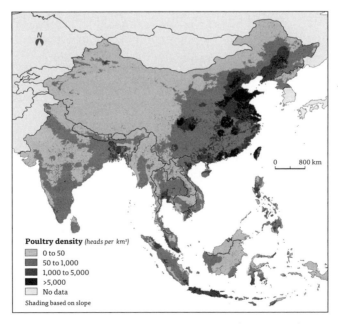

Figure 4.2. Density of poultry farms in Asia. (Gerber 2006)

The first observation woke me up to the accomplished fact of globalized industrial food animal production, dispelling any illusions I had that this was something that was about to happen. Globalized industrial food animal production was here and now. The second observation had important implications for the intermittent emergence of influenza A viruses—from H5N1 to H1N1, H7N3, H7N7, H7N9, and H9N2—which, after decades of relative quiescence, were reported with increasingly short periodicity and were thought by many experts to require passage through both avians and pigs to acquire genes that increased virulence and, most important, enabled the virus to make the jump from zoonosis to human disease.

When I finally met Pierre in 2012, the year I started to write this book, he was remarkably fresh and optimistic in his outlook on global agriculture, a contrast with the gloomy implications of his maps. A Belgian, he had earned a master's degree in the United States, and he looked like an American graduate student in economics or engineering, sporting not the sloppy combination of bedroom and gym wear, but a look that said "sharp" in the sense of an engineer. He was well put together, not flamboyantly, distinctively, or expensively dressed, but rather prudently priced and generic.

I should digress a bit and talk about FAO, as it is not one of the better known parts of the UN family of international agencies devoted to both research and international development. FAO is a major source of information in this book for its libraries and its documentation of agriculture big and small. FAO, if Americans think about it at all, is probably lumped in the liberal mind with the agribusiness camp, promoting "big farming" and destroying smallholders throughout the world. This is not entirely inaccurate, as it is funded by the big agriculture-producing nations, and its policies are generally in line with their interests. But FAO is also home to important research and support for agriculture and nutrition at all levels. From a book I found in a church thrift shop in Cape Cod, written by Josué de Castro, one of the founding directors of FAO, the concept of an agency on food and agriculture was raised in the original talks among the Allies of World War II in 1943 about building international organizations for the postwar world. FAO was established as a UN agency in 1945 and now has 195 member countries. From an original focus on food and nutrition, it is now involved in development, health, poverty, food security, sustainability, climate change, water resource management, organic farming and agroecology, gender studies, and cultural integrity—in short, all the concerns that are attached to agriculture.

Not everyone thinks that FAO manages all items in this diverse portfolio equally well, and, in the worlds of nongovernmental organizations (NGOs) and academia, there are plenty of suspicions about FAO's real objectives, given its ties to the big-producer countries and the influence of big-producer industries. Like many UN organizations, FAO has an industry cooperative program, which (according to some) makes it inherently opposed to its founding goals of bread for the world (the translation of its motto, *fiat panis*) and "likely to preserve, reinforce, and indeed worsen the inequalities that exist between the over-developed and underdeveloped parts of the world," in the words of one of its critics. There are numerous examples of the consequences of FAO adoption of the World Bank policies, and terms bundled together as structural readjustment. As an international organization reliant upon development bank funding, FAO had little choice but to adopt these terms, which the World Health Organization (WHO) summarized succinctly:

> Structural adjustment programs and policies reflect the neo-liberal ideology that drives globalization. They aim to achieve long-term or accelerated economic growth in poorer countries by restructuring the economy and reducing government intervention. SAPs [structural adjustment programs] include currency devaluation, managed balance of payments, reduction of government services through public spending cuts / budget deficit cuts, reducing tax on high earners, reducing inflation, wage suppression, privatization, lowered tariffs on imports and tighter monetary policy, increased free trade, cuts in social spending, and business deregulation. Governments are also encouraged or forced to reduce their role in the economy by privatizing state-owned industries, including the health sector, and opening up their economies to foreign competition.

These dry words need to be quoted, for they conceal the human costs of complicity (or complaisance) of FAO in increasing access to national markets and resources for the big multinationals like Heinz, Nestlé, Cargill, and Gulf and Western Industries Inc. Of greater concern is that its programs continued an old colonial model in these industry cooperative programs, whereby the "overdeveloped" countries and their industries take resources from the underdeveloped countries, leaving little investment, expertise, or hardware behind. In the name of economic development (and with the complicity of the World Bank), FAO funded programs that displaced local food crops with cash crops, for example, bananas in Central America and soybeans in Africa. Throughout the UN system, coziness with industry has only increased as member states' contributions have decreased, as I know firsthand from the sad decline of environmental health programs at the WHO.

Nonetheless, FAO remains an agency largely staffed by earnest people, like Pierre Gerber, who have forsworn much more lucrative opportunities to accomplish the near-impossible goals of mutual transfer of knowledge on agriculture among the nations of the UN. Pierre and his colleague Joachim Otte (with whom I worked on a project concerning the implications of the coincident spread of the poultry and pork industries) at the time both worked for the Pro-Poor Livestock Policy Initiative. Unlike some scientists and managers at the FDA and the USDA, fewer of these international civil servants seem to retire and go on to lucrative positions in the private sector after their time at FAO.

Pierre's maps were the first depictions I had seen of what the USDA calls "chickenization," or the spread of the industrial model of food animal production, in homage to the lead role of broiler poultry production in this process. His maps showed chicken and pig production in Asia—including China, India, and the Southeast Asian countries—in a dense array of black dots as thick and indistinguishable as on the USDA maps of chicken and pig production in the United States by 1979, after the industrial revolution in food animal production was mostly complete. It was a visual statement of the rapidity with which this new technology has been taken up as it moved overseas. Since the 1930s, when Arthur Perdue first began the transformation of poultry production in Delmarva, the world is a "flatter place," to quote Tom Friedman. As a result, innovations and their accompanying risks and benefits now spread rapidly from localized and modest beginnings until there are so many dots on national and global maps, that the only way to see each individual dot is by blowing them up. The industrial model is rapidly displacing local agricultural practices in many countries, resulting from a speeded-up pace in events otherwise not different from the changes that un- folded over half a century in the United States from 1930 to 1980: economic consolidation of smallholder and small-company operations into larger economic units; the adoption of the integrated model, including many of the stages in production; transfer of technology from US production (including intensive production and marketing, confinements, specially formulated feeds with additions of antimicrobial drugs); as well as supplanting of traditional breeds (especially in poultry) with breeds developed in the US specifically for the conditions of intensive production and rapid growth.

Unlike other waves of innovation and technology in the past, global chickenization has not been primarily driven by the expansion of US companies into other countries but rather by the activities of national companies within each country. Some US companies have contributed to chickenization (particularly multinational feed companies such as ConAgra Foods, Cargill, and seed and fertilizer companies such as Syngenta and Monsanto, as well as breeders such as Cobb-Vantress Inc.). The Cobb-Vantress strains of broilers deserve special note, as that company's penetration into the worldwide industry changed the ecology of poultry production in substantial ways. The original company (Cobb) responded to the chickenization of poultry production in the United States by developing its White Rock breed in 1947, an all-white chicken bred to survive life in confinement and to efficiently consume the new diet of finely ground formulated feeds. The White Rock took over broiler poultry production in the United States, and the company continued to develop strains for the conditions of industrial production and for US consumption preferences for white meat. In 1974, the company was separated into two component companies, which were bought by the Upjohn Company and Tyson Foods, such that the world's largest breeder incorporated the interests of both the major poultry integrator and the pharmaceutical industry. In 1994, Tyson purchased Cobb from Upjohn. Cobb, now part of Tyson, has a dominant presence in most regions of the world, with breeding facilities and partnerships in Latin America (notably Brazil), northern and southern Africa (Egypt and South Africa), Asia (China, Japan, Korea, and Thailand), the EU, and Russia.

What drives the chickenization of the world? The answer is not hard to guess. Many of the same forces that drove industrialization in the United States are at play globally: increased demand for meat-based protein as a result of increasing affluence and changes in food preference and patterns of consumption as well as increased urbanization. In addition, in many developing countries, there is an increasing role of food animal products for export as part of deliberate national economic policies. Affluence and urbanization are historically connected with upscale changes in diet, with increasing consumption of the food of elite populations, including meat. This is clearly true for poultry, which as of 2012 became the leading source of meat-based protein in the world. In fact, Marcus Upton, an FAO economist, has calculated the relationship between increases in income and consumption of poultry and eggs. He found that in low- and lower-middle-income societies (not the lowest-income countries, where the socioeconomic base for dietary change is not yet present), a 1 percent increase in income is associated with a greater than 1 percent increase in poultry meat and egg consumption. Some cultural differences affect this increase as well; for instance, in Brazil, poultry meat constitutes nearly 50 percent of total meat consumption, but only 18 percent in China, while poultry is still only rarely consumed in India. In those developing countries that have emerged as major producers, such as Brazil, as of 2005 per capita consumption of poultry meat has outstripped that in many high-income countries.

When I started to look at the history of industrial food animal production in the United States, I found some fuzzy uncertainties (like the legend of Mrs. Steele in Delaware) as well as fairly clear indicators of the factors that have driven and accommodated change by the industry and adoption by the public. There are conundrums in understanding the international story as well. On the one hand, the increasingly global nature of the consumer food basket supports common methods of production and industrialization throughout the world. Moreover, global markets influence national economies and industries such that they are not immune to the choices and preferences of populations in the United States or their neighbors. As well, the partial liberalization of trade barriers protecting national agricultures has reduced obstacles to the entry of foreign agricultural methods and products. As evidenced in several recent rounds of international trade negotiations focusing on agriculture, however, no country is willing to abandon entirely its national right to support and protect its own agricultural sector.

There is a backstory to the spread of industrial food animal production that has its roots in the destruction of national agricultures in many countries during and soon after the Second World War. To offer a compressed history, in Europe and much of Asia, local environments were damaged by warfare, the workforce was reduced, and even those countries not directly affected by total warfare were in disarray. The Soviet Union had already lost much of its agricultural manpower during Stalin's campaign to crush the traditional small farmers, or *kulaks*. Its five-year plans for agriculture still held to Lysenko's anti-Darwinist theories applied to agriculture. Trofim Lysenko held that evolutionary theory contradicted Marxist-Leninist theories of society, and with the adoption of his views by Stalin in the 1930s, biology and agronomy research in the Soviet Union and later in China came to a halt under political control, with consequences that included decades of crop failure and famine.

Shortly after the war, national revolutions in India and China disrupted traditional social organization and economies, to a much greater extent in the latter than in the former. During this period of unsettled and needy economies, the United States became the major patron of postwar economic and social aid. Of necessity, food and agriculture were major components of aid programs, and this remained the case through the Cold War and into the post-Gorbachev era. The US Agency for International Development (USAID), which incorporated much of the more scattered foreign aid programs prior to the Kennedy administration, has continued its programs for food aid and agricultural development, along with the USDA. Industrial and intensive agricultures in the production of food animals and crops were a clear showcase for the triumph of American capitalism and a strong card in the Cold War competition with Soviet influence, insofar as the example of Soviet agriculture was an eloquent rebuttal to collectivist alternatives, Lysenkoism, and the abolition of economic incentives for productivity. So the seeds of industrialized agriculture were dispersed globally in the postwar period as a matter of foreign policy.

The dependence of the industrial model on fossil fuel sources of energy and chemicals was also consistent with US economic interests because US corporations dominated the production of both gasoline and agrochemicals. Some companies—such as Chevron Corporation—actually produced both. This kind of foreign aid redounded to domestic profits and was thus highly prized politically. This is not to ignore the additional aid in the form of technical expertise, in which many US farmers, agronomists, and agricultural scientists were sent to advise foreign governments in the adoption of industrial techniques. Key foreign nationals were funded by the USDA to study at US agricultural institutions, including some seven hundred researchers from sixty-four countries who were awarded the esteemed Norman Borlaug Fellowships of the USDA, named after the American agronomist whose research was foundational to the Green Revolution.

I do not accept the idea that this strategy was entirely self-serving; aid organizations and foundations could justifiably conclude during this period that the methods developed in US agriculture could, in fact, feed the world. The competing countries of the COMECON, the economic association established by the Soviet Union with its satellites in 1949 as a response to the Western allies' OECD, intended to facilitate trade and development, but COMECON could not claim that the Communist model was successful, as they were patently unable to feed their own populations. The United States remains the major source of commodity food aid in the world, and the transfer of US agricultural products through international food aid is a key part of government support for domestic agricultural production.

DIFFERENT PATHS TO CHICKENIZATION

To understand the commonalities and differences in the adoption of industrial food animal production, I focus on several of the countries selected by FAO for its analysis of the revolution in poultry production: Brazil, Thailand, China, and India. These countries gained or lost their positions through different strategies. With the exception of India, these countries have become major producers of poultry for both domestic consumption and export. On a relative basis, however, although poultry production has increased most rapidly in India, absolute amounts of production are still very low. India is a special case in the story of global chickenization and is thus included. Different strategies and strategic mixtures have been adopted by these fast-growing countries, but common to them all is that increases and changes in demand and changes in production methods have driven chickenization. Just as in the United States.

The spread of chickenization has changed national standings in production and export. In 1970, the United States dominated production and was second in export. By 2005, the United States still dominated production, a place it has recently lost to Brazil.

THE POWER OF RESEARCH: BRAZIL

Brazil followed the US model of government funding of research and development to achieve success in agriculture. The US commitment to public-private partnerships in agricultural research began in 1862 and remains in force, as reiterated by the President's Council of Advisors on Science and Technology in its December 2012 review of agriculture:

> Meeting these challenges requires a renewed commitment to research, innovation, and technology development in agriculture. Private industry will continue to play an important role meeting these challenges in areas directly related to commercial developments and commodities. But many of the developments necessary to meet these challenges are public goods and not easily monetized. These challenges require a strong public commitment to agricultural research, one that fosters a culture of innovation and excellence to address some of the greatest threats to U.S. long-term prosperity and security.

This may seem like boilerplate rhetoric, but Brazil and the United States are alone in their implementation of these principles to guide agricultural development. Just as investments in research and education in agronomy and related sciences through the establishment of the land-grant university system by Congress during the Civil War drove the modern revolutions of agriculture in the United States, Brazil increased its federal investments in agricultural research and development and engaging government, academic institutions, and private consortia in these programs.

Some analysts assume that the expansion of Brazil's agricultural sector followed and was dependent on the political and economic reforms in the 1980s. This is not the case. The adoption of a strategic commitment to agricultural research preceded these important events. In 1973, the military dictatorship (which did not yield power until 1985) established its own agricultural research institution known as EMBRAPA (Empresa Brasileira de Pesquisa Agropecuária, the Brazilian Agricultural Research Corporation) as a focus for public and private partnerships in research and development, with an emphasis on soil and plant science. As in the United States,

EMBRAPA has worked through coordinated university research teams of academic and industrial scientists as well as government agencies.

The creation of EMBRAPA was critical in meeting the particular challenges and opportunities for agricultural expansion in Brazil. It adopted two strategies: a strong commitment to advanced technology and independence from importing technology developed in and held by patents in the United States. These investments quickly proved their worth. EMBRAPA's first phase of applied research enabled discoveries in soil and plant science that resulted in the "miracle of the *cerrado*," transforming the vast center of the country, formerly considered impossible for crop growing, into one of the major food production regions of the world. The Brazilian minister of agriculture, Alysson Paolinelli, and an EMBRAPA scientist, Edson Lobato, were awarded the 2006 World Food Prize for these achievements. Since that time, Brazil has continued its aggressive investments in research, including in molecular methods to sequence the genomes of key plants, such as eucalyptus and coffee, and major plant pests. Since 2000, EMBRAPA has registered nearly two hundred patents for the development of bioengineered strains of carrots, corn, beans, cotton, rice, and cassava with improved resilience to tropical conditions as well as enhanced nutritional value.

Political and economic reforms starting in the 1990s under Fernando Henrique Cardoso and continued by Lula da Silva stimulated domestic demand for higher-level agricultural products through the expansion of an affluent middle class in Brazil. According to the USDA, between 1968 and 1998, poultry production in Brazil increased twentyfold, and it has continued to grow since that time, to almost 12 million tonnes in 2009. Domestic consumption tripled over that same period. These policies included market reforms and a deliberate opening to foreign investment, enabling the arrival of external sources of innovation in food animal production with the entrance of Tyson and Groupe Doux, two leading poultry integrators from the United States and France, respectively.

Although in the early 1980s my friends in Belém claimed that Brazilians would never give up their traditional *galinha* (or older stewing chicken) for the North American chicken, an onslaught of advertising from Sadia (the first large integrator in Brazil) played upon the images of the new *frango* (a broiler) as a symbol of abundance and emulation of North American ethnicity.

Brazil rapidly adopted the industrial model of poultry production, and, by 2010, over 90 percent of domestic broiler chickens were produced in this manner. As in the United States, the market has become substantially consolidated with three mega companies, JBS, Marfrig Group, and BRF, dominating the domestic and export market. In June 2012, JBS took over the operations of Doux when the French company declared bankruptcy. JBS and BRF are now acquiring businesses in the EU and United States. On October 31, 2012, *World Poultry News* announced that BRF was expanding into integrated production in China as well.

Through its decision to adopt research and technology to stimulate agricultural production, Brazil has expanded its advantages in the international context of industrial food animal and crop production, building on its natural advantages of water and land in a manner similar to the United States. The investments and strategies of EMBRAPA focused heavily on improving the basic constituents of animal feeds, notably corn and soybeans.

Because Brazil was an early adopter of biotechnology starting in 2003, it now has sizable national research investments in plant and animal genomics. According to the International Service for the Acquisition of Agrobiotech Applications, or ISAAA (an international organization supported by industry, governments, and international organizations), as of 2010, Brazil was the second-largest producer of genetically modified crops after the United States. This decision, according to ISAAA, contributed to its rise in global soybean and corn production in 2012.

The Amazon is now considered the "soybean frontier," to quote the USDA. Few persons engaged in Amazon protection saw this coming. The Amazon was assumed to be a poor region for intensive agriculture, but this view did not consider the power of biotechnology and chemical fertilizers to compensate for natural limitations on arability. Susanna Hecht, a longtime scholar of the Amazon, wrote, "it has been soybeans that destroyed the Amazon."

To travel south through the state of Mato Grosso to the center of Brazilian agriculture in the state of Goiás made me rub my eyes, thinking I had somehow wound up in Iowa. The view is quite similar: fields of corn and soybeans, fat animals grazing in vast holdings, grain elevators, and farmers in jeans with big belt buckles, many wearing class rings from the great land-grant universities of the United States. The same long buildings dot the landscape, housing chickens and pigs. A hundred kilometers north of Goiás, I stopped at a Ralston Purina feed store and saw the same antimicrobial feed additives for sale. *Como America?* the owner asked. "Like America?" *Mesmo*, I replied. "Exactly the same."

In contrast to mining and logging, public reaction to the encroachment of soybeans seems relatively undisturbed by concerns about the rain forest, in part because the soybean frontier is somewhat south and more central than the heart of the contested jungle. The political impetus of often lawless owners of large tracts of land displacing indigenous communities, sometimes killing their leaders, is not usually attached to expansion of farming, although there have been rumors surrounding the methods used by Blairo Maggi, the self-styled King of Soja (*soja* means soybeans in Portuguese), to acquire land in the state of Pará. The new farms generate steady jobs instead of the sporadic employment in slash-and-burn agriculture or logging or gold mining. The interior towns are flourishing. Santarém has a new branch of the federal university and a new hospital. A road now connects the Tapajós to Mato Grosso. I think of the little girl in Brasília Legal, a tiny village between Santarém and Aveiro, sitting on her mother's lap at one of our community meetings. She was blissfully clutching a Barbie doll, a signifier of the new linkages between this sleepy *caboclo* settlement and the shops to the north.

THAILAND: THE MULTINATIONAL CORPORATION'S ROLE IN INDUSTRIAL FOOD ANIMAL PRODUCTION

The rise of the Thai poultry industry tells another story, a story of both the advantages and disadvantages of industrialization. Thailand became and remains a major regional poultry producer through the singular growth strategy of the Charoen Pokphand Group (CP), a multinational enterprise started by Chinese refugees in the 1920s, coupled with strong state support.

Chickenization has taken a different course from the US and Brazilian experience by jumping over the early stages of development seen in these two countries. CP did not participate in or benefit from a deliberate national research policy to modernize agriculture or from the domestic poultry industry. Like other multinational enterprises in Asia, CP was a conglomerate with many subsidiaries prior to its involvement in poultry production, a distinct contrast with Perdue and Tyson, which grew from small-business beginnings by its founders into multinational corporations. CP had some holdings in agriculture in its portfolio prior to 1997, mostly in selling animal feeds. In 1970, CP formed a partnership with Arbor Acres, a US poultry breeder and the leading global supplier of the Cobb-Vantress breed for broiler production. CP now manages these subsidiary companies for most of Southeast Asia as well as in India and China. Within a few years after expanding into poultry, CP adopted the integrated model of both poultry and swine production, including contract farming. CP also resembles the US corporate giants Tyson and Perdue in its family ownership of multilevel cross-holdings. Like them, CP expanded its feed production activities and established partnerships with US firms to import hybrid seed. CP then moved into neighboring countries, notably Indonesia in 1972, and then into China soon after the opening of foreign economic zones. By 1997, CP was operating feed mills and production facilities in twenty-seven Chinese provinces, and by 2002, it was producing 27 percent of China's broiler poultry. Their toehold was feed production, followed by contracted poultry farms and, finally, the processing plants. Theirs was the same strategy of expansion and integration used by Perdue and Tyson some sixty years earlier.

CP's rapid implementation of the integrated model along with industrialized methods drove the expansion of poultry production in Thailand starting in the 1980s. As in most countries, increases in production went hand in hand with increases in incomes and consumption, such that from 1970 to 1992 per capita poultry consumption increased more than tenfold. Increased demand influenced both production and marketing, with the formal market sector supplied by the large integrators selling through "hypermarkets" and other large retail outlets. At the same time, what FAO refers to as "semi-industrial" production has persisted in Thailand, in the form of farms that are smaller than the intensive operations but still raise the international broiler breeds and are linked into the integrated system. These farms sell through smaller segments of the retail market as well as in so-called wet markets, where live animals are sold and slaughtered on site (with significant health risks, as exemplified by the outbreak of SARS in a wet market in Guangdong, China). There are also some independent smallholder operations that support families and local markets. These sectors raise indigenous breeds and some crossbred animals as well.

The smaller operations drastically lost numbers and market share from 1993 to 2003, by about the same percentage as the industrial operations gained. These changes affected rural economies and society in ways that resembled the experience in the United States. Then, in 2003, the Thai poultry industry suddenly collapsed in the wake of the avian influenza outbreaks that swept through Asia from China. A virtual boycott of poultry products from Thailand and other affected countries devastated the regional industry. Production and exports fell drastically (over tenfold) from 2003 to 2004. The Thai industry was severely affected, with the greatest losses experienced by CP after they were required to cull more than 64 million birds in 2004 and 2005.

At first, reaction to the H5N1 outbreak was strongly supportive of industrialization under the Farm Standard regulations issued by the Thai government (with similar programs put in place in other countries). Based on the assumption that the cycle of avian influenza dissemination went from wild avian species to domesticated avians in small backyard or community operations open to contact, these regulations almost destroyed traditional poultry production and the livelihoods of smallholder farmers. These regulations were supported by a fiat from international organizations—the WHO and the World Organisation for Animal Health (OIE)—as well as national authorities to industrialize the industry in the name of health.

It was at a conference on the ethical implications of the avian flu programs of international and national institutions that I first met Joachim Otte. Like others at FAO, Joachim is a serious and dedicated scientist with a tendency to doubt official wisdom. A senior scientist at the Pro-Poor Livestock Initiative at FAO, he had long expressed concerns about the impacts of these assumptions and policies on smallholders, particularly women, in the poorest of the poor populations in developing countries. There is something incongruous about conferences on poverty amid the Italian luxury of the Rockefeller villa, commanding the heights of Bellagio, a playground for wealthy expats or pass-through tourists, but this did not detract from the seriousness of the organizers and attendees at this meeting.

I had and have little expertise in zoonotic viruses, but I found myself one of the few persons with much experience in the actual operations of industrial or "confined" poultry production. These are not confined operations in the public health sense of biosecurity (keeping housed flocks safe from external pathogens) and biocontainment (preventing releases of pathogens from these flocks to the external environment). As a consequence, I had some doubts about the evidence supporting the WHO policy of encouraging "confined" poultry operations over traditional smallholder farms. I expressed these doubts to Joachim, and we agreed to work together on a reevaluation of the evidence using data from Thanawat Tiensin of the Thai Ministry of Health. This was an important question. If the basis for global highly pathogenic avian influenza (HPAI) prevention was not scientifically justifiable, then not only were we failing to prevent future outbreaks, but we were also potentially enabling unnecessary and devastating impacts on poor growers around the world, especially in Asia.

After Joachim and I left Bellagio, we began our work, for which we enlisted the assistance of two biostatisticians who had worked on analyses of HPAI with FAO. One of them, after being contacted by me regarding his interest in collaborating on a reconsideration of the role of industrial-scale poultry operations on avian influenza outbreaks, informed me tersely by e-mail, "Of course, you are wrong." I like that much more than a team of true believers. Within weeks of analysis, he e-mailed me again: "By God, you're right." To his great credit, when we briefed him on the results of our analyses, Thanawat also requested to join us as a coauthor. The resulting paper has been widely cited since its publication and continues to be a major talking point in the discussion about pandemic flu prevention. However, I still find myself having to describe and illustrate the lack of real confinement that characterizes industrial food animal production in practice.

This event effectively derailed chickenization in Thailand. Since that time, CP has ceased almost all export of fresh poultry and diversified its investments into aquaculture, telecommunications, and chemicals manufacture, among other ventures. Its telecommunications ventures involved a partnership with Thaksin Shinawatra, later prime minister of Thailand, whose support for CP remains a controversial aspect in the collapse of the Shinawatra government amid charges of nepotism and corruption. Within the national market, after the avian flu outbreaks, the industrial sector has become more concentrated and increased its percentage of production and market share, with only 10 percent of production from smallholder commercial or backyard operations. Most of this production at all levels now involves the international standard broiler breed (Cobb-Vantress), available primarily through the integrated system to intensive large-scale farms. The remnants of the smaller poultry production sectors have survived by focusing on local markets. They have been able to enter the major urban markets—and, to a limited extent, the export market—through aggregators. These entrepreneurs are a phenomenon in several developing economies; they are independent of the integrated system but function similarly by linking farmers to markets. Some may also supply slaughter and processing facilities in addition to transport to market vendors, which is what enables this sector to extend their sales outside their immediate regions. This provides something of an expanded alterative market for farmers outside the integrated system, but it is relatively small. CP's current profitability lies outside Thailand, mainly in China.

FAO's analysis has a less than optimistic future for this sector because of barriers related to the economic dominance of large-scale production by integrators, their superior access to information (including new technology), their access to feeds and medicines, and their production of a product that is preferred by internal and external markets.

CHINA: IMPORT THE INDUSTRY AND THEN BUY THE ORIGINALS

The history of chickenization in China dates from the opening of foreign investment zones in 1978 to achieve, among other socioeconomic goals, increased production of food for a rapidly urbanizing population. Prior to economic reform, rural agriculture and life in China had changed little, which is still largely true outside the major cities and off the tourist tracks. But what skills remained in traditional agriculture were disrupted several times since the Maoist revolution by the use of rural exile and farm labor as punishments for political reasons. Like Stalin, Mao had strong political views about the class of independent agriculturalists, and, like Stalin, Mao used rural development policies directed to extinguish this class. In China, agronomy was forced to abide by the same erroneous biology of Lysenko decreed by Stalin. In both countries, these policies precipitated disastrous falls in production with widespread famine and death. The Great Leap Forward from 1958 to 1961 was a period of economic stagnation, decline in agricultural production, and the deaths of between 18 and 35 million persons. For political reasons, the Chinese government refused to admit the catastrophic crop failures of the late 1950s and turned down offers of food even as it continued to export wheat as a matter of national prestige.

Unlike Khrushchev, Mao never visited an American farm to be confronted with the evidence of the successes of industrial crop and food animal production in the United States in the postwar period. Change came only in 1978 with the economic reforms of the post-Mao period. One of the first reforms was to end collectivization of agriculture, followed by opening the country to limited and highly controlled foreign economic investment.

The model of chickenization in China followed a different path owing to politics. Lagging behind developments in other countries, China did not independently develop its own industrialized food animal production industries, as Brazil and Thailand had; rather, government policies allowed foreign companies to operate within China. US and European firms brought the fully integrated and industrialized model to China and, along with CP, profited under these policies for almost three decades. In 2004, the government changed its policy concerning agricultural and rural development to emphasize the role of a national sector in livestock production. With its expanding economy, China shifted from growing its internal industry through foreign transplants to supporting domestic companies and discouraging the autonomy of foreign businesses. National enterprises bought up many of the foreign holdings, with government encouragement. As a company founded and still run by Thais of Chinese ancestry, only CP retained its advantages in competing for a place in agribusiness in China.

In 2013, this policy was amended to explicitly endorse transition to larger-scale operations, including contracting arrangements between farmers and food industries. Production of pork and chicken grew rapidly. By 2008, China was producing over 450 billion pigs, nearly eight times that of the United States. Consumption also increased, and as a consequence China has become a powerhouse of pork and poultry production in less than ten years.

Economic bumps in national economic growth due to policy shifts and poor central management reduced growth of the agricultural sector and was designed to encourage consolidation of food-producing companies. In addition, Chinese industries were hit by HPAI and swine flu outbreaks as in Thailand, but with less impact on the indstry because China was not and is not an exporter of poultry. Additional events have also affected consumer confidence, such as several highly publicized incidents of adulterated food containing deliberate additions of melamine and other agents. These concerns have stimulated investments by national companies as well as by the remaining international companies, such as Tyson, to achieve more complete integration in order to control all aspects of production, including farms.

Despite these advances, China remains a net importer of meat and poultry products, largely fueled by increasing demand as the population increasingly relocates to cities. Despite national investment, production is not expected to keep up with these demographic trends in consumption in light of constraints on water and other resources. These constraints have stimulated yet another transition in chickenization in China. As with other resources, China is dependent upon other countries for feeds and is rapidly becoming a multinational player in food animal production through acquisition of companies in other countries, including meat- and poultry-processing operations. In September 2013, the US government approved the acquisition of Smithfield Foods by Shuanghui Group, the largest meat-processing company in China. Shuanghui has had a meteoric rise since its founding as Leohe Meat Processing in 1984. In 1998, Shuanghui merged with its leading competitor, Henan, becoming the largest pork producer in the world. It was privatized in 2006 with underwriting by the Goldman Sachs Group Inc.

China has followed a distinctive path to industrialization of agriculture. In some ways, the transition was eased by the destruction of traditional agriculture methods and social reorganization during collectivization. China emulated the path of Japan in terms of initiating its industrialization of agriculture by allowing foreign companies to enter the domestic market and then using its economic power to quickly adopt industrial methods and organizational principles in its own industry, moving China into the lead in food animal production, including acquisition of foreign corporations. This strategy has supported the most rapid chickenization process in any country, contributing to the social and economic transformation of China, including urbanization and privatization of the consumer market.

The largest and still indeterminate factor in China's agricultural expansion is its impacts on the environment. Unlike the United States, where environmental concerns relate to the impacts of industrial agriculture on ecosystems, in China, there is popular concern and finally official recognition that industry—metal smelting, chemical production, textiles—has affected human health through contaminated land and water. Agriculture is not insulated from these concerns over pollution. Hunan Province, which produces much of the rice for the country, is also a leading producer of lead, cadmium, and other metals. An official report issued in 2010 acknowledged that heavy metals and pesticide overuse contaminates millions of acres of arable land and millions of tons of food crops. (Destruction of soil resources cannot easily be reversed, as the Romans knew when they plowed salt into the ruins of Carthage after three wars in order to prevent its rebuilding. Livy describes these wars best. Ironically, it was the Romans who rebuilt Carthage and established it as capital of the province of Africa.) Water quality is possibly worse; official reports indicate that more than half of the surface and groundwater systems are undrinkable. Water quantity is also a looming issue. China has one of the lowest amounts of water per capita in the world, and it is contaminating and withdrawing these resources rapidly for urbanization, industry, and farming.

These trends demonstrate the importance of locating chickenization and other forms of increased agricultural production within a national system that balances needs (for safe food and water) with wants (the products of a consumer economy). As a recent program on National Public Radio stated, we were once China. And, as others have said, if you don't like the EPA, go to China.

INDIA: TRADE RESTRICTION, RESISTANCE TO SOCIAL CHANGE, AND POULTRY

The history of chickenization in India is rife with contradictory policies and trends. One could be misled by the fact that, in terms of percentage change, India is home to the fastest-growing poultry industry among all these countries. But overall poultry production and consumption in India is still small on a per capita basis. The first integrator, Godrej Agrovet, began operations in 1999 at the point in time when trade restrictions on importation of chicks were lifted. The contract system has since taken root most extensively among growers in the south of the country, where up to 80 percent of poultry consumed is produced within the integrated system. But the regional concentration of India's poultry industry is indicative of the conflicting influence of increasing affluence and changes in dietary preference and the brakes applied by culture and politics. In some parts of the country, consumption of poultry meat and eggs appears to be socially favored or acceptable in this shift, as compared to the "red meats" of beef, pork, goat, and lamb, but chickenization on a national scale remains limited by cultural and religious traditions concerning meat consumption, particularly under the Narendra Modi government.

The poultry industry in India has also been significantly burdened by political decisions favoring protection of traditional production methods. Government policies to support poultry development began in 1955 and, prior to economic reform in 1991, utilized two instruments: direct support of the existing poultry sector and import restrictions on foreign projects. The All India Poultry Development Program extended this support by design to protect the small producers. After economic reform, government support to poultry production grew almost tenfold by 2007, but policies continued to protect its domestic industry through import bans on the Cobb broiler and high tariffs. These policies are counterproductive because, unlike Brazil, India faces limits on the availability of feed components. Indian agriculture does not produce sufficient grains (notably corn and soy) to support an enlarged poultry sector. There has been relatively little increase in productivity of the crop sector. Other limits holding back growth are unresolved problems in transportation and energy supply.

As a result of these policies and conditions, there is relatively little foreign investment in India's poultry production beyond CP from Thailand. Overall, the fully integrated system has yet to develop to any great extent. At the consumer end, most broilers (95 percent in 2007) are still purchased by consumers as live birds at wet markets rather than through an integrated value chain controlled by large enterprises.

The rationale for these government policies is the concern that without restraints, the poultry production system will be increasingly integrator dominated, and these changes will affect the livelihoods of India's rural poor as well as the ecology of poultry production itself. Recent history in other countries (such as Thailand) demonstrates the reality of these concerns in terms of adverse economic impacts on the traditional economy of rural smallholders. Like other countries that have undergone this change (especially the United States), farm incomes in both Thailand and India have fallen as industrialization has spread.

Traditionally, raising poultry has been a critical element in survival among at least half of the landless poor. This is still a large economic sector, with over 14 million persons involved in animal husbandry as independent small-scale farmers contributing to almost 30 percent of gross domestic product (when combined with fisheries). In certain regions, this sector accounts for as much as 75 percent of household incomes. These figures indicate the continuing importance of traditional smallholder agriculture for the life of the country. The Indian government provides major support to this sector through a poultry venture capital fund, which supports self-described "low-technology investments," including conservation of threatened breeds. There has been no support for technical innovations, imported breeds, or more intensive modes of production. In many ways, this is an anti-industrialization policy, which comes at a considerable cost to both farmers and consumers. In poultry production, these smallholder operations continue to produce a local bird, using methods that are considerably less efficient in terms of feed conversion and time to market weight. Growers of these birds cannot compete with the industrialized sector because of its lower costs and higher productivity, including the use of an American breed.

India's policies of food sovereignty through protecting the domestic industry have succeeded in their stated goal of impeding chickenization. Although India is the third-largest egg producer and among the top twenty broiler producers in the world, over the past thirty years, poultry production has increased only about 2 percent annually, lagging far behind population growth, urbanization, and consumer demand. As noted by the Associated Chambers of Commerce and Industry of India, production must increase to meet rising demand, increasing 15 percent per year, related to the usual drivers of an expanding middle class and increasing incomes, the increased presence of fast-food outlets, and changing diets to include meat products.

It remains to be seen whether India can continue to hold out against the industrialization of its industry and impose on consumers the costs of food sovereignty politics, a highly inefficient agricultural sector, and continuing problems in infrastructure for transport and storage from processing to markets.

SUMMARY

Industrialization of agriculture was invented in the United States, and, like many of our exports, it engenders a complex mixture of love and hate when it comes to many foreigners' attitudes toward the United States. On one hand, there has been considerable antagonism to the expanding American hegemony, including the wars that have littered history since 1945; on the other hand, there is considerable love for and imitation of the cultural artifacts of American life. Many others have written on this apparent paradox in depth; I am interested only insofar as it seems to carry over into food. It was exemplified for me in an exchange at an OECD meeting in Paris, when I served as a member of the US delegation to its environment program. The subject of food and agriculture came up, and, at a break, one of the French delegates said to me, "We can't listen to a country that eats Cheez Doodles" (a statement that told me he had been in the United States for some period of his education). The same interlocutor remarked on a later day, "my children adore MacD, and the frites are not bad." Less anecdotally, when I first started attending these meetings, there was one Casino *supermarché* in the neighborhood of the OECD amid many small *boucheries, fromageries, laiteries, boulangeries*, and the like; ten years on, the Casino was joined by two other large chains, which were always crowded with French shoppers. The *supermarchés* were open nonstop from before work to early evening, but the small shops maintained the rhythm of an earlier Parisian life, closing at noon and reopening at about 3:00 p.m. for another three hours at most. Convenience, price, and availability: these characteristics of the food system are universally desired by consumers.

We all live in the industrial and postindustrial age of agricultural production, whether we choose to recognize it or not. My European colleagues insist that although this may be the case in the United States, in Italy or France much of the food supply is still produced in a preindustrial, artisanal manner in line with cultural preferences. Statistics from the EU tell a different story.

Some of the most vociferous assertions of allegiance to traditonal agriculture were expressed to me while I wrote this chapter in Bologna, an epicenter of traditional foods. As in the United States, Italy has an inverse relationship between farm size and production levels. Although it has preserved a larger number of small farms, they contribute less and less to the national market basket, as the proportion of broilers produced by industrial-scale operations in Italy is about the same as in the United States.

It takes time for most of us to recognize that industrialization has happened, that traditional modes of work have disappeared and that traditional social organizations have been displaced. But there is an urgency to acknowledging the extent to which agriculture has become an industrialized activity. What we think about when we think about animals and our food is not what is really happening to animals or in the stages between growing and producing packages of meat or poultry or fish. These are not easy things to look at clearly and fully. It is easier to accept the ambiguous morality and ethics of food animal production and consumption through selective remembering and forgetting, connecting and disconnecting, and visibility and invisibility. This is why we want to accept the manufactured reality presented in images posted by food producers like Tyson and Perdue. These pictures of small farms in beautiful landscapes are consistent with an agrarian and Arcadian memory that permits us to connect in our imaginations with an equally manufactured Edenic time of innocence. The food industry assists us in making this choice by its use of images to invoke a collective memory that protects the reality of food animal production from confronting and disturbing the pleasure of our daily meals.

Pierre Gerber's maps shocked me into writing this book. We do not have the luxury of much more time to dream about agriculture as it was, if we are to change the working of agriculture as it is. I wrote this book to confront the power of these misleading memories, because they continue to fortify the exasperating challenge of persuading government and all of us—including you, the reader—to remove all lenses (rosy and otherwise) and to see the current state of food animal production. We do not want to see the reality because it is our food. My job is to lead you past these images to the reality of food animal production so that we can discern paths to improvement. So long as we fail to realize its extent and largely irreversible status, we cannot pursue change.

Winston Churchill once said of making public policy that it is not good to examine it too closely; it is rather like querying what goes into a sausage. Food animal production is exactly what goes into the sausage. We are horrified, rightly, by exposés of wanton cruelty such as workers beating injured animals to force them into the abattoir. We do not want to think very deeply about the everyday conditions that animals endure, laying hens in cage boxes and nursing sows confined so closely that they cannot turn around. It is surely easier to think of food as items that arrive in packages, ready to prepare or ready to eat. We are alarmed and angered by outbreaks of food poisoning, but we do not want too much information about the daily lack of control of foodborne pathogens. In addition, as Upton Sinclair lamented, we rarely think about the workers involved in producing our food, preferring to believe the bucolic images of entrepreneurial country folk.

Like Virgil leading Dante through Hell to Paradise, my other challenge is to lead you through these discouraging realities toward real and sustainable change. Powerful works have been written on these matters, and some gain attention for a limited period. Why do these messages lack permanence? First, they lose in competition with the more powerful manufactured memories of Arcadia. Second, most of the messengers have been much less compelling in offering explanations as to how we got to the way we raise animals as we do, and what alternative paths might be available to us without major costs in how we live and eat.

The argument is also too often framed as "either/or"—either a radically different agronomy or industrial food animal production. In this book, I consider a road to the future that is more likely to be of the "and/and" variety, perhaps less satisfying in terms of scope and ambition but probably more feasible and acceptable. I have participated in too many international meetings on agriculture, on climate change, and on zoonotic disease, where a great deal of value is placed on strong representations from those who can afford expensive food as well as stakeholders advocating smallholder agronomy, in the face of the fact the world has become flattened before the power of chickenization. So look at Pierre's maps again.

5

THE COMING OF THE DRUGS

Growth-promoting antibiotics or antimicrobials (GPAs) are what the FDA calls drugs that are added to feeds to increase growth rates of pigs, chickens, and other animals that are raised for human consumption. (I choose to use the term *antimicrobials* instead of "antibiotics" because it is recommended by the WHO; for all practical purposes, the words are interchangeable. I also choose to continue using the term *growth-promoting* in the face of new coinage invented by the industry without objection from the FDA that the same use and conditions formerly known as GPAs can now be called "disease prevention" by the industry.)

GPAs have had a major impact on human health through the eroding effectiveness of the same "wonder drugs" that we use for treatment and prevention of infectious diseases caused by bacterial pathogens. Most persons alive today do not remember what it was like before the coming of the drugs, rightly referred to as the "golden age of medicine." We will probably live—or die—in the twilight of this brief period, when we could cure diseases, keep wounds from festering, support cancer chemotherapy, protect infants and mothers during childbirth, and ensure the best outcomes from transplants. In recent times we have seen the negative effects that the overuse of drugs has brought, and there is a continuing cascade of information on doctors and parents as the cause of this overuse in notices from writers on health, the US Centers for Disease Control and Prevention (CDC), and others. But almost all health-oriented books and announcements, even the most recent, fail to identify agriculture as the major contributor to misuse and drug resistance. This chapter corrects this long-overdue accounting with the unexamined history of how antimicrobial drugs came to be used in animal feeds; chapter 6 is about why this particular use has been the major driver of the end of the antimicrobial era.

How did antimicrobial drugs get into animal feeds on the claim of promoting growth? Why has it been so difficult—impossible in the United States—to get them out? The history of how these drugs got into the feeds is not secret, but neither has it been carefully examined. Most of the accounts were written decades after the fact by uncritical industrial scientists, some of whom, like Thomas Jukes of Lederle, were involved in the early history and wrote to elevate their own role in this history. Jukes will figure in this chapter. Others, including historians, have accepted the industry's story of how events unfolded without much analysis. I found myself weaving back from each starting point that I identified to discover that the story begins much earlier than is commonly recognized, well before the rise of industrialized food animal production. This topic has delivered the greatest surprises to me, and for that reason I think that this earlier history can help us discern opportunities for alternate paths that were previously ignored.

The reasons usually asserted for the coming of the drugs are not entirely satisfactory. The industry and the USDA claim that the rationale for the introduction of drugs into feeds was the result of the success of the first wave of the new model of poultry production, roughly from 1924 to 1946, because it stimulated increased consumption of poultry, ever-increasing production goals, and intensive competition to lower production costs. Without something new to increase productivity without increasing costs, it is claimed, after the fact, there would have been a crisis in the food supply.

Was there really a "crisis" in productivity? Were antimicrobials essential to the continued intensification of food animal production? In fact, long before the introduction of the first antimicrobial drug to animal feeds, even before the discovery of antimicrobials, poultry production in the United States had expanded mightily. From a few thousand broilers produced mostly in Delmarva in 1925, the US industry was producing nearly 300 million broilers by 1943. A related argument advanced in the official history is that a looming corn shortage threatened the availability of feeds and continued growth of the poultry industry. But there is no basis for this claim, either. There is no evidence of a dearth of corn for feeds to an extent that limited poultry production. I looked into crop data from the USDA, which indicate that there was little change in corn production over that period and that prices for corn actually fell, suggesting that there was no shortage.

What is true is that government policies supporting the rise of industrial poultry production included little scrutiny of the means to these ends. From the beginning, the contract system of economic and structural integration of poultry production was never successfully challenged, despite early protests and even government lawsuits that this system clearly disempowered farmers and debilitated rural society. And it is still the case that communities have been legally blocked from imposing few if any regulations on siting poultry or swine houses, or on the impacts of intensive food animal growing operations.

This same acquiescence figures in the history of how antimicrobial drugs got introduced into animal feeds. With stunning rapidity, almost immediately after the identification of the new "wonder drugs," the FDA approved registrations one after the other for using antimicrobial drugs as feed additives in the new model of broiler poultry production. Other industries, such as pork production, and other countries coming later to the game adopted the same permissive pattern without independent analysis. This record of government approvals is clear (although it took me digging through the FDA archives and its reluctant librarian to find it). But a major mystery remains as to the evidence that GPAs actually promoted growth and reduced feed intake, as claimed from the beginning.

Critical evidence-based questions were never really addressed in the speedy process by which industry proposed and governments around the world approved this practice. This negligence raises some important questions. What was, and is, the evidence to support the advantages of antimicrobials from the industry perspective? How do these drugs support animal growth in the artificial space created by industrial methods of production? What kind of assessment was done in terms of drug resistance? Making the case for change—in this instance, banning use of antimicrobial drugs as feed additives—depends upon the answers to these questions.

In the introduction to this book, I admitted my lack of knowledge about this aspect of modern food animal production until I was alerted unexpectedly to the role of foodborne infections in the rapidly growing burden of drug-resistant infectious diseases. As I thought at the time, and continue to think, *this cannot be a good idea for public health*. But if it is a good idea for the economics of food animal production, then these competing goals need to be scrutinized fairly and fully. To explore this key issue, I followed the same road map I have used in other highly contested issues: know the origins of the issue, understand all perspectives and interests, reduce or counterbalance impacts of change, make alliances wherever possible, and isolate from discussion those who reject scientific evidence and will never agree. I know every step of this road map firsthand, as all of these factors came into play during my research on the risks and benefits of adding lead to gasoline. I thought that a similar analysis might prove valuable in breaking the deadlock on the issue of GPAs in food animal production.

It turns out that the drugs were added to animal feed because of the continuing determination of poultry integrators to reduce production costs, not because of any limitation on corn or other constituents of feeds. The industry had already cut the incomes of farmers and workers through the contract system, and the time required for chicks to grow to market-weight chickens had been reduced by more than half through breeding and modifying housing conditions. Now the most obvious variable left in the search for increased profit was reducing the amount of feed chickens needed to consume to make market weight. This is known as feed conversion efficiency. In 1925, it took 4.2 lbs. of feed to attain a 1-lb. increase in live weight chicken, for a feed conversion efficiency ratio of less than 25 percent; today, the average feed conversion efficiency ratio is more than 50 percent, meaning that for every pound of feed, a chicken will gain a half pound of body weight.

ORIGINS: THE TALE OF DR. LUCY WILLS

The story behind GPAs in animal feeds begins not only before the actual discovery of antimicrobial drugs but also before the industrialization of poultry production. It begins with a remarkable woman named Lucy Wills and her forgotten contributions to the scientific understanding of nutrition. She deserves to be in this book, not because of the connection between her research and the coming of the drugs, but because had her research been correctly understood, the support for the necessity of using drugs would have not been so convincing.

Nutrition has always been an empirical science, even to this day. We still indirectly collect observations on human diets through surveys and interviews and then attempt to draw conclusions about how what people say they eat may or may not be associated with health and disease. The weakness of this method is revealed when we undertake more controlled studies to test the effect of a specific nutrient using a clinical trial, which is considered to be the best form of evidence in medicine. The strength of any clinical trial depends on a rigorous design in which people are randomly assigned to a specific drug, diet, or medication containing a nutrient or to a dummy or placebo agent, without participants knowing what treatment they are getting. (This approach can be applied to chickens as well, as we will see.) This method is a lot more dependable than asking people to recall their diets or even to keep diet notebooks over a long period during which they are observed or asked to report on their health. People don't always accurately remember their diets, people sometimes tell interviewers what they think is the "right" thing to say (suppressing the number of soft drinks they consume, for example), and at the same time people in these studies may engage in other behaviors that are good or bad for health that researchers do not ask about. Such factors introduce what epidemiologists call bias, or problems of unmeasured events that can influence the outcome. Our suspicions about these indirect studies of what people eat are raised by the failure of most clinical trials of specific nutrients to support the results we get from asking people. Vitamin E, beta-carotene, and a whole list of likely nutritional candidates have not survived the test of a clinical trial. What people eat is just a part of what people do and how they live, and often people who report eating healthy diets are also more likely to exercise, to reduce intake of alcohol, and to engage in many behaviors that support health. A current fad in the United States is the Mediterranean diet, but I know from living in Italy for seven months that those who eat a Mediterranean diet mostly have a different social and psychological outlook on life than the harried working mother trying to juggle work and childcare in a busy American city.

Lucy Wills was one of the first to try to bring order to nutritional research. She was a remarkable person in many ways, including being one of the first women qualified in medicine in England. She could not get a hospital appointment suitable for her training, however, so she took an appointment in chemical pathology (an experimental science), which gave her a somewhat unusual competence in both clinical medicine and experimental sciences. In 1928, she left England for India, where she stayed for four remarkably productive years. Upon her return to England, she was appointed to the faculty of the London Free Hospital, where she was a highly recognized teacher. After World War II, she was elected to Parliament as a Labor MP.

In India, Wills received funding to study pernicious anemia, a disease of the blood, from the Tata Trust, by then already a major philanthropic force in the British Raj. Colonial leaders in India had an interest in pernicious anemia because of its effects on the productivity of women working in the textile mills of the Empire. Wills observed that this often fatal disease was associated with poor diets, and that the risks of severe anemia were much greater among Hindu women than among Muslim women. Because Hindus did not eat meat, but Muslims did, she hypothesized that this disparity could be related at least in part to a dietary deficiency in animal protein. She began with experiments involving additions of liver extracts to the diet and reported substantial improvements in her patients. She then undertook what nutritional researchers still do: testing the constituents of liver to determine which might confer these observed benefits. She examined the effects of vitamins A, C, and D in both her patients and in experimental animals and observed no effect. Wills then considered the potential role of the B-complex vitamins, which had recently been identified in liver extracts. She knew that these vitamins were also present in extracts of yeast, and so she began new studies of the effects of yeast extracts on pernicious anemia.

The nutritional value of yeast extract had long been recognized in England, and a product based on it had been commercialized in 1902. Thus began the manufacture of Marmite, the bane or triumph of British food fabrication, depending on which side of the pond one hails from. Wills conducted painstaking studies of this product, comparing liver extracts, wheat germ, and a range of fractionations. The results were striking. She concluded that some but not all B-complex vitamins had the property of reversing pernicious anemia.

Now, with Lucy Wills in mind, let's return to the story of the developing poultry industry in the United States. These paths will intersect. Nutrition for chickens was recognized as a problem in raising poultry even before industrialization. From the late nineteenth century on, the US government supported a great deal of experimentation at land-grant universities on nutritional strategies to prevent conditions of decreased growth and weakness that were commonly observed in livestock and poultry. Much of the research and experimental work in this area involved dietary modifications in trace elements as well as other nutrients.

After the advent of high-density production in the first broiler houses of Arkansas and Delmarva, these newly confined animals experienced additional problems, notably lameness and failure to survive. These problems threatened expansion of the new production model. The discovery of vitamin D and its role in bone growth is said to have made broiler house production possible in its early days.

The rapid growth and spread of industrial methods throughout the Southeast and Mid-Atlantic regions continued to drive federally funded research in poultry nutrition. The production of poultry increased remarkably, even spectacularly, from 1940 on, with government support to meet the wartime and postwar demands for food for troops and the home population. By the early 1940s, it was recognized that feeds composed solely of finely ground corn and other grains were insufficient to achieve adequate survival and weight gain in poultry raised in houses. In traditional practice, chickens would have had access to a range of consumables, including insects and other animals. There was talk in the literature about some unidentified "animal protein factor" that was needed, but no one knew what that could be.

Some historians write as if there was an easy jump from this point to the notion of adding antimicrobial drugs to poultry feeds. In reality, the process seems to have happened in a much less straightforward manner, and the trail of facts is not easily discerned. Early in my work on poultry production, colleagues at the School of Poultry Science of the University of Maryland told me that the use of antimicrobial additives was coincidental, connected to using fermentation wastes from the pharmaceutical industry in New Jersey as a convenient source of nutrients. Although I have found no source for this information, it did not seem improbable, as there is a long history of using fermentation wastes—mainly from making beer and cheese—to feed livestock and other domesticated animals. The pigs of Emilia Romagna, the source of the finest prosciutto of Parma, are still fed wastes from the manufacture of the equally renowned *grana parmigiana* cheeses in the same region.

Enter the pharmaceutical industry. Thomas Jukes, a nutritional bio-chemist at Lederle Laboratories, claims to be one of the early researchers on antimicrobials and animal growth. In his later writings, he has influenced writers on the history of poultry production through his highly cited re-views of the early events, including the use of pharmaceutical fermentation wastes. He noted that observational studies in the 1930s had pointed to some powerful growth-promoting agent known as the animal protein factor. It was not present in feeds composed solely of plant products but was present in liver and other animal by-products. Recall, however, that Lucy Wills had already shown the importance of the presence of animal protein factor in her studies on nutritional interventions to prevent pernicious anemia in women. This is the connection that links animal protein factor, Lucy Wills, and antimicrobials in animal feeds. The animal protein factor, or APF, was eventually identified in liver isolates in 1948 as vitamin B12. But to discern this connection requires integrating the history of nutrition research, as exemplified by Lucy Wills, with the history of antimicrobial discovery and the advent of drug production for clinical medicine.

MARCH OF THE ANTIMICROBIALS

Alexander Fleming is generally recognized as the primary discoverer in 1929 of the bactericidal properties of a natural product present in his microbial cultures that killed *Staphylococcus aureus*. It was ten more years before two scientists working in England, Howard Florey and Ernst Chain, identified the causal agent and demonstrated its potential clinical value in treating bacterial diseases. Progress from this point to the modern antimicrobial era required one further step: mass production of reliably active products. Mass production was achieved in both England and the United States, but the larger amount of funding from the USDA enabled M. J. Johnson and F. G. Jarvis at the University of Wisconsin to take the lead in developing large-scale fermentation methods for producing and purifying the antimicrobial product. With these methods and other incentives from the US government, Merck and Co. began industrial production of penicillin. The volume of penicillin production increased from 2,300 kg in 1945 to 3 million kg in 1963, and, over the same period, the cost of production fell from $11,000 to $150 per kilogram.

Back to Lederle. In 1938, Robert Stokstad, another nutritional researcher at Lederle along with Jukes, confirmed Wills's earlier findings in humans and mice by showing that liver and yeast extracts could prevent pernicious anemia in chickens. Wills had shown that APF, the so-called animal protein factor first identified in liver, could also be produced by yeast, which drew Stokstad's attention to bacteria as a potentially cheaper source for this undefined compound. But before the discovery of microbial products as treatments for bacterial disease, there was little work on developing methods for producing large amounts of bacteria. In the 1940s, extracting liver tissue was the only way to obtain APF (which we know as vitamin B12), and it was expensive. That changed in the mid-1940s with the commercialization of antimicrobial production. According to Jukes, the availability of fermentation by-products from large-scale antimicrobial production going on at Merck and other industries led him and Stokstad to compare the efficacy of liver extracts to that of fermentation by-products from antimicrobial production. They thus integrated the results of Wills's original studies on yeast within the new pharmaceutical industry.

Jukes and Stokstad claim primacy in reporting that the antimicrobials alone were as effective as the fermentation "mash" in supporting animal growth. They were working with fermentation cultures producing another antimicrobial, aureomycin (later named streptomycin), and they reported that additions of this fermentation mash increased growth rates beyond that associated with liver extracts alone. To explain these results, they first suggested the existence of an "auxiliary growth factor" in addition to the APF that had been associated with liver or with yeast extracts. They then went further to claim that the active agent was not a microbial product at all, but rather the drug residues present in the mash. Looking at the data from short lab experiments using a few chickens, however, it is far from clear that the mash from antimicrobial production actually increased growth rates over liver or vitamin B12 supplementations. They were nowhere close to Wills's methodical approach in terms of the carefulness of their studies, as will be seen. More crucially, they did not cite her work.

But such were the pressures on the poultry industry to reduce the costs of production by increasing feed conversion efficiency, that these claims were immediately accepted and quickly translated into practice. The first application for the specific addition of antimicrobials to animal feeds—as distinct from pharmaceutical process wastes—was made to the FDA in 1949, and the agency approved this first registration in 1951. Multiple approvals rapidly followed, granted almost as fast as the applications were submitted. Within one year after Jukes's first report, and on such a slender reed of information, an entire industry was shaped, and the economic alliance between what my Hopkins colleague John Boland calls "Big Farm" and "Big Pharma" began. By the end of 1951, growers and feed suppliers were spending millions of dollars on antimicrobials as feed additives, and the practice was quickly adopted for raising hogs. I once asked an FDA official why, unlike most other countries in the world including in the EU, the United States had never approved the use of vancomycin, a powerful multipurpose antimicrobial, as a feed additive. He looked a bit puzzled and finally said, "I guess they never asked us to register it."

There are some other loose ends in this history that challenge the claims of priority by Jukes and Stokstad. Four years before the work of Jukes and Stokstad at Lederle, Moore and colleagues at the College of Agriculture of the University of Wisconsin published a paper in 1946 reporting on the effects of adding three antibiotics (two sulfa drugs and streptomycin) to poultry feeds. They followed the growth of chicks for nine days and observed what they termed "unexpected" results, that is, growth stimulation, with the drug-containing feed. What is most interesting about this paper is the limited scope of the study, considerably less than the lifespan of producing a broiler chicken, and its lack of critical information, such as the number of chicks in each study group. Evident from the results but noted in neither the title nor the text, they observed a similar effect on weight by adding only liver extract to the feeds, similar to Stokstad's later paper.

More important than primacy, these earliest papers by both groups make clear that adding liver extracts as a source of APF produced results as impressive as using either drug fermentation mashes or the drugs themselves. And no one looked at the efficacy of Marmite, which Wills had demonstrated to be effective in both clinical and experimental research. _These observations have never been reconsidered in the argument over the essentiality of GPAs._

Possibly because of the economic interests of the pharmaceutical companies, possibly because of the inability to patent Wills's growth factor, and possibly because of the lack of scientific rigor in evaluating the evidence submitted to the FDA—once established, it has been impossible to dislodge antimicrobials from their role in food animal production.

Without questioning or opposition, the industry was quick to call attention to the benefits of GPA use, including reductions in the need for crop-based constituents for animal feeds and assuring reliably uniform rates of growth as a prerequisite for product standardization, which in itself was critical to the assembly line model for production of food from animals. The information required by the FDA to support the claims of industry in its applications was minimal; efficacy was defined as increased rates of growth and decreased consumption of feed to support growth. Evidence in support of these claims came from relatively small and short-term studies, almost all conducted in laboratory conditions, such as the original studies by Jukes and Stokstad, who used twelve chickens, and by Moore, who used seven chicks. Neither study followed the birds over their entire grow-out period; in fact, the length of most of these experiments was shorter than one month at best. Moreover, the early papers claiming efficacy do not provide sufficient data to determine whether their observations were statistically reliable. That was not unusual back in the 1940s and 1950s, but it should provoke reconsideration nearly three quarters of a century later.

WHAT'S THE EVIDENCE THAT GPAS WORK?

Despite decades of hypotheses, no clear scientific rationale exists to support GPA use in animal feeds. Early on, it was assumed that the antimicrobials might alter or deplete the populations of bacteria normally in the gut (known as the microbiome) and by this way somehow reduce competition for food between the host animal and its microbiome. With today's more sophisticated knowledge of the complexity of host–microbiome interactions, this hypothesis is now being explored.

Others have suggested that GPA use reduces low-level infections, but, as we will see, there is little or no evidence for this effect. Actually, the low concentrations of antimicrobials permitted by the FDA for GPA use in feeds—below the therapeutic dose—argues against a true "antimicrobial" effect. Some studies, including those by Moore and Jukes, suggested that changes in bile biochemistry and retention of nutrients are involved, but little evidence has been consistently developed to elucidate these points.

This fact is not unimportant. If antimicrobials are not working through their well-recognized properties to affect microbial communities, then it is possible that other interventions could achieve the same goals with lower risks, without the negative effects of GPAs on the prevention and treatment of human infections.

The industry continues to claim that continued access to GPAs as feed additives is essential to the survival of the industry and the availability of affordable food in the United States and worldwide. In 2015, following the announcement by Tyson that it would "strive" to reduce antimicrobial use in feeds, Sanderson (another poultry giant) announced that it would never stop using drugs in their feeds. To sort through the actual evidence for or against the use of antimicrobials in feeds, we need to consider a phenomenon that is important in any study of changes over time. This is the secular trend, or the tendency for things to change over time independent of what we may do to intervene. In biomedical research, many outcomes often improve over time independent of the specific factor or intervention that is being tested. A secular trend in terms of animal growth was reported by Libby and Schaible, who noted remarkable increases in growth rates in chickens and pigs over the period from 1950 to 1954, regardless of the presence or absence of antimicrobials in feeds. They were among the minority of researchers who actually conducted their studies in broiler houses rather than in the lab. Their results are consistent with a secular trend; that is, their observations suggest that there are other beneficial factors independent of GPAs. These factors could have included continued improvements in both breed and feeds as well as changes in housing conditions and management.

What, then, is the evidence for the efficacy of antimicrobials in promoting growth of animals, including rates of growth and feed conversion efficiency? The USDA did an empirical study that used growers' self-reports on the effects of using feeds with antimicrobials for growth promotion and feed consumption in swine. The studies were inconclusive, which is not surprising because these types of studies can be biased by the self-selection of people who participate. The studies did not even collect real information on measured outcomes such as growth rates and feed consumption.

Let's be stricter. Are there any studies now available from real-world settings over the entire period of raising a reasonable number of chickens or hogs? This is a critical question, as conditions within a broiler or swine house are clearly quite different from those in a laboratory or experimental animal holding facility. Moreover, these studies need to be large enough to determine whether there is *any* effect, because of the known variability among animals in growth rates and feed consumption. And all this information needs to be documented. That is why the failure to find such studies and information in the literature used to support antimicrobial use makes it difficult to accept the claim of the "essentiality" of GPAs.

But there is one study available, and it is even more robust than the early report by Libby and Schaible. This study is actually close to a true randomized clinical trial, the gold standard for evidence in medicine. This very large study was conducted on real chickens in real poultry houses that were randomly assigned to treatment or control groups. It was an experimental study, in that the chickens were assigned to either of two conventional feeds, with or without GPAs. Nothing else was done. Such a research design is known as a placebo double-blind trial, where neither the chickens nor the scientists running the study knew which house was fed which feed. Clinical trials are particularly important in testing nutritional claims, for humans as well as for poultry, because, as evident in Lucy Wills's work, so many other things are often going on, besides what either humans or chickens are eating, that could influence outcomes.

It may come as a surprise that this study comes from the industry, namely, Perdue Farms. A scientist working for Perdue referred me to it on the grounds that it would "explain why we use GPAs." I was excited; we had been looking for this information from a real study that would tell us the size of the benefit (in this case, reduced costs of production and eventually reduced costs to consumers) that would have to be considered if GPAs were to be removed. It is important information because if the removal of GPAs from feeds would cause production costs to increase for the industry (and thereby for consumers), these costs would need some compensation or other adjustment in government policies (such as subsidies), or the poultry industry could lose its market share as the main source of meat-based protein consumed by American consumers and the cost of a popular food item would be increased. Discovering this study had the potential to change my entire approach to this issue, and I was not sure which way when we started to look at the study.

Hank Engster conducted the Perdue study. It took more than 2 years and involved 27 million broiler chickens raised in 158 houses at 13 farms in Delmarva and 6 farms in North Carolina. The experiments ran for the natural flock growing cycle, or a little over 7 weeks. Apart from the presence or absence of GPAs, there were no other changes in operating conditions or management at the houses, and switching the houses in terms of feeds for a repeat of the study ensured that individual house management differences were not influencing the outcome. Dr. Engster measured all the outcomes of importance in broiler production: growth rate, feed consumption, deaths, illnesses, and "condemnations," or birds considered unacceptable for transfer to slaughter and processing at the end of the growth cycle. Impressively, the Perdue study demonstrates that it would have been possible to undertake this type of study earlier in the history of GPAs and to get information that would have been truly informative on this important topic.

The results of the study surprised me. The study found no or very small benefits of GPAs, nothing on the order of the double digits of increased growth reported by Jukes and others that had been cited in both the general literature and in the arguments of the food production and pharmaceutical industries. On average (which is how the data were reported), without GPAs, mortality rates were slightly higher (between 0.2 and 0.14 percent), whereas weight gain was slightly lower (0.03 to 0.04 lbs., or about 0.5 oz.). Feed conversion ratios were slightly higher with GPAs, at about 0.02 percent, and total condemnations did not differ between the two conditions. Engster also examined the effect of removing GPAs on the uniformity of broilers, which is an important variable for the efficiency of assembly line production. He reported some increase in size variability but not a significant difference—a less than 2 percent coefficient of variation, which is very small, statistically speaking.

These data are consistent with the influence of a secular trend over the period from 1950 to the present. Interestingly, the Perdue investigators also assessed another intervention, cleaning the broiler house in between flocks. This is not the usual practice in US poultry production; at most, houses may be thoroughly cleaned once a year. The beneficial results of cleaning the houses between flocks were, in fact, greater than the effects of GPAs on reducing mortality and increasing feed conversion efficiency. There was no significant effect either way on weight gain.

This is an extraordinarily powerful paper, and one that has been little noted by the industry (including Perdue), the USDA, or really anyone until we were made aware of it. It continues to amaze me how the limited and inadequate the information we have relied on has allowed an enormous misuse of the critical medical resource of antimicrobial drugs, and the extent to which all these parties have continued to resist any change.

It would have been nice to have all the data from this study, and we asked for it. Perdue refused. It would also be nice to have an independent replication of the Perdue study. We made such a suggestion to the USDA, and they were not interested. It would be even nicer to see similar data on swine production. At the very least, it would be nice to see the FDA reconsider its decades-old approvals of drugs in feeds. But unlike the EPA, which is legally required to carry out periodic reevaluations of pesticides for safety, the FDA has never issued a requirement to submit additional data on either the claimed efficacy or hazards of antimicrobial feed additives.

Is this justifiable? Think about the original rationale for investigating microbial fermentation for the elusive APF and the trail of omitted or forgotten knowledge from Lucy Wills that led Jukes and Stokstad to turn to antimicrobials. That rationale was developed prior to major advances in animal nutrition that have led to extensive reformulation of animal feeds, which now include the agents first identified empirically by Wills as effective in preventing disease in animals and humans. In an unintentional tribute to Wills, all feeds now contain additions of cobalamin, which is vitamin B_{12}. In fact, cobalamin's main use is as a feed additive; over 50 percent of its total production in the United States is intended for that purpose.

TWO WRONGS

Now facing some calls to stop using antimicrobials as feed additives, the industry through its trade associations continues to argue that antimicrobials are added to feeds not so much for growth promotion but to prevent disease, particularly under the conditions of raising animals in confinement. This is a nice way of saying that they need to compensate for what is accepted practice in poultry and swine houses, which I prefer to analogize to badly run and overcrowded hospitals. Unfortunately, this is not a minor footnote in the discussion, but rather at the forefront as a justification for this new purpose, as the solid evidence has melted away for the essentiality of antimicrobials for sustaining rapid growth along with low costs for the consumer and profits for the industry. So the industry now wants to claim that the same use of antimicrobials in feeds for growth promotion is now intended for disease prevention. This claim has even less validity than their claims for growth promotion. The industry has never previously advanced adequate evidence in support of this claim (probably because it was only required to support the regulatory claim of growth promotion, which is something different). Once again, the Perdue clinical trial provides the best evidence: in that study, where no change was made in the conditions of raising chickens except to use feeds without added antimicrobials in one group, no increases in disease, deaths, or condemnations and no need for preventive treatment were observed in the unmedicated group. And this finding is not surprising. If improvement in animal welfare is the goal, the industry could follow the Perdue study and require cleanouts of animal houses after each herd or flock. The Perdue study found such measures to be more effective than GPAs.

There is a more fundamental problem. The terms under which the FDA originally registered antimicrobials for use in animal feeds are specifically described as "subtherapeutic." Prevention of an infection requires therapeutic doses. The American Veterinary Medical Association makes this clear in their 2015 statement about antimicrobials in agriculture: "one antibiotic might be administered in the feed at a low level labeled for growth promotion/feed efficiency, at a slightly higher dose for prevention and at higher doses in feed or by injection for control and treatment," contradicting the assertions by the FDA, the industry, and its experts that the low dose approved for GPA is somehow now sufficient to prevent disease. Studies of GPA exposures to animals fed at approved rates indicate that few, if any, receive therapeutically effective doses. So the industry has adopted a special word, "metaphylactic," to cover mass administration of subtherapeutic dosages of GPAs through feeds, supposedly to prevent disease, even without indications of disease in the flock or herd. When I have had these debates about disease prevention with industry people, I have asked them, "What is it about the word 'subtherapeutic' that you don't understand?"

By using such medicalized terminology, the industry in several countries has attempted to evade new rules and guidelines related to the use of antimicrobials in feeds for growth promotion. Only the Scandinavian countries saw through this redefinition scam and adopted the clearest possible statement: no drugs in feeds. If the conditions of animal husbandry necessitate routine administration of antimicrobials, then agriculture agencies can intervene to require improvements in these conditions rather than acquiescing to the claims and excuses of farm and pharma. In the United States, the industry has succeeded in evading the recent FDA guidelines to cease the use of antimicrobials for growth promotion by dropping the term "growth promotion." Some companies have gone further. In the fall of 2014, Perdue announced that they were no longer using antimicrobials in feeds at all, a claim made by several other companies after feeling the pressure of consumer concern. The FDA remained silent. Despite these claims, however, intrepid investigative journalism by three reporters for Reuters uncovered systematic use of drugs in feeds by Tyson, Pilgrim's Pride, Perdue, Georges, and Koch Food. They discovered this information by collecting the feed tickets issued by the mills that made poultry feed, which list the names and amounts of each active drug in each batch of feed. The FDA already had access to these tickets. They chose not to comment.

The data from the Perdue study are remarkably important, so much so that it is incredible that a similar study has yet to be conducted in other sectors of industrial food animal production or required by the USDA or the FDA in support of their regulations permitting GPAs. In our economic analysis of the Perdue study, we concluded that there is certainly no evidence that removing antimicrobials would raise costs to both producers and consumers. Yet from this practice, many of the most difficult challenges to public health have arisen and moved from farm to fork and from farm to ecosystem. For what, then, are we risking the loss of the crown jewel of modern medicine, the ability to prevent and cure deadly infections with antimicrobial drugs?

RESISTANCE

I remember one of the first meetings I attended on industrial food animal production as an environmental issue, organized by the EPA; I entered the convention hall about ten minutes before my talk to hear a veterinarian from the industry opine that he wasn't really sure there was a problem with drug resistance in human health. When it came time for me to speak, I scrapped my opening sentence and said instead, "I assure you there is a very great problem with drug-resistant infections in human health; the only question is, how much of it are you responsible for?"

The hazards of misusing antimicrobials were evident long before agricultural benefits were claimed. Alexander Fleming observed the evolution of drug resistance in his laboratory cultures of *Staphylococcus aureus* that were exposed to what was later identified as penicillin. In his Nobel Prize speech in 1945 (awarded for medicine, shared with Chain and Florey), he warned against the loss of effective treatment unless uses were carefully controlled.

These risks of GPAs were also observed early in the history of introducing GPAs into animal feeds. One of the architects of this practice, Thomas Jukes, recognized quite clearly what the consequences were likely to be and admitted with appalling glibness that it was "a given" that feeding chickens drug-containing diets would result in selection for drug resistance in their gut bacteria. A study of poultry in 1951 quickly confirmed his nonchalant comment; it concluded, "We hope that those charged with the protection of the public health will objectively evaluate this situation," but—as with Cassandra, who received the power of prophecy but was condemned by the gods never to be believed—no one heeded this warning for decades.

This hope has been a long time in coming, and too many in influential positions in the public and private sector have still not acknowledged the truth of these early warnings. This issue, like too many others, illustrates the difficulties put in the way of sensible change and our ability to get beyond what David Gee of the EU Environment Agency has called "late lessons from early warnings." Our modern system of regulation is based on a gross imbalance between the weight of evidence needed to permit a new practice or product to enter the marketplace and the much heavier burden of proof demanded to stop or ban it, even after harm is evident. Put more simply, there is a greater weight of self-interest in perpetuating policy than in changing it. Once something is being made and sold, there are economic interests in its perpetuation, just as the lead industry spokesman explained to me a long time ago: "Of course we know that lead is dangerous, and we recognize that our product is exposing children to lead, but"—and here he leaned in close to impart wisdom he knew I had never learned in school—"every year we can sell tetraethyl lead, we make over $1 billion." Just so, the pharmaceutical industry can sell both old and new molecules for additives to animal feeds with minimal requirements for information, compared with going through the process of approval of the same drugs for clinical medicine.

The other problem is liability. Acknowledgment of the need to change is too often seized upon as tantamount to an admission of guilt for not doing it earlier or doing it in the first place. In the legally charged domain of public discourse in the United States, these are real impediments that originate from the problematic process of having to rely on tort law as an instrument of policy making to protect human health, because the costs of legal liability can be very high.

This is not a risk-free debate. "That which does not kill us makes us stronger," said Nietzsche, and bacteria can well adopt this statement as their mantra. There is no question that antimicrobial use in food animal production is a major driver of resistance to treatment of infectious diseases. It is far and away the major use of antimicrobials produced in the United States, over 70 percent according to the latest FDA data. If experts in clinical medicine and public health fully recognized the way antimicrobials are employed in food animal production, they would rank this issue at the top of misuses and abuses of antimicrobials and the main reason why we are at the end of the antimicrobial era—and the end of medicine as we know it. These are not my words, but those of Dr. Margaret Chan, director of the WHO, and Dr. Sally Davies, chief medical officer of the United Kingdom. Our health officials have been silent by comparison. As it turns out, there has been a short grace period in which we changed the balance of biological power between our species and the much larger kingdom of bacteria, no more than the blink of an eye in our joint history, but greatly important to the progress of medicine and public health.

In 2013, CDC published some vivid data on the current state of the crisis. Overall, CDC estimated that there are at least two million cases of disease caused by drug-resistant microbes, with 23,000 deaths. For the first time, the agency acknowledged the important role of agricultural GPAs in driving this crisis, concluding that "simply using antibiotics creates resistance. These drugs should only be used to treat infections." No "metaphylaxis," no GPAs masquerading under another name.

We cannot continue this flagrant misuse. As we lose each existing drug to resistance, we are discovering and synthesizing only a few new molecules. We have even thrown away new drugs before we could use them by allowing them to be used first as GPAs prior to approvals for clinical uses. Then when we came to use them in medicine as the last line of defense, we found the cupboard was bare. Synercid, a powerful combination antibiotic, is the glaring example of our profligacy: when we began to use it to treat the very pathogens for which we had no effective treatment, it turned out they were already resistant to our latest discovery because we had thrown this latest pearl literally before swine . . . and chickens. As if this were not bad enough, we are also creating new strains of pathogenic bacteria resistant to multiple drugs, a highly dangerous trend that is strongly connected to agricultural use of multiple GPAs.

We have a catastrophe on our hands, and the damage is accelerating. It is a catastrophe caused entirely by our own ignorance and cupidity. In his wonderful analysis of human stupidity, historian Carlo Cipolla distinguishes between the stupid person, who "causes losses to another person or to a group of persons while himself deriving no gain," and the bandit, who can also be stupid but "takes an action which resulted in his gain and in our loss." Of course, as the bandits in this account are eventually also at risk of exposure to untreatable infections, perhaps they are fundamentally stupid and only temporarily bandits. There was no good basis for the approval of GPAs starting in 1947, and there has been no demonstration since that time that GPAs are necessary to industrialized food animal production.

The only acceptable study on this topic, conducted by industry, refutes all claims for both increased productivity and improved disease prevention. Yet the argument continues to be made by industry and too many government officials that there is no proven connection between GPAs and the train wreck occurring before our eyes in veterinary and human clinical medicine. Contrast that confidence with CDC's conclusions. Or with an article by Dr. Thomas O'Brien of Harvard, who wrote an article in 2002 about the emergence, spread, and environmental effects of resistance with the subtitle "How Use of an Antimicrobial Anywhere Can Increase Resistance to Any Antimicrobial Anywhere Else."

6

WHEN YOU LOOK AT A SCREEN, DO YOU SEE LATTICES OR HOLES?

Industrial food animal production is called "confined." But what first impressed me was how unconfined it really is. *Porous* is a better term. You can look at a screen and see either the lattice or the holes. But no one would call a screen confined. This struck me the first time I was in a poultry house, during a visit arranged by two senior poultry scientists from the University of Maryland (before I began to wear out my welcome at that land-grant institution). In Maryland's part of Delmarva, around the small city of Princess Anne, you can smell the chicken houses before you can see them, a sure indicator that confinement is not complete. As you approach a chicken house on foot or by car, you can usually make out a path of dust and feathers leading to it.

What first hooked me into research and policy on industrial food animal production was not food safety, although it was a casual remark about food safety that first opened my eyes. From the beginning, I was impressed by the geography of the industry, its intensity and density, and I was struck by how little the environment figured in discussions or research on pathways of exposure to the pathogens flowing out of these factories that produced more waste than chickens. This is not unique to the issue of industrial food animal production—environmental health and infectious disease parted ways as an unintended consequence of the rise of environmentalism as a social movement and policy focus in the early 1970s. Prior to that time, environmental health was strongly connected to preventing infectious disease. My department at Johns Hopkins University was among the first in the School of Hygiene and Public Health, as it was known at its founding in 1916, and its research was preeminently important to preventing infectious disease. It was, after all, where Abel Wolman developed chlorination of water as the frontline defense against microbial contamination of drinking water.

This holistic view of environmental health changed with the creation of the EPA. When new agencies are formed by legislation or executive order (as in the case of the EPA), they come into political existence because of real or perceived gaps in existing mandates and institutions. So it was with the EPA, whose origins were largely driven by the gaps in regulation of pesticides by the USDA and of air pollution by the Public Health Service. The EPA is not, contrary to a recent book on environmental policy, something totally "new under the sun." New agencies usually take authorities and personnel from existing agencies, and the actual scope of their authority is fit into the existing brickwork of government. But sometimes things get left out or get stuck in an uneasy place between laws and agencies. Therefore, even though the enabling executive order and subsequent legislation fitting out the EPA contain the grandiose mandate "to protect human health and the environment," in practice, its responsibilities are bounded by the preexisting authorities of the FDA and the USDA in terms of food and agriculture, and by the US Department of Health and Human Services (HHS) in terms of infectious disease. This was little noted at the time, because the photographs of dead birds and the Cuyahoga River on fire were the images that generated public demand for a new environmental agency in the early 1970s. To be sure, the EPA regulates and funds plants for wastewater and drinking water treatment in American cities and towns, but these regulations until recently were pretty ancient when it comes to pathogens. The EPA supports relatively little research on pathogens as compared to its support of research on chemical toxicology and air pollution. I say "ancient" because the EPA's regulations for pathogens are stuck in methods that were old by the time the agency was founded. EPA requires testing for "coliform bacteria," which it calls "a simple rule for effective performance" of water quality assessment and wastewater management. The test is simple and cheap, requiring minimal investment in resources or expertise. But that is the problem with the test. By the EPA's own definition, total coliform is "a group of closely related bacteria that are generally harmless." This has been partly modernized by requiring testing for *Escherichia coli* (*E. coli*), but this still does not confirm or exclude the presence of very toxic strains of this bacterium. Moreover, while increases in total coliform counts from water generally indicate that the system may be or has been contaminated by gut bacteria from animal (and human) wastes, it does not provide information on other waterborne pathogens, including viruses or parasites such as norovirus and cryptosporidium (a virus and a microparasite, respectively), which are the most frequent causes of serious waterborne infections. Moreover, the presence of these pathogenic organisms is not related to coliform bacteria. These same limitations also undermine our confidence in the way we test for pathogens in swimming pools and beaches. The wall of demarcation created between environmental health and infectious disease has important consequences for research as well, not least of which is the difficulty of funding work on a topic like industrial food animal production.

My particular perspective was to look beyond food, a view that was reinforced by meeting Patrick Harmon at a dinner honoring the accomplishments of his organization, the Delmarva Poultry Justice Alliance. Patrick's job was to catch chickens, put them into wire crates, and load them on the trucks that took them to slaughter. He was the courageous worker who was the lead plaintiff in a lawsuit that overturned a common practice by the poultry industry in Delmarva of defining workers like him as contractors, which made them ineligible for the benefits and protections given to full-time employees, at least in the state of Maryland. Patrick exemplified everything about the risks of industrial food animal production that is not limited to consuming food—he lived and worked around chickens in Pocomoke City in the southern part of Worcester County, and he fished in the Pocomoke River, a few miles from the state line between Maryland and Virginia, a boundary that is signified by two things not seen in Maryland: a legal fireworks store and a huge sign reading "Welcome to Dixie." He was most certainly not a person who was able to buy heritage free-range chickens at a cost of more than ten times what he was paid to catch chickens inside the broiler houses. Descended from an African American family with deep roots in Delmarva, Patrick, like many others in rural Delmarva, had gone to work in poultry production because it was one of the few employment opportunities available.

We spent the first months over in Delmarva getting to know who and what we should study in our research. A lot of that time was with Patrick and Carole Morison, an equally fearless poultry grower with a farm outside Pocomoke City, who cofounded the Delmarva Poultry Justice Alliance. This period of getting to know each other was critical. Since then, I have spent hours with workers on other farms as well as in slaughter and processing plants in Maryland and the Carolinas. Many of my colleagues in scientific research, even in public health research, do not always go to see the problems they are studying. That's where I start whenever possible, and I have always learned something unexpected by being there. I have gone to the largest primary lead smelter in the Americas, where I insisted upon being taken up its enormous slag pile (the Monte Nero of the Peñoles smelter in Torreón, Mexico). At the top, I jumped out of the company SUV to determine whether the accumulated bag house dusts could be respirable by rubbing my palm on the top of the dust. They were.

In the same way, I knew that I needed to see how chicken houses were built and operated to understand what the conditions of work were really like. These visits to industrial broiler production operations were not only key influences on our research, but they also prepared me to respond to attacks from the industry. At one of the first talks I ever gave on the topic of environmental risks of industrial food animal production, I needed to convey this eyewitness experience. It was at a meeting of the American Public Health Association, the leading organization for public health researchers, educators, and practitioners in the world; I have been a faithful member for most of my academic and public service career, and from the association I had received the Barsky Award for my work on lead. This time, however, my talk was scheduled in a session organized by the Veterinary Medicine Section, which I did not know was mostly populated by veterinarians tied to the industry. I quickly realized the tenor of the audience—not so different from the lead industry I had faced down as a young postdoctoral researcher— when Dr. Liz Wagstrom, then scientific director of the National Pork Board, interrupted me when I referred to swine houses as "unhygienic." I am sure she was confident that I had never actually seen a swine barn or confinement house. In fact, I had, and a prepared slide permitted me to respond, "Dr. Wagstrom, if you think this is hygienic, then I suggest that the next time you go into a hospital you ask for a room with a bedpan for a bed." That response is legendary among my students.

My mantra as a scientist is "only look." Look at the world you want to study, and look at your data while your eyes are still fresh. If the data tell you something is the case, check it out. An FDA official told me that it was not possible for "just anyone" to buy antimicrobial drugs sold as feed additives. I checked it out in the company of a reluctant student at a feed store in Princess Anne, Maryland. We walked in, with no pretense of being poultry farmers or even from Delmarva, and I asked the woman behind the counter if we could buy some antibiotics. "What do you want?" she asked. I thought for a second and replied, "Oh, some tetracycline and some penicillin." "How much d'ya want?" I thought about how much money I had in cash before answering. "What have you got?" She led us to a shelf on the back wall. "Here's the tet—it's in 1 lb., or 5 lbs., or 40 lbs.—and here's the penicillin—it's in 5 or 10 lbs." We purchased 1 lb. of tetracycline and 5 lbs. of penicillin. They remain on a shelf in the lab, as silent witnesses to the imperative to check things out. Two years later, at a WHO meeting on antimicrobial resistance and feed additives, the head of the Center for Veterinary Medicine of the FDA, in response to some justifiable criticism from a Swedish delegate about the lack of regulations on antimicrobial feed additives in the United States, said the same thing, that one cannot just walk into a store and buy antimicrobials in the United States. At the coffee break, I went over to him with three colleagues from Scandinavia, and said, "That is not true, and if you say it again, I will stand up and call you a liar." He was too surprised to reply; my Danish friend Henrik Wegener, head of the division in the Danish research institute that has studied drug resistance in foodborne bacteria, asked, "Is this true?" I replied, "Of course it is. I wouldn't say otherwise."

So-called confined animal houses for swine and broiler chickens are not and cannot be truly confined. It does not matter if they are old, with openings on the side as in traditional animal house design, or modern, with no side openings at all. In all cases, in order to keep the animals alive, these houses have to be equipped with large fans at the end of each house in a design known as tunnel ventilation. In a 2012 document, the University of Florida extension service details the requirements to reduce heat and humidity. According to this source, 25,000 chickens (a small broiler operation by today's standards) can generate 1 million BTUs and 40 gallons of moisture per hour.

It really does not take an engineer to figure out that a lot of air has to be moved into and out of these houses to keep the animals alive. The operating conditions for ventilation are stipulated in the contracts between integrators and poultry farmers, such that fans must be installed to move air through the houses at rates between 350 and 400 cubic feet per minute. This creates a wind velocity of some 4–5 mph. These same contracts stipulate that screening sufficient enough to keep dusts and other airborne material inside the house cannot be used because of the rapidity with which they are clogged by the mass of suspended dusts. Similar operating conditions are necessary for hog production, because pigs cannot regulate their body temperature through sweating.

There are usually at least three, and often as many as six, of these large fans at one end of each poultry house, operating twenty-four hours a day, seven days a week. No wonder there is a visible exit trail from the houses of all the dusts and materials swept out by this system. No wonder, as we learned, it is possible to measure pathogens that came from inside poultry houses at a distance of at least one football field downwind from the fans.

It is not possible for 35,000 to 100,000 birds to survive the heat and buildup of ammonia in an enclosed space, especially in the summer heat of the Broiler Belt, where temperatures can stay above 90°F for days at a time. Owing to the actions of a drunken intruder in a chicken house in Maryland in August of 2012, we have real data supporting that, under such conditions, tens of thousands of chickens in broiler houses can die within fifteen minutes after ventilation stops. In science we call this an experiment of nature. The story about the drunken intruder went viral after being reported by the *Salisbury Times*. One day a man entered a broiler house near Delmar, Maryland, and before he passed out, he managed to shut off the electric power for the large fans. All the chickens died before the police were called. The local sheriff concluded, "Quite frankly, he was probably in a condition where he really didn't know what he was doing." Bill Satterfield, head of the Delmarva Poultry Industry Association, was stunned, saying, "I have never heard of a drunkard going in and killing chickens."

It should go without saying that the growers have to pay for the purchase, installation, and maintenance of these fans, whose design and capacity are stipulated by the integrator, as well as the costs of energy to run them. The recurring nightmare for growers is a power failure, which causes mass die-offs. Although the integrators (from whom the growers obtain the young chicks or pigs) are usually insured against such losses, the growers are not because they do not own the animals. Moreover, they have no way to recover the labor or other costs they have already incurred during grow-out. "It takes a tough man to raise a tender chicken," claimed Frank Perdue, referring to himself as an integrator, but the real toughness and endurance are required of those who actually raise all Perdue's chickens.

I have spent the time to describe these details because of the widespread assumption that industrial food animal production is conducted in confinement, such that pathogens cannot enter or escape. I have encountered this stated as fact at government meetings, at WHO meetings, and at too many scientific conferences to count. Under conditions of zoonotic disease outbreaks, such as highly pathogenic avian influenza or porcine epidemic diarrhea (which ravaged the US industry in 2015), containment measures are often imposed—mostly on movement of farmers and workers—but the inability to prevent spread of these diseases demonstrates that these measures are incomplete.

Another bit of evidence is the presence of wild birds around poultry houses. During another early visit, I noticed that wild birds flocked around the outside of the chicken houses, a factor that had never been noted by students of avian influenza, who had assumed that housing acted as a completely effective barrier separating wild and domesticated birds. A poultry farmer explained why the wild birds were present: "Because they know there's food there." Inspired by a similar curiosity, Jay Graham, at the time a PhD student in my lab, noticed that his car was covered with flies when he left a poultry farm, so he did a study of flies trapped around poultry houses and demonstrated that they were carrying pathogens traceable to the poultry waste.

The industry and the USDA both know these facts. Yet they continue to insist that their operations are "biocontained" (keeping biological agents and biotoxins inside) and "biosecure" (keeping these same hazards outside). This is not an argument about terminology; the concept of "confined" animal feeding operations is a misnomer that has resulted in false assurances and mistaken policies in disease prevention. Is it deliberate? Probably not. The original meaning was to distinguish the raising of animals within the defined and loosely confined space of a building. Further elaborations to claim biosecurity are dishonest, however. They are problematic because these claims form the basis for industry and government assurances as well as international guidelines recommending conversion of smallholder animal production into industrial-scale "confinement" to prevent the spread of diseases such as swine and avian influenzas. It is more accurate to acknowledge that food animals are held in buildings that are open sources that provide little or no barriers to the release of what is inside or the entrance of what is outside. Moreover, the lack of real confinement in housing construction and operations is augmented by other aspects of production that create additional porosities, particularly the other products of industrialized food animal production.

Chicks and shoats are put into these houses, and chickens and hogs are taken out. But they are not the only products of industrial food animal production, just as electricity is not the only product of a coal-fired power plant. Wastes are the major output of food animal production and, from an engineering perspective, most of the porosity in these operations is the waste. Over its short lifespan of some 7 weeks, each chicken produces about 10 lbs. of waste, which is considerably more than the weight of a fresh broiler chicken at the supermarket (about 4 lbs.). For swine, the amount of waste produced per hog also far exceeds its market weight of 200–300 lbs. To reach that weight, each hog produces about one ton of waste. Contrast these figures with humans. Each American produces about 5 lbs. of waste a day, or about 1,600 lbs. per year. With a lot more pigs than people in states like North Carolina and Iowa, that means a lot of waste. The other difference is that human waste undergoes stringent management. But because animal waste is not a direct part of the food chain, it is largely unnoticed and, consequently, there is little regulation of animal waste management.

As in other aspects of animal husbandry, the industrial model has substantially changed by the generation and management challenges of handling these large amounts of animal wastes. When animals were raised in open areas, their density was limited by the availability of crops for forage and for storage after harvest. The limits of crop agriculture constrained the density of animals to a level that also permitted natural processes to absorb and utilize their wastes. But those natural bounds no longer apply to an agricultural production system in which tens of thousands of animals are raised in houses that are densely located in clusters (as demonstrated in the USDA maps of poultry and swine production in the United States today), because they can survive on manufactured feeds that are trucked in from other regions, sometimes across international borders. Held in buildings for their lifetimes, these animals have no place to excrete their wastes but onto the flooring of poultry houses (usually hard-packed ground or concrete) or onto the slats that form the flooring above cesspits in swine houses.

It is a lot of waste. In a short-lived advertisement run by Perdue Farms, the current company chairman Jim Perdue is shown standing next to 1,500 tons of poultry waste that is meant to represent the "other product" of his industry. The ad is captioned with an echo of his father's boast "It takes a tough man to manage all this . . . manure." It is an understatement; as the caption indicates, the yearly production of poultry waste by Perdue is about seventy times this amount by Perdue alone. And Perdue does not even manage it—that responsibility is handed off to the farmers.

"Manage," like "confinement," is another one of those words that deserves close scrutiny. First is to identify who must manage these tons of waste. The integrators do not have any responsibility to deal with waste from animal houses, because this is one of the steps in the process that has been conveniently (for the business model) outsourced to the contractors. The farmers, who raise producers' animals to market weight and receive a pittance of the profit, are responsible.

To understand what needs to be done to manage these wastes, we need to take a closer look at what constitutes animal house wastes. (This is where in real life my children would cry, "Mom's taking us to a sewage treatment plant," one of the many travel adventures they dubbed "Public Health Tourism.") In poultry production, wastes are called "house litter," which is not a very informative term. Litter is the bedding placed on the ground of the house, often sawdust that may be mixed with other ground-up plant materials. But house litter also consists of what the birds excrete over their lifespan, spilled feed, dead animals, and feathers, mixed together with the bedding material. What the animals excrete is feces, along with the drugs and other feed additives they have eaten. They also excrete bacteria and other pathogens in their waste, along with the genes that make bacteria resistant to antibiotics.

The poultry flocks live out their short lives amid this mixture (remember, the house floor is either packed earth or concrete), a practice that endangers their health as well as that of consumers of poultry products. The litter contains many types of microbes, some of which cause major poultry diseases, including Fowlpox, Newcastle disease, and Marek's disease. Because it is common practice in the United States and many countries not to clean out or disinfect the house between flocks, the accumulation of these pathogens acts as a reservoir within the poultry house for bacteria that cause human disease, such as *Salmonella* and *Campylobacter.*

The usual practice in the industry is to remove only the top layer of litter—known as the "crust"—which becomes caked with dried liquid waste and water. This is not a complete cleanout. Based on growers' reports, a complete cleanout may occur once every twelve to eighteen months, unless there is a disease outbreak, which would necessitate an earlier cleanout. Parsimony is the reason for this seeming carelessness, as growers are responsible for the management of wastes, they have to bear the costs involved. There is no decontamination of this waste, and growers usually store the house wastes in an open-sided shed until its eventual disposal on land, either by the grower or by someone else after transfer off the farm.

Swine wastes also contain excreta, feeds, and their constituent drugs and pathogens. They are collected in open cesspits under the floor slats of swine houses, which explains the overwhelming smell inside and close by swine houses. When the building cesspits are filled, the wastes flow into open cesspits, usually located near the swine houses. These are called, in one of the most extraordinary euphemisms of the industry, "lagoons." No palm trees here; only open waste holding. When the lagoons need emptying, the wastes are transferred into trucks that spray the liquid wastes on fields in most instances, but not for fertilizing. At all stages of holding and disposal, the odors and irritant aerosols from this process can be staggering in intensity.

There are few regulations on the placement or management of these impoundments. They do not have to be lined to prevent leakage into the ground, and they are often poorly managed, such that heavy rains can cause spills and overflows. When Hurricane Floyd swept through the dense swine production lowlands of North Carolina in 1999, the contents of thousands of lagoons were swept into nearby rivers. "We do have a practical problem here," the governor, James B. Hunt Jr., said one month after the hurricane. But with the efforts of Senator Jesse Helms, the same whole infrastructure was rebuilt, with no changes to the vacuum of management. With federal aid, the industry replaced the waste impoundments in the same locations.

Whether we are concerned about nutrients, drugs, bacteria, or genes, what we have now is not waste management, but waste holding and dumping. The major porosity of industrial food animal production in the United States is the absence of any regulations requiring real management of its enormous waste streams. Enormity is not simply a matter of total mass but also denotes the geographically intense impacts of waste generation by intensive food animal production, which is an unavoidable consequence of its extreme regional intensification. USDA maps of poultry and swine production demonstrate vividly the density of food animal production; now, imagine this as a map of waste generation and dumping.

There are no regulations and no monitoring. There are *recommendations* from the USDA about handling animal wastes, such as holding times before disposal on land, and some guidance from some states as to how often and where wastes can be applied to land. But neither reduces the hazards present in the waste. Most people know what "recommendations" from government agencies means—have a cup of coffee and pray, as the workers say about health and safety recommendations in slaughter and processing plants.

We would not tolerate this situation if these populations of animals were cities of humans, with enough people living in Delmarva to generate millions of tons of raw sewage. We have demanded and gotten enforceable laws, not recommendations, to deal with human waste. Under the Clean Water Act, the EPA requires cities and towns to install approved waste management technologies and to ensure their effectiveness. These rules are frequently updated to require more and more sophisticated treatment. For example, a current discussion at the EPA is about the need to prevent water contamination by pharmaceuticals, including antimicrobial drugs that enter rivers and streams from household waste and are not removed by conventional wastewater treatment methods. Ironically, of course, the vast majority of antibiotic use in the United States is not by humans but by industrially raised food animals. Antimicrobials in animal wastes have been detected in rivers and streams.

Our rules on human waste management do not stop with the raw sewage; the EPA also requires extensive management of human "biosolids," or the solid materials that remain after treatment of sewage. Biosolid management requires a great deal of technology and monitoring as well as requirements that must be met before further disposal or use. Among these requirements is testing to ensure that there are no infectious disease risks in the material. None of these rules applies to wastes from industrial food animal production. This industry slides through the traditional loophole of regulation as a "nonpoint source"; that is, its waste does not come from an identifiable pipe. If intensive food animal production were recognized as the industry that it is, we would end this fantasy and regulate its activities just as we regulate industrial waste generation. We also would not tolerate shifting the burden of responsibility from the industry to its contractors, as demonstrated by our collective refusal to accept just such a defense offered by Allied Chemical to escape liability for the contamination of the James River by a subcontractor involved in packaging its pesticide kepone.

The array of hazardous waste management laws implemented by the EPA clearly assigns responsibility for downstream management to the industry that produced the wastes. But this concept of corporate responsibility has not been adopted for animal wastes, once again because of the general refusal—in which we are all complicit—to recognize that agriculture has become industrialized and to accept the convenient divisions that have been created by the integrated structure. The integrators bear no responsibility for animal wastes. Individual farmers are responsible for meeting any state regulations (such as limits on land disposal in Maryland) or the short-lived EPA regulations related to obtaining permits for releasing animal wastes into surface waters (not soils). Individual farmers have been sued by citizens groups for failure to comply with these regulations. In a case brought in Maryland by the Waterkeepers Alliance, an environmental NGO, the judge ruled that Perdue Farms had no responsibility for any pollution arising from poultry houses run by its contract chicken growers. This was an ill-considered lawsuit insofar as it only served to confirm the legality of integrators' shifting of the burden of waste management to farmers and to insulate the integrated system from any requirement to change its operations.

The USDA and the EPA have the authority to impose standards for management of agricultural waste. Neither has stepped up to their obligation to regulate. For the USDA, the basis for its silence on waste management is its persistent allegiance to the long-gone traditions of small farms producing limited amounts of wastes that can be locally recycled for improving soil quality for agricultural benefit. There is no recognition of the changes in volume or constituents of this waste stream. As a result, the USDA does not actually regulate waste management but only *suggests* that wastes should be composted 180 days prior to land disposal in areas where crops are grown for human consumption. That is a nice thought, but the word "compost" means much more than simply heaping up waste material for some period of time. And the USDA knows the difference, with its detailed descriptions of adequate composting for households and for use in raising crops that meet its organic standard.

Composting as practiced by the poultry industry basically consists of piling wastes, sometimes under a roof, until it is hauled away. Not much happens in terms of reducing hazards in the waste. *True* composting, on the other hand, is a defined process of highly controlled temperature and moisture conditions as well as regular turning or stirring to support actual degradation. This process is evident at wastewater treatment plants, where giant stirrers are active in the secondary treatment stage. In composting, the conditions are closely monitored to ensure that temperature and moisture conditions are maintained. Proper aeration is maintained by regularly turning the mixture. Worms and fungi further break up the material. Aerobic bacteria manage the chemical process by converting the inputs into heat, carbon dioxide, and ammonium. Otherwise, it is a bit hard to understand how composting would reduce bacteria, as bacteria are the engine of successful composting. The only way that some of the pathogens can be killed off is by sustaining high temperatures for a substantial period of time and by mixing the material being composted.

Anyone who passes by poultry waste heaps next to poultry houses and swine lagoons next to swine houses knows that these are not managed or monitored processes. My group of student researchers has studied what happens to poultry waste over the USDA's recommended period of 180 days before land disposal, under empirical conditions at a poultry grow-out operation in Delmarva. We took samples every week and measured the parameters recommended for composting. As might be expected, in the absence of any formal method that would ensure the right temperature and moisture controls and in the presence of lots of bacterial nutrients, the numbers of bacteria increased, as did the numbers of drug-resistant bacteria and resistance genes. Other researchers have measured the survivability of bacteria and viruses in wastes and in soils where wastes are applied. With swine waste, the lagoons cannot be confused with secondary waste treatment as required for human wastes. Without control over the conditions and with continuing additions of raw waste, once again concentrations of pathogens increase. This is a feast for the microbiome, the realm of bacteria.

A side observation: we need an ombudsman to flag the use of misleading words to describe industrial agriculture, such as "confinement," "family farms," "swine lagoons," "waste composting," and "chicken houses." This ombudsman could also flag claims that have not been verified, such as growth promotion and biosecurity. I suppose that is what I am doing in this book.

In late 2013, the FDA broke ranks with the USDA in response to the outbreaks and concerns about the health implications of their ineffective composting recommendations, on the basis of the risk of food contamination by antimicrobial-resistant pathogens. This welcome development could signal a possible change in the balance of power in this part of managing industrial agriculture. The FDA has proposed but not issued regulations to require standards and treatment to reduce microbial contamination of animal wastes (including documentation of composting; limits on land application in fields where crops are produced for human consumption; rules on storage, transport, and handling of wastes; and recordkeeping). But the FDA still buys into the concept that time alone will reduce the presence of pathogens and drug resistance in animal wastes as well as in soils treated with these wastes. Time—in the absence of action—only allows bacteria to increase in nutrient-rich ecosystems like waste and soil. But it is a start. Unfortunately, the organic producers who have long utilized wastes from industrial food animal production are strenuously resisting these proposals. Small may be beautiful, but small is not necessarily safe.

After holding wastes in heaps or open septic ponds at production facilities, the final step of "management" of animal wastes involves complete transgression of any containment that might exist within animal houses, swine waste lagoons, or poultry house litter sheds: the wastes are applied to land. Land disposal is confusingly called "land amendment" (another term for the language ombudsman) to suggest that something beneficial is being accomplished. It also invokes the natural cycle of traditional agriculture, the utilization of animal wastes to add nutrients to soil for growing crops to feed the next batch of animals. This is another illusion arising from our failure to replace our visions of traditional farming—images of pigs in sties and chickens in coops, producing modest amounts of waste that can be easily stored and used as "manure," a word that originally meant "to work by hand."

This is not what is happening. The intensive localization of the industry means that the local volume of waste far exceeds the local carrying or absorptive capacity of soils in the same location. Moreover, in many areas where intensive operations are increasing, such as central West Virginia, there is little or no use of land for agriculture, such that there are no fields waiting for nutrient additions. Even where there are arable fields available for use, the sheer volume of wastes exceeds what agronomists know to be appropriate levels of inputs such as nitrogen and phosphorus that are natural constituents of animal wastes. Overloading soils with these nutrients (and other materials that are not useful for agriculture) results in what can only be called *land pollution*. In lower Wicomico County, Maryland, a small field next to an array of poultry houses directly abuts the Pocomoke River. The excess nutrients and other contaminants in poultry waste are only partly constrained by intermittent trees and shrubs from moving into the river and then into the Chesapeake Bay.

Some modest alternatives to land disposal are under development, but the overwhelming volumes of wastes from poultry and swine are still applied to land. Experiments are being conducted to see whether poultry waste can be combusted to generate energy, but the heterogeneity and dampness of the wastes are impediments to implementation on a reasonable scale of return. For swine wastes, attempts have been made to capture methane emissions for energy utilization with no updates as to applicability. Another disposal method that Perdue and some other producers are marketing is the sale of dried poultry wastes as fertilizers for consumer use, marketed under names such as Cockadoodle-Doo. Biosolids from human waste can be used for fertilizers, but with two major differences. These products cannot be used for growing crops for human consumption, and they must meet stringent tests prior to sale. When we tested some of these products, which we purchased at garden stores, we found recoverable drug-resistant bacteria in them along with arsenic. Arsenic, as an element, is resistant to control by either proper composting or burning. With the removal of arsenicals from poultry feeds, this problem has been dealt with for once properly at the source, but arsenicals are still approved for use in swine feed.

OTHER POROSITIES: HUMANS AND ANIMALS ON THE MOVE

People and animals also move through the porosities of intensive food animal production. Growers, their families, and animal house workers are all
at risk of contracting and then carrying a range of problems from working and living near these operations. Proximity counts as much as direct
involvement. Dr. Beth Feingold in our research group took data from the
health system in the Netherlands and found that the risks of exposure to
animal-related pathogens (in this study, it was methicillin-resistant *Staphylococcus aureus*, or MRSA) are not limited to people who work directly with
animals (such as farmers or veterinarians or truck drivers taking animals to
slaughter). Simply living in an area with a high density of hogs is sufficient
to increase these exposure risks. People can carry infectious agents in two
ways. First, when infected, we can transfer pathogens through personal contact, sneezing, or other normal activities. Second, people can also function
as surfaces for carrying bacteria without being infected—acting like what
are termed *fomites*—through contamination of the surfaces of clothing and
skin that are a means of transporting pathogens from one environment to
another. This is how a lot of hospital infections get spread: on the gloves and
coats of healthcare personnel. Relatively few growers and other workers
have access to or use the type of protective clothing that is disposable or
kept at the workplace, as is now common at hospitals, to prevent this type
of diffusion.

The animals are also moved about during their short lifespans, from
house to house (in the case of pigs) and from farms to slaughterhouses.
Almost universally, animal transport is done in slat-sided trucks or in cages
stacked on the back of trucks, with no controls on pathogen releases. The
process of transport is highly stressful to the animals. They are packed into
pens or cages, and, so like all stressed animals, they defecate. One consequence is that, by the time animals are moved from house to slaughterhouse, almost all of them are contaminated by the same pathogens. The
other consequence is that, because all of this traffic in live animals takes
place on public roads, the materials flying off the back of transport trucks
are highly contaminated. "We were trapped behind a chicken truck on our
way back from the beach," recounted one of my colleagues at Hopkins with
a rueful look. "What a stinking mess! The windshield was covered with

feathers and chicken shit." (These are exciting words to a public health scientist. As my children know, to their regret, nothing tempts their mother more than the words "stinking mess.") So we carried out a study in Delmarva in which we chased chicken trucks to the slaughterhouse, with air samplers in our cars. We found extensive release of drug-resistant bacteria and pathogens from the trucks onto surfaces *inside* the cars, including on a soda can in the beverage holder. The industry complained that the greater risk was chasing their trucks, which was arguably true given the excessive speeds with which the trucks ran through the small towns of southern Delmarva.

The field known as *industrial ecology* was developed to understand material flows in production processes like automobile production and microchip manufacture in order to identify opportunities for more efficient use of inputs and more effective reductions in pollution. The industrial ecology of intensive food animal production allows us to see plainly why it is not just a food safety problem. This is why interventions such as irradiating food at the end-stage of production, as proposed by many concerned solely about consumer safety, is not enough to prevent the public health impacts of this industry. We do need to aim at the heart as well as the stomach.

Although industrial food animal production has decoupled animal husbandry from the constraints of the environment and place, its operations are not sealed off from the environment and place. The failure to recognize or acknowledge the porosity of industrial food animal production has warped programs to prevent transmission of zoonotic diseases, and it has impeded policies and regulations on the density of locating animal buildings, which could otherwise be important means of controlling some of the external impacts of these operations. We need to consider food animal waste to be an environmental pollutant. We need to think even more deeply what goes out in food animal waste, beyond drugs and bugs to antimicrobial resistance itself.

Jose Martinez, a microbiologist in Madrid, first proposed the concept of antimicrobial resistance as environmental pollution. This idea challenges both microbiologists and environmental health scientists to consider "resistance" as a material and then environmental aspects of its behavior as a material. This is key to understanding much of the problems of the "other product" of industrialized food animal production. Antibiotic resistance is a material; it is first a gene and then a protein that is made from the genetic template—these are both materials that you can, if not quite hold in your hand, see after extracting, purifying, and using the high-resolution detection methods of modern molecular biology—such as polymerase chain reaction (PCR), which is like a highly efficient copying machine for genes and then other new tools to separate and identify the protein product of the gene. Both genes and proteins are properly defined as substances and in fact they can be patented in the United States.

So, as substances released into the environment mostly through animal wastes, we can think of their properties in the same way as the material properties of more conventional contaminants, such as pesticides. Two characteristics that are important in environmental health are hazard and persistence. First, regarding hazard, does the substance in itself possess properties that could harm human health or organisms in the environment? (Later we get to dose or how much it takes to cause harm.) Regarding persistence, does the substance remain unchanged in the environment—in air, water, soils?

We can certainly say that an antibiotic resistance gene is hazardous to human health when it is present in bacteria. This is a bit more complicated than the usual hazard identification for chemicals, which don't have to be incorporated into an organism to be hazardous. But it is not so different from thinking about chemicals that do get incorporated into organisms— such as methyl mercury in fish—because it is this incorporation that often brings us into contact with the chemical. Just as we think about mercury apart from fish, it is important to think about the resistance genes apart from their presence in specific bacteria. Resistance genes can survive in soils for long periods; think of the studies in which DNA is extracted from prehistoric mammals, for example. Bacteria also survive in soils and biofilms, and those that are robust may become the reservoirs of resistance for the microbial community.

It is a bit more of a stretch, but resistance genes can also be bioaccumulated—like pesticides such as DDT or polychlorinated biphenyls (PCBs)—in the environment, in the sense that they can be amplified through the growth of microbial populations. That is, once a novel gene is taken up and incorporated into the bacterial genome, when that organism divides, its daughter cells each contain the new gene. Given the rates of bacterial growth, this process is far more efficient at increasing the total amount of the hazard than the traditional trophic food web by which (again, think of methyl mercury) a toxic chemical accumulates through consumption. In fact, bioaccumulation in the microbial world is conceptually quite different: the movement of a chemical up the food chain does not increase the total amount of the chemical but rather results in higher concentrations in predators that have consumed prey, such as osprey—or humans—feeding on fish. Unlike chemicals, resistance genes are actually increased in number through uptake by bacteria and subsequent biological expansion of the bacterial community. This is where biology and chemistry diverge, and why our concerns about bioweapons are so much greater than our concerns for chemical warfare agents.

So we have persistence and accumulation in common across microbiology and toxicology. Environmental perspectives can also help us with exposure assessment or how substances in air, water, or soil reach individual people. These same pathways are important for antibiotic resistance, with the notable addition that the hazard—resistance genes—can be shuttled among organisms, rather like a game of Australian rules football, where the ball can be propelled by running or by foot or hand in any direction up and down the field in the course of the game. In contrast, chemical exposures are usually more like American football, with forward movement being all that counts. Thus, if a bacterium carrying a resistance gene is killed (downed), the gene may be picked up by another organism and moved through the community of bacteria in our guts or in the environment. Gene transfers among bacteria are not only multidirectional but more complex than simple movement along a linear path of organisms. There are teams of a sort among bacteria, making up networks of gene transfer like teams of football players passing the ball within the team.

The inextricable relationship between industrial food animal production and the environment challenges us in two ways. First, we are all at risk—not just those of us who consume the products of industrially raised animals—and second, decontaminating food products will not contain the public health problems of this industry. It is time to think about industrial food animal production as an industry in terms of environmental pollution, and it is long overdue to recognize that its pollution footprint, like its production, is industrial in scale.

7

ANTIMICROBIAL RESISTANCE

How Agriculture Ended the Antimicrobial Era

Like the many pollutants in food animal waste, resistance genes can and should be defined and thought of as environmental pollutants. Genes are, after all, chemicals like pollutants, specialized in function for directing the cellular production of proteins, which are also chemicals. Resistance genes encode changes in proteins that enable bacteria to evade the toxicity of antimicrobial chemicals, including our drugs. Defining resistance genes as pollutants encourages us to focus on the environment as the location where these genes are released, accumulated, transferred, and become part of the resources for bacteria to survive our best efforts to prevent disease. Even so, resistance genes are not exactly like other environmental pollutants.

In understanding how and why resistance genes are different, it is useful to adopt the perspective of the bacteria. After all, as Martin Blaser reminds us, most of our cells are bacteria—that is, if we define ourselves more completely as all that is part of us, not just within us. We are, of course, made up of the cells of our bodies, but our bodies are also home to billions of bacteria on the external surfaces of our skin, our ears, our armpits, our noses, our throats, and our guts. All of these surfaces are external—that is, coextensive with the outside of our bodies—even the lining of our gut. We are host to these multiple resident bacterial communities or *microbiomes* that are defined by their locations. This is all new stuff, and it is one of the most exciting ideas in current medicine and biomedical research, challenging our ideas about how we become who we are and the nature of health and disease over our lifespans. Because what and who we are is not separable from those billions of bacteria that reside in these spaces of our bodies, we need to understand the bacterial perspective, which will also help us to understand how bacteria see antimicrobial drugs and antimicrobial resistance. I don't apologize for giving bacteria "sight" and much more.

From the bacterial perspective, we can more clearly realize how dangerously we have wasted antimicrobials, nature's gift to the survival of our species. We are on the brink of the end of the antimicrobial era, of losing the ability of these natural products to change the balance of power between our species and the microbial world. It has been a short truce between the time we opened nature's treasure chest and today's crisis in antimicrobial resistance. In the early days of antimicrobial production we released both good and evil into the world, much like Pandora, although not out of curiosity but because of our greed and profligacy—traits that seem to be hardwired into our species.

Greed abetted by ignorance is a dangerous driver of destruction, as Isaiah noted. Greed may always be part of the human condition, but we can and should do something about our ignorance. In this story of greed and ignorance, there are certainly those in decision-making positions who should have known better, and who should have acted on that knowledge. Like so much of the history of industrialized food animal production, the mixture of politics and self-interest has trumped the science and blocks action to this day.

But the usual suspects in industry are not the only ones to blame. The medical, veterinary, and public health communities have failed us as well. They have not spoken out, and this failure encourages the excuses and denials by politicians and regulators. Consult most websites on antimicrobial resistance—those from federal and state governments, international groups, NGOs, and major medical providers—and agricultural use of antimicrobials does not register at the top of leading causes of drug resistance. The biomedical and public health communities are silent, too. There are a few rare and compelling voices to the contrary, such as Dr. Sally Davies, the chief medical officer of the United Kingdom, and Anthony van Bogaard of Belgium, one of the first to insist upon the biological drive for resistance in agricultural settings. But not a one, really, in the United States.

The central problem is a failure to recognize what we are really up against and how agricultural use has become the major driver for the rise of resistance. We do not fully appreciate the complexity and versatility of the bacterial world. We think it is some kind of contest between us and the bacteria. We are prone to talk about "wars" in medicine and public health, against diseases and conditions—cancer, AIDS, poverty—because using bellicose language seems to signify that we take these issues seriously, demonstrating the strength of our commitment to control them. But wars against bacteria are quite literally wars against ourselves, which is why we urgently need to fully appreciate our "enemy." Bacteria are not really our enemy, but part of ourselves. They constitute communities of organisms, some of which are friendly and some of which are unfriendly, that live within and all around us. That is the meaning of the microbiome: the recognition that bacteria live in and among us, in populations that function not so dissimilarly from ourselves. To know thyself, understand the microbiome.

Like us, bacteria form communities in which different groups know different things. Like us, the bacteria talk with each other. This is not a trivial statement; until recently, we did not consider that bacteria "knew" things or that they lived in communities. We have tended to think of bacteria as separate organisms or at most groups of identical organisms, or clones, derived from one organism. We did not think of bacteria as having the types of social interactions—including communicating—that define communities. We thought of bacteria as hermitic and solitary organisms, each surviving as monads by sensing and responding to environmental signals and nothing more.

As a result of this misunderstanding, we have made a fundamentally dangerous mistake of defining bacteria by our perspectives, as being "good" or "bad" for us, ignorant of the fact that each bacterial strain, like each group of people, is part of a larger community existing on and within our bodies, in spaces as large as the solar system is to us. It is rather like the Trojans mistaking the wooden horse for a single organism rather than a structure housing a dangerous group of soldiers.

If we define community as an association of individuals that both serves individual needs and combines individuals into something more resilient and effective at survival than a dissociated set of individuals, it becomes clear that bacteria are most definitely communities. But we are only just beginning to recognize the communal nature of bacteria. Bacterial communities are called microbiomes in recognition of their being a large population in one location made up of groups of heterogeneous individuals, just as we refer to a city by its location and its neighborhoods composed of different sorts of people. Like groups of humans, a microbiome is defined by its common interests and often by its location, but, like web-based groups, microbiomes are not necessarily limited by geographical proximity.

E. O. Wilson has made a strong case for insects as the pinnacle of social evolution, but nothing exceeds the bacterial microbiome for communitarianism, both in the extent of its socialization and its versatility in using the machinery of evolution to advance community interests in controlling us and our planet. As Lewis Thomas wrote, "our microbial ancestors, all by themselves, laid out all the rules and regulations for interliving, habits we humans should be studying now for clues to our own survival." We are not used to thinking of bacteria in this way; most scientists still consider bacteria as living "unicellular lives," like anchorites in the desert in early Christianity, devoid of social contacts. The community-based interactions and alliances among bacteria are similar to but vastly more effective than ours, and, because of this, bacteria have succeeded in occupying almost every niche of our planet, with the possible exception of some extreme environments (although they can hunker down to survive ice, fire, drought, and the ocean depths to colonize almost every extreme habitat of our planet). It is for bacterial life that we now search the solar system. The second important aspect of bacterial communities is that they coexist and comingle with human communities, although we are late to notice this. The microbiome–human connection has existed throughout the evolution of life on earth. Bacteria were here first, appearing between three and four billion years ago.

Forget invasions of alien life forms from outer space—bacteria have always been here and always within us. Our relationship is well described by the Beatles in their song "I Am the Walrus": "I am he as you are he as you are me and we are all together." Our relationship is totally and mutually essential: bacteria contributed to our evolution, and today all of us carry within our genomes the contributions of bacterial evolution fundamental to our survival. Mitochondria are the engines of life for all cells. The mitochondria in our cells were originally incorporated from bacteria residing within the cells of the first multicellular organisms. These mitochondria were eventually transferred through evolution of species to our primate ancestors and then to us. So, when we talk about mitochondrial genes, which indicate the contribution of matrilineal inheritance, we should acknowledge that the mothers of us all are the bacteria.

Our relationship with bacteria did not end in the distant evolutionary past, however. Our present existence continues to be influenced by the bacterial microbiomes that are resident with us, populating the external surfaces inside and outside of our bodies. This kind of intertwined living is called *symbiosis* when it is mutually required or beneficial. The continuing coexistence of humans and bacteria is not always an even balance or symbiosis, and microbiomes have had and continue to have more influence on humans as a species and as individuals than we have previously realized. The growth and development of these microbiomes shape our own growth and development. Their stability and resilience define our own health and disease. Bacteria are the first gatekeepers at the entry points for the external world that we contact by eating, drinking, breathing, and touching. For this reason, some have called bacteria the "fourth portal" (after the skin, lungs, and gut). Gut bacteria not only digest our food, they also transform other chemicals that enter our bodies through ingestion, with potentially more impact than the pathways of internal metabolism in the liver and lung that we have spent the past century studying in much of biomedical research. The state of our internal microbiome affects not only our physical state of health but also our thoughts and intentions.

A DANGEROUS CONFIDENCE

It is entirely appropriate to think about ourselves and our world from the bacterial perspective. Adopting this perspective is not pathetic fallacy or ascribing human emotions to nature, but an urgent need as we fall farther and farther behind in the struggle for who controls what. As a first step, we must discard some long-held notions about us and the bacteria. Of these, one of the most dangerous is our assumption that bacteria can be divided into two groups that are defined by our interests rather than theirs. Bacteria that we have assumed share an equal interest in our survival we call *commensal*, or, literally, eating at the same table. We can, and in some cases must, live with them—or, more accurately, they live in and on us—without notably harming us, that is, by causing disease. From this relationship, we receive the life-giving benefit of their eating at the same table because these gut bacteria process our food, and they receive the benefit of plentiful food supply without having to find it. The other group of bacteria we call *pathogens*, the bacteria that cause disease and death for us. We make the effort to identify and name them when we recognize their roles in causing specific diseases.

But this distinction between commensals and pathogens is a creation of our own thinking. The distinction between "good" (commensal) and "bad" (pathogenic) bacteria has nothing to do with the interests or functions or social structures of bacteria. The spreading of bacterial diseases, such as tuberculosis and MRSA, has much more to do with our behavior than with theirs. Nevertheless, because this distinction is enshrined in medical and public health microbiology, it encourages us to focus only on the "bad" bacteria. We persuade ourselves that eradicating pathogens is what we need to do to prevent disease, that we can ignore the rest of the community, the microbiome. Such thinking is particularly dangerous when it prevents us from understanding and anticipating the emergence of bacterial strains that are highly virulent or resistant to antimicrobials. Take, for example, the case of *E. coli*, a large group of bacteria that populate our gut along with much of the external environment. Because many *E. coli* strains contribute to life as we know it, we call most of them commensal, or helpful, attesting to their useful presence in our gut. But certain strains of *E. coli* are highly virulent and can cause life-threatening human disease, including diarrhea (from enteropathogenic *E. coli*, or EPEC) and urinary tract infections, particularly in women and children that can progress to kidney failure (from extraintestinal pathogenic *E. coli*, or ExPEC). Some of these virulent communities of *E. coli* are also resistant to multiple antimicrobials. We call these strains pathogenic, the bad bugs. But from the bacterial perspective, all of these *E. coli* strains are part of the same community or microbiome. New strains of virulent and drug-resistant *E. coli* arise continuously within the broader community of *E. coli* in our gut and the guts of animals, including the highly virulent *E. coli* 0157:H7 and the newly reported multidrug-resistant strain of New Delhi metallo-β-lactamase *E. coli* (NDEC). If you haven't heard about these strains, you will. These emergences appear to be recent, but it only seems that way to us because of the time it has taken us to recognize their association with human disease. The important fact is that no hard and fast line exists between communities of so-called good and bad bugs, and we will always be late in recognizing virulent strains until we drop this distinction.

How do good bugs become bad (in our perspective), how do these newly recognized strains of pathogenic bacteria emerge, and how does drug resistance spread like wildfire throughout the bacterial world? By exchanging information. Just like our social groups, bacteria organize their communities and respond to their world by trading information. And, within their communities, bacteria exchange information much as we do, by sending and receiving signals relevant to the survival and well-being of the community.

Bacteria use two types of communication: short-duration signals and more durable mechanisms of information transfer. Short-duration signals—like tweeting among humans—are readily diffusible signals using small proteins and molecules that can be released and move among organisms. Some of these are signals for mating (yes, bacteria mate in terms of forming pairs and exchanging more complex information, including genes, by—here is a telling word—conjugation). Among bacteria, many of these signals are referred to as *quorum sensing*, using the word "quorum" in the same sense as we do, to indicate the communal nature of this chatter.

The longer-duration signals involve exchanges of genes among bacteria, often within what Elizabeth Skippington of Oxford University calls "cliques," remarkably similar to a close circle of adolescents (usually girls, in my experience) that define exclusionary sets of chatterers. There is relatively little new in our own social evolution in terms of these types of chatter; in fact, Rod McNab and Richard Lamont referred to the bacteria as "the chattering classes" that have "microbial dinner party conversations." It's hard to resist these analogies to our socialization, and perhaps we shouldn't, since the bacteria came first.

Of course, bacteria do not really talk or write—they do not even use a waggle dance for communication like the honeybees, as first described by Karl von Frisch, who won the Nobel Prize in 1973. There are now reports that suggest that bacteria, like the bees, may move in coordinated motions and patterns, which is a pretty good definition of dancing. We don't yet know if this activity is intended to communicate information like the bees' waggle dancing.

Bacteria communicate speechlessly by using the most fundamental language of all, the biological building blocks that underlie human language and insect dancing: DNA and the proteins encoded by DNA. Bacteria "talk" by sending specific molecules and genes through their highly efficient social networks. They also store this information for themselves and their communities in the form of DNA.

Compared to bacteria, humans are belatedly recognizing how to use DNA for information storage and transmission. Computer scientists are just starting to propose the use of genetic language as the basis for the most efficient computing machines possible. Bacteria are way ahead of us, having used DNA-based language for billions of years in order to talk for the same reasons we do, to establish social circuits and to ensure the survival of their communities. Like us, the most critical information for bacteria is for survival, to make social connections, and to recognize and send alerts about threats.

Among the most significant threats to the microbiome are antimicrobial molecules, those same natural products that we only recently "discovered" and learned how to use but that have been deployed as weapons of mass destruction among competing microbial communities for billions of years. Like hostile armies, that is enough time for bacteria to have developed a large amount of information needed to fend off these weapons. This information forms the blueprints that bacteria use to make new proteins that enable them to resist antimicrobial weapons launched by other microbes, including other bacteria. This store of information is what we call *antimicrobial resistance*; it is encoded in DNA and written, stored, and communicated within the microbiome in a library of genes called the *resistome*. This is a bacterial resource analogous to our armories—rocks and sharpened sticks in Neolithic times, swords and lances a few hundred years ago, and lines of missile defense and aircraft equipped with warning and control systems today. But the bacterial resistome is much more nimble and responsive to change than any of these comparatively anachronistic human systems, which require decades of adaptation and construction.

In addition to enabling a community response to external attack, the microbiome is highly self-protective. For example, it regulates its own population size by detecting cell density and the availability of critical nutrients and oxygen. The community thus regulates its own expansion to fit the resources available—the ideal of avoiding demographic crashes described by Thomas Robert Malthus, who predicted an inevitable crash of human societies unless we too learned how to recognize these limits and accordingly adjust their reproductive rates.

The bacterial system of communication and storage is also much more efficient than ours, using less energy and being based on a universal language of DNA that needs no translation. Moreover, communication among bacteria, like that of E. O. Wilson's social insects, is not confounded by those traits of egotism, paranoia, and the other ills of the so-called higher organisms, such as humans, that cause our communities to divide against each other.

There is also no premium for spreading misinformation among bacteria as there is in human societies. Bacteria would never create junk bonds or deceptive mortgage-backed securities to advance the short-term interests of some individuals, because doing so would damage the interests of the community as a whole. This is to the great advantage of bacteria; unlike humans, they do not act against their own self-interest, which is the primary definition of stupidity in Carlo Cipolla's great book *The Six Laws of Human Stupidity*. There are no stupid bacteria by his definition.

Bacteria use DNA not only for communication of information throughout their communities but also, as we do, for the transmission of information across generations, from parent to offspring. Both humans and bacteria accomplish this in part through the transmission of genes to offspring at reproduction, and in part by communications from elders to younger members of the community. For human populations, information flow through genes is how we solidify experience over the long term, in the form of heritable and nonheritable or epigenetic changes in our genomes that have been proven to confer successful survival and reproduction. But in this generational form of information transmission, the advantage also goes to bacteria. Unlike our species, bacterial reproduction is rapid and efficient, not tedious like human reproduction, which requires years to attain sexual maturity and months to produce offspring. Within minutes and hours, bacterial communities grow exponentially (that is, by doubling) through cell division to produce "daughter cells." As a result, important information can be quickly propagated throughout the community by these high rates of cell division as well as by weeding out those groups of individuals that do not possess this critical information. The same processes for selecting genes in humans in response to external stress take much more time. It has been estimated to take thirty thousand years for a spontaneous mutation in a critical human gene to appear at high enough frequency to result in a genetic change that improves our survival. Moreover, we are unable to adapt quickly to the removal of the same pressure for selection so that we continue to carry a gene or genes that formerly conferred a survival advantage but at a cost. Sickle cell anemia, for example, a genetic change that encodes an important change in the cell wall of our red blood cells, is thought to have been selected evolutionarily over many generations as a bioprotection against malaria, an ancient disease in our species' history. But with the subsequent movement of peoples from malarial regions in Africa to cooler northern climates, this evolutionary response was no longer necessary for survival and revealed its disadvantages in terms of increasing vulnerability to sudden cardiac death by persisting among populations in whom malaria risks were greatly reduced or absent. In these circumstances, the evolutionary advantage becomes a burden to us, as sickle cell anemia also decreases the efficiency of red cells to carry oxygen from the lung to the hungry tissues of our organ systems. Fortune favors the nimble, in terms of evolution—nimble to respond, nimble to shed the response.

The high reproduction rates of bacteria provide another advantage for evolutionary responses to stress. High rates of spontaneous genetic change or mutation are associated with high rates of cell division, which is why, within hours, a significant number of mutant strains of bacteria appear spontaneously within the microbiome, particularly under conditions of stress. Think of this as a poker game, in which we can advance our fortunes by waiting for a new hand to be dealt; bacteria get new cards within seconds, and the dealer deals faster when danger is present. We think of increases in mutation as often being harmful to human health (causing cancer, for example), but they are also critical to evolution and in any case much less costly to bacteria (which do not get cancer), which confers on bacterial populations the ability to either shed or adapt to mutations that carry a cost (like the sickle cell mutation in humans). In human terms, it would be like holding onto the sickle cell gene in case of the reemergence of malaria in a given area but acquiring another mutation that would reverse the impact of sickling on oxygen transport. By hedging their bets, anthropomorphically speaking, bacteria are prepared to respond more quickly when a threat (like our use of antimicrobials) appears.

We do not have the capacity to emulate the ability of bacteria to use another strategy of DNA-based communication for intergroup exchange, one that does not require reproduction. "So what?" we might ask. We humans have other ways to store and transmit knowledge among each other in ways that work over time and distance, without the limitations of reproduction or anything else that requires person-to-person interactions. We can read and write. That is how we have built knowledge over the centuries and why it is not necessary for each child to recapitulate the entire history of human knowledge. As we became more adept at generating information, we developed methods for storing this information outside our own brains, in material objects such as tablets, scrolls, and books; then in libraries; then in computer-based devices; and, finally, in the apotheosis of externalized knowledge—the cloud—an Internet-based system that we can now use only as needed. These achievements, many claim, are unique to our species: "Humans, but probably no other species, have the socio-cognitive capacity to engage in 'ostensive' communication," declared a recent article published in a Royal Society journal. We may believe this and we may say this, but we would be wrong. Bacteria have utilized methods for storage of information for billions of years. For bacteria, as for all forms of life, the fundamentals of life knowledge are stored in the genome as a collection of data that can be read out when needed (think of DNA as a book and RNA as the photocopy of information in the book, which enables the manufacture of usable information in the form of a protein). Humans are just starting to emulate how cells make things, for example, by using three-dimensional printing to directly translate stored information into objects (proteins are also three-dimensional structures).

If not communication, some philosophers point to empathy as a characteristic that is uniquely human and therefore cannot be present in androids or in bacteria. But even humans with limited empathy are still considered human, as Peter Singer argues, and some nonhuman animals demonstrably express empathy. We may not know what empathy means in bacteria, but bacteria clearly act in the interests of their community. *Do Androids Dream of Electric Sheep?* asks Philip K. Dick in the title of his most famous sci-fi novel, which explores the blurred distinctions between humans and nonhumans. Do bacteria "dream" of their friends?

We need to get over ourselves as the center of creation, a fixation that is common to creationism and evolutionary biology. We need to reconsider these claims that we use to separate us from bacteria. We talk about communication as a hallmark of human sentience, the ability to exchange and store knowledge among each other and even apart from each other in books and libraries and electronic devices. We do refer to animal communication, including that of insects and worms, and we do talk about "thinking machines" in terms of an ability to accumulate and share experiential knowledge. But bacteria? Once again, as with community, we need to reconsider what we mean by communicating. Bacteria are very small, and, as individual organisms, they do not possess the cellular machinery of a nervous system or memory. That might be the strongest argument in favor of the position that they cannot really think or communicate. But wait: we live in the age of technology, when intelligence can be distributed among machines. Why not among organisms? We have invented the superior power of what computer scientists call "parallel distributed processing" and "cloud storage" of information, but bacteria got there first. Parallel distributed processing was first proposed as a model of human cognition, based on neurobiology, in which the power of the human brain is in its network of physical units that interact and connect. The invention of the cloud indicates that there is no requirement that networks of thinking and communicating have to be housed inside one organ or organism. In computer science, we have developed the power of linking large computing machines into a network that performs operations and stores computerized information. We now store information outside ourselves and beyond our individual computers or networks of computers.

Like us, but once again long before us, bacteria had their own version of cloud computing, or externalized systems of information storage. What makes a cloud system work is the rapid and universal availability of the data, removing the need for each user to download or store or (horrible to contemplate) print out the desired information when we need it. This revolution changes what we mean by *knowledge*. Is a knowledgeable person someone who has memorized (transferred information to the brain) a great deal of information, or is a knowledgeable person someone who knows how to find information when it is needed? I am coming to understand that the latter definition may be more appropriate, and that conversations punctuated by "Let's Google that" are not annoying but rather a sign of our new connectedness to an enormous storehouse of knowledge far exceeding that of even the most remarkable idiot savant.

By storing information about resistance to antimicrobials in the form of DNA, bacteria are not limited to accessing and exchanging this knowledge vertically, that is, through reproduction and genetic inheritance (from parent cell to daughter cell) or even through social verticality (among each other or from parent to child). Like us, bacteria can deal information horizontally or laterally by shuttling genes among each other and within their communities. This capability greatly amplifies their ability to rapidly adjust to and resist threats like antimicrobial drugs. Very recently, for example, we humans invented a new class of antimicrobial agents made of silver, in the form of nanomaterials. Within months—a short time of use in water and food—much shorter than the time it took us to develop and make nanosilver—bacteria have selected and stored a new genetic mutation that makes them resistant to it.

These resources of resistance exist in an information cloud that Gordon Wright has called the resistome, independent of but accessible to each user. We recognize the power and danger of externalized information—our massive databanks and distributed systems—and in the same way we need to recognize the power and danger of externalized bacterial information. The implications for biosecurity are the same as for national security. If we are to protect ourselves against the inevitability of widespread resistance, we must constrain its movement through the microbiome at the level of the cloud.

In my experience, regulators and industry experts are unaware of most of the above information, which is why I include it in this book. It is discouraging to read statements from government agencies in the United States that still claim that there is insufficient evidence to link antimicrobials in food animal feeds with increased risks of drug-resistant infections in humans. Attempts by groups, such as the American Veterinary Medical Association and the Animal Health Institute (an industry trade group), to narrowly stipulate the rules of evidence—that a specified use must be shown to be associated with measurable increases in risks of specified drug-resistant infections by specified bacteria—are willful denials of the reality of cloud computing and a refusal to see beyond the narrow question of resistance in one specific bacterial strain that happens to concern us at a particular point in time.

HOW AGRICULTURE BUILDS THE ENVIRONMENTAL RESISTOME

Where is this cloud that holds the resistome for the microbiome? Unlike our commercialized, proprietary systems of cloud computing, the bacterial cloud that holds the resistome is highly dispersed. It is replicated and shared within the many environments in which bacterial communities reside, including the landscape of soils, sediments, and water as well as the landscapes inside and on us humans. Like Google, it is everywhere. This is why, to paraphrase the words of Tom O'Brien of Harvard University, the use of any antimicrobial anywhere can promote resistance everywhere. This global dispersion also confers strength; unlike our privatized systems, the multiplicity of bacterial clouds buffers the problems faced by cloud computing, such as business failures, localized power outages, or earthquakes in Silicon Valley. The bacterial cloud does not depend on external power sources or carefully controlled temperatures. DNA can survive for millions of years inside bacteria that have gone into their sleeper cell phase or in sediments and ice long after bacteria die.

At the same time as we are mindful of the level of genes and the microbiome, we must move back to the world as we think we know it, to understand the flow of information, more like a mighty river of drug resistance that flows mostly from agriculture into an expanding cloud of information that informs bacterial resistance to antimicrobials. The sheer volume of antimicrobial use in agriculture, its deliberate ineffectiveness at controlling bacteria, creates the single largest driving force for building the cloud. Food animal production takes place within a set of environments or ecosystems, starting with the farm and ending with us in our world. All of these systems are highly porous; they are in contact with each other through the movement of animals and humans, transport systems, air, and water. We enhance this movement by our failure to manage wastes from food animal production and by the globalization of our food supply.

The cloud contains complex packets of information, defenses that are triggered by one of the many antimicrobials in the mixtures added to feeds. For that reason, there are no differences between "expendable drugs" and "critical drugs"—another anthropocentric concept that conveys an anthropocentric perspective on the priorities of disease—as regulators as well as industry worldwide like to assert as justification to permit the continued use of such drugs as erythromycin and tetracycline, drugs whose utility in clinical medicine has already been reduced by overuse and widespread resistance. Even expendable drugs can act as a tag identifying and enabling information exchange by driving the ability of bacteria to access and transfer multivalent packets of information, which contain multiple genes that confer resistance to many drugs, including the ones we consider critical.

Agriculture is a major player in the expansion of the resistome and the shuttling of information among bacteria via the resistome. Our decision to feed food animals multidrug mixtures produces a continuous and widespread onslaught of antimicrobial stresses on microbiomes within animal guts and the environments, driving the closely linked emergence of multidrug resistance and also contributing to the persistence of resistance within the microbiome. Persistence is important. In the absence of antimicrobial pressure, the advantage of carrying a resistance gene is lost, and the population of susceptible organisms should be at least equally fit as the resistant ones. More careful experiments began to cast doubt on this finding, which is what I like about microbiology—it is often a ready transition from theory to observation. These experiments, by Bruce Levin from the University of Georgia, and others, reported that resistance did not always go away within bacterial populations after antimicrobial pressure was withdrawn. He hypothesized that a population of resistant organisms under the conditions of nothing to resist had two evolutionary "choices." They could revert to susceptibility and lose whatever the costs associated with resistance, or they could maintain resistance and acquire another genetic change that compensated for the cost of resistance. The choice is analogous to carrying a heavy rock up a hill. One could decide to drop the rock, or one could obtain a wheelbarrow and continue to hold onto the rock. Why choose to find a wheelbarrow? If one anticipated a need for the rock, then one would find a way to get around the burden of carrying it until it is needed by using a wheelbarrow or another aid. One would be inclined to do so if experience had indicated that the rock would be needed many times in the future. This is not a completely appropriate analogy, as all anthropomorphizing in biology is imperfect, but it is arguable that, in a sea of antimicrobials—which is what we have created—it is biologically prudent at the community level for bacteria to maintain an arsenal of genetic defenses by stockpiling something akin to what the US Department of Defense likes to call "multivalent missiles," in this case, multiple-resistance genes. Bacteria are highly prudent organisms, which is why they have survived.

In this chapter I have used science to challenge the limits on our current debate over continuing the use of antimicrobials in animal feeds. Thinking about only a small fraction of the microbiome and separating bacteria into friends and enemies (*commensals* and *pathogens*, respectively, in medical terminology) is inadequate. Building a regulatory response on the basis of preventing resistance to "critical" drugs while ignoring the drugs whose efficacy we have already destroyed is completely out of whack with how bacteria chatter.

Some recent proposals have generated the hope that we can reestablish our edge in the battle with bacteria by manipulating their communities on a large scale rather than trying to kill specific pathogens. Ideas about using probiotics, or good bacteria, to outcompete the bad bacteria are fashionable at the present time, but little data support either the theory or the practical implementation of these concepts. Setting up competitions among bacteria is not as easy as it sounds, as both "sides" have means to adapt to each other's presence by parceling out the resources of the environment. Also, we do not yet have a comprehensive understanding of the microbiome within our guts, for example, or of the factors that can determine death or survival of a given set of bacteria. We are not going to win this battle in such a simple fashion. We have no choice but to reexamine what we are doing with antimicrobials and to build prudent defenses to prevent leakage between the domains we want to target, such as human disease and the broader environment. We have to adopt the notion of a community for bacterial events, just as we have done in studies of social ecology and environmental health. We understand that community-level characteristics of resilience may be more important than individual characteristics in the survival and growth of both individuals and communities. We have to accept the fact that bacteria are expert communicators; therefore our priority must be to understand their communities and their methods of communication. We must go beyond defining the problem—as the US Centers for Disease Control and Prevention and the World Health Organization still do—in terms of "good" and "bad" bacteria or "critical" and "expendable" drugs, not even in terms of individual resistance genes. This is a problem of gene flow within communities and their clouds of information. We must recalculate our policies to identify sources and pathways to the microbiomes within the environments inside and outside our bodies and those of other animals.

Industrial food animal production has an inextricable relationship with the environment, despite all claims to the contrary in the definition of industrial food animal production as "confined" or as "separated from" the environment. We are all at risk, not just those of us who consume the products of industrially raised animals. Vegetarians and vegans, for example, consume plant products grown with animal manures. Moreover, decontaminating food products by radiation or other methods at the end-stage of processing animals into food will not contain the public health problems of this industry. This is a process that leaks all the way.

Achieving these goals is a daunting challenge, but we have faced it before in coming to grips with microbial risks. Over the past centuries, we had to give up our notions that miasmas, witches, cadavers, and evil winds caused infectious disease. When we accepted Louis Pasteur's evidence of germ theory, we took up the task of learning how to detect and control microorganisms rather than witches. Today, we have to accept the new science on bacterial societies and bacterial chatter to develop the right molecular tools for tracing outbreaks and anticipating the transmission of infectious diseases. And we must climb out of the depths of ignorance in which our policy making has been trapped.

8

COLLATERAL DAMAGE

Taking and Putting

Agriculture is unavoidably connected to the environment. Agriculture is unavoidably situated in the environment, even industrialized agriculture. Unlike some other human activities, like electronics manufacturing, which can be done in sealed operations such as in clean rooms for microchips, agriculture cannot be entirely sequestered from the broader ecosystem. Or, actually, ecosystems, if we expand this concept to human ecology, the relationship of humans to their environments, such as the built environments of houses, towns, and cities. In all these systems, agriculture takes from the environment and puts materials into the environment that cause collateral damage. The scale of agriculture—and its industrial production of catfish, poultry, swine, and salmon—is now so large that it indents a new, artificial, and visible patchwork on the landscape as well as an invisible footprint on the environment.

Is this a vision of ecological hell, or do we need to look more closely? As with everything in agriculture, it depends upon the glasses we are wearing. Clearly, the environmental footprint of industrial food production is large and it can impact ecosystems and regions, as in the case of the midwestern United States and the San Joaquin and Imperial Valleys of California. But looked at in another way, density, which is one of the attributes of industrial production, greatly reduces the amount of land needed for raising animals as compared to raising animals that are fed by foraging. Some argue that the use of land displaced by intensive food animal production structures includes the large amounts of land needed to produce the crops to feed large numbers of animals with processed feeds. But the evidence suggests otherwise. From 1990 to 2005, land use for crop production fell in Canada and the United States, and, globally, increases in land used for crops has lagged behind increases in crop production as well as in population, leading to the claim that agriculture is among the industries that have "dematerialized" in terms of their requirements for physical inputs and their environmental footprint. But this is a limited form of dematerialization—occurring in one dimension only—one that does not include the increased burdens on animals and humans.

If we move to lower-density methods of food animal production, there is likely to be an unavoidable trade-off between output and use of natural resources. It is not really fair to claim that one agroecological farm has a "lighter footprint" than one industrial farm; the real question is whether the size of their footprints differs at the same level of production; that is, how many agroecologically managed acres would be necessary to produce the same amount of animal products for human consumption? The case has been made that to achieve similar levels of production of crops and animals using alternative methods would require considerably greater resources of land—to say nothing of human labor—as compared to the industrial model.

Alternative methods have not yet made a compelling case for meeting the same consumer demands in an economically sustainable manner. In weighing these methods against the industrial model, it is appropriate to examine whether they can accomplish this large goal in a more ecologically sustainable manner. Even if we assume that these methods can produce enough food to meet national demands, at current levels of productivity, traditional methods of food production—both crops and animals—would require a great deal more land and considerably more human labor to yield enough to feed consumers at anything above a small population scale. It would not be possible to provide meat-based protein to the average US city within the local system much prized by proponents of alternative agriculture. Reducing meat consumption is another thing altogether.

But the lack of restraints on the density and location of intensive crop and livestock production tips this argument on its head. The impacts of intensity and density can be seen at the regional and international scale, as typified by the Chesapeake Bay region, an ecosystem heavily impacted by broiler poultry production in Delmarva that has created a large dead zone in which the water is depleted of oxygen to the extent that the normal ecosystem of plants and animals cannot survive. Like climate change eating away at the glaciers, the impact of industrialized agriculture is undeniably visible in the estuaries and bays that receive the accumulated inputs of these operations in a large watershed. Similar impacts exist in the Pamlico Sound of North Carolina, impacted by swine production in its watershed, and in the estuarine outflow of the Pearl River in Guangzhou, China, which similarly sees the impacts of swine and poultry production.

TAKING

Industrial food animal production is not just about animals. To satisfy our appetites for meat, the enormous appetites of billions of chickens and millions of swine require the production of enormous amounts of feed crops and water. These appetites have their own collateral impacts on the environment. Accompanying them are major increases in the basic feedstocks of animal feeds—corn and soybeans—which, in turn, have exerted demands for land and water as well as the ancillary inputs of synthetic fertilizers and pesticides. How this happened, and with what consequences, is one of the main focuses of this chapter, with the story of how industrial agriculture "tamed" the Amazon rain forest for human use.

THE AMAZON: THE SOYBEAN FRONTIER

"We were wrong," concluded Susanna Hecht, a longtime researcher and advocate for the preservation of Amazonia. In 1993, like other keen observers and participants in the struggle to save the Amazon, Hecht assumed that a principal driver of deforestation was the "hamburger connection," that is, clearing land to produce beef. Until recently, Hecht and others had worked to call attention to the government policies in Brazil and Bolivia that encouraged migration into Amazonia, supported the building of roads that sliced up ecosystems, and largely ignored uncontrolled resource extractions, particularly of gold and timber. But the main cause of deforestation in the Amazon was none of these. Something in itself much smaller but much more devastating succeeded where these big events did not: soybeans. The Amazon, according to the USDA, was to be the "final soybean frontier," not just for Brazil but for world agricultural production. This was a prescient call in 2004 and went largely unnoticed by those of us who were unaware of the three decades of investment by the Brazilian government in agricultural research. By 2010, Brazil had become the world's leading producer of soybeans and the major supplier to the growing Asian market.

The word "soy" is not even mentioned in Hecht's landmark 2010 book *The Fate of the Forest*. It was a fatal oversight, as she later noted. Because no one thought about soybeans, the proposals and recommendations developed by ecologists, activists, and others to preserve the Amazon were powerless to stop the march of the soybean frontier. Particularly vulnerable was the long-standing claim by many Northern Hemisphere ecologists and ecological economists that a true valuation of the Amazon forests would support their preservation. But they made a mistake. They only compared the economic value of the forest and its services in terms of the value of clearing land for the purpose of smallholder livestock and crop production. From an economic perspective, this analysis supported forest preservation because of the relatively inefficient and low yield of this type of agriculture. It was possible to argue that the worth of a standing forest for such "products" as natural pharmaceuticals and carbon sequestration would greatly exceed the worth of expanding multiple smallholdings of peasant agriculture. But it was the wrong comparison.

What happened?

Brazil had started programs in the 1970s to become a world player in intensive agricultural production of livestock, poultry, and crops as a matter of national economic policy. To support this activity, the Brazilian Ministry of Agriculture supported research to develop a new strain of soybeans with traits enabling production in Amazonia and the Sertão, the vast and arid region of limited arability. And not just Brazil: similar activities supported a similar agricultural transition and expansion in Bolivia in the early 2000s, where soy and corn began to supplant the traditional sustenance crops for indigenous communities and local markets. Just as in Delmarva in the 1950s, market gardens of tomatoes and beans for local consumption are falling to the profitability of soy production, an example of the interacting ecosystems of nature and human society.

The economic value of soy production far outweighs the valuations placed on the forest, even in the most optimistic analysis. Moreover, instead of displacing the local population, farmworkers in soy production earn real wages, rather than just subsistence food, and with these wages their socioeconomic standing exceeds the livelihoods they were able to achieve in the preindustrial days of smallholder agriculture and resource extraction from the forest. With such economic benefits, the community base in support of preserving the Amazon eroded. As a result, the predictions for continued settlement and expansion of agriculture are for more.

I saw this for myself over the course of twenty years of field research on small-scale gold mining in the watershed of the Tapajós River in the Brazilian Amazon states of Pará and Mato Grosso. On my last field trip, in 2006, the jungle had vanished from the lower Tapajós, and a huge loading dock for soybean shipments had been built by Cargill Inc., at the port town of Santarém, where the Tapajós meets the Amazon. I did not recognize the landscape as the plane landed. When I walked down the steps from the small Embraer plane, I felt further disorientation. The air had lost its limpid humidity. The smells were different. All was dry, and all was cleared. It was no longer the gold mining town that I had studied over those two decades, and the transformation did not occur because of the sporadic attempts to relocate poor rural populations to Amazonia or the even more sporadic attempts at improving transportation links among the small settlements of the regions. Soybeans triumphed over all. With soybeans came a stability that had eluded the small riverside communities of *caboclos*, the Brazilian term for the admixture of European, African, and indigenous ancestry. With soybeans came a much better life, from the perspective of their residents. Now there was a branch of the Federal University of Pará in Santarém, new primary and secondary schools, large stores selling fresh meats and vegetables, a library, two movie theaters, and housing constructed of bricks and cinderblock in the center. The flimsier structures made of salvaged wood and metal were in the periphery of new settlements, similar to many cities in Brazil. Inside many buildings there was air conditioning. There were families walking the new streets. The church was freshly painted. And the residents welcomed these changes.

There were very few small family plots of subsistence crops to supplement wild fruits and fish. Some eighty years earlier, the industrialization of agriculture in the United States drove a similar shift in crop farming to meet the corn and soybean diets of pigs and chicken in specific regions of the United States. Traditional market gardens have been displaced by soy and corn production, crops that are grown with considerable chemical inputs for fertilizers and pest management, certainly as compared to grazing lands in traditional agronomy.

PUTTING

The physical extent of land use is only one measure of an ecological footprint. In the case of agriculture, shrinking the physical space occupied by animal and food animal production may actually increase the weight of its environmental footprint. Intensity matters extremely because the health of ecosystems is determined at a small scale, expressed by the concept of *carrying capacity*, or the characteristics of a river or forest or soil system to absorb and utilize inputs without sustaining damage. In regions with intense and dense food animal production, the microbial systems of soils have been damaged, and the habitability of surface waters for much aquatic life has been reduced. Reducing these inputs to a manageable level at some other point along a landscape does not prevent or remediate damage at this place. It therefore matters if there are 600 million chickens within a small area of a small state (such as Maryland), as compared to the same number of chickens spread throughout a larger region (such as the state of Goiás in Brazil). The challenges resulting from high density at a local scale are inherent to the industrial model, as concentration is one of the economically and organizationally advantageous attributes of industrial agriculture. As a result, as the USDA maps show, the shrinking space occupied by industrial swine and poultry production may matter more for the environment than the overall increases in numbers. Concentration is what pollution is all about; the reverse of the old adage in environmental engineering, that dilution is the solution to pollution. Take animal waste, billions of pounds of it produced every year by pigs and chickens in the United States. Animal waste is a source of important nutrients for plant production, and, like a well-managed compost heap, it can be highly valuable for raising crops. But the key to the proper use of animal waste is good management, which includes composting and ensuring the appropriate rate and amount of application to the land. The industry will argue the former but ignore the latter.

The vastness and concentration of food animal production makes the option of using animal waste from billions of chickens and millions of hogs unfeasible in much of the United States where these animals are produced. Moreover, given the concentration of chicken production in a small region of the United States, transporting animal wastes to other regions would be prohibitively expensive. In my state of Maryland, for example, where we raise some 600 million chickens that produce about 2 billion pounds of waste each year, "land farming" all that waste would far exceed all the arable land available in the state. A ton of chicken waste contains 60 lbs. of nitrogen and 60 lbs. of phosphate, which is why it is a valuable resource for growing corn and soybeans. Even though some claim that it is impossible to overapply chicken waste to cropland, ecologists would disagree.

Ecologically, overloading soils with waste-borne nutrients results in overloading surface waters with these nutrients. With rains and runoff, as much as 50 percent of the applied nutrients are lost before they can be absorbed into soils. This results in enriching surface waters, which is a major contributor to the degradation of these systems. In many regions, food animal production is the major source of adverse impacts on the health of surface waters and coastal waters. The EPA estimated in 2007 that intensive food animal production was associated with 35,000 miles of ecologically damaged rivers in the twenty-two states with appreciable numbers of these operations. The impacts can be chronic, impairing the habitability of waterways for aquatic life and their utility for human recreation, or acute, resulting in massive fish kills and harmful algal blooms.

This is where my story started, and my focus on poultry waste in the environment began with the 1999 outbreak of *Pfiesteria* (the microorganism held responsible for those fish kills and algae blooms). But in addition to nutrient loadings, these operations release pathogens, antimicrobial drugs, and animal hormones into surface and groundwater sources. Land quality is also reduced by phosphorus overloading in animal wastes. And air emissions from animals held in confinement and from waste holdings (such as swine lagoons) are sources of noxious irritation as well as methane, a greenhouse gas, and nitrogen compounds.

Intensity creates some of the ecological problems in agriculture, but it can also point the way to solutions. There are economies, even ecological economies, of scale in which efficiency can beat the performance and lower the costs of disaggregated systems of production. Inputs, such as energy and water, can be reduced and outputs can be more effectively managed, although few of these inputs are currently acknowledged. On this point, critics of industrialized agriculture are right that our implementation and toleration of the process of industrializing agriculture rest on a failure to close the ecological circle in terms of including its high externalized costs to environment, health, and society. These critics argue compellingly for inclusion of both unvalued and undervalued costs, including impacts on health (and concomitant burdens on healthcare systems) from foodborne and zoonotic diseases, workplace health concerns, environmental impacts on terrestrial and aquatic ecosystems such as ecological services and reductions in biodiversity, animal welfare, soil erosion and loss of arability, wasteful uses of water, greenhouse gas emissions, and reliance on fossil fuels for energy. All of these debts to nature constitute a "vast series of implicit subsidies to cheap industrial food" as well as a failure to manage these externalities as if they mattered. Some in the alternative methods movement do themselves no good to argue for exemptions from regulation (as in resistance to the new food safety laws in the United States). They may be seeking "equal justice under law" given the benign neglect of the USDA, FDA, EPA, and Occupational Safety and Health Administration (OSHA) in regulating industrial agriculture, but the right answer is equal enforcement, not equal exemption.

HUMAN ECOLOGY

The transformation of agriculture into industry has also impacted human ecology, particularly in rural communities. This is not in itself new; as noted earlier, rural communities have been in continuous flux throughout post-Paleolithic history, but it is a significant threnody in the complaints about industrialization of agriculture as well as of other human works and days since the earliest steps in technology.

It is indisputable that the traditional social structure of rural communities has been altered over the past seventy years, mostly for worse. But this is only the most recent chapter in a long social and economic history of farming in America, following a sudden, sharp shock to the system delivered by industrialization starting in the early 1920s. Farming by smallholders or independent entrepreneurs is valued because it sustains a local focus for rural communities, whereas sharecropping and contract agriculture insert physical and socioeconomic distance between producers and communities. In a way, we have reverted to an earlier social arrangement of agriculture, similar to the hegemony of absentee landowners in premodern society (and in late modernizing countries such as Portugal and Russia) and in societies subject to foreign domination by colonial powers. Those arrangements were almost exclusively to the economic benefit of landowners, in line with the distribution of other forms of power.

But not all farmers in preindustrial times were self-employed entrepreneurs. Salaried workers have always augmented the efforts of owner-operators and their families in agriculture. Prior to wage labor, forced labor was imposed by peonage or slavery or by economic means of indenture and land rents. The latter has vestigial traces still evident in some of the first colonies in North America, such as Maryland, where it is possible to own a house but to have to rent the land on which it was built. Centuries of a tradition—a harsh one—have created two opposing forces, a drive for emigration that has powered movement of peoples from the country to towns and cities since the Neolithic Age and, at the same time, for others, robust and meaningful ties to rural life and agriculture. The folk traditions of Ireland exemplify this tradition: the desperation of the rural poor tied to absentee landowners and the movement off the land to cities and other countries contrasted with the deep emotional life of some of these communities such as the Blasket Islands. One does not obliterate the other, but often the memory obliterates the reality of what has been left and lost. Returning children of the émigrés often experience these tangled feelings, from the great-grandchildren of the Irish famine to those of the southern Italians who emigrated after being forced off their land by local despots. Now the condition of farm ownership today in the United States is more often one of rental or lease, replacing family ownership.

Industrialization has imposed a rough bargain between farmers and capitalists. The new sharecropping regime shifts much of the risks of independent farming to corporate enterprises (by guaranteeing payments for the product), but it removes the traditional autonomy of independent farmers and their direct engagement in the marketplace. This new arrangement has been a driver in the loss of economic focus for rural communities, and in many countries, rural villages and towns are disappearing. But it would be wrong to ascribe the full momentum for these trends solely to industrial agriculture. Many social and economic drivers have been at work. In some places, the pressure for alternative land use increased, driving up the value of farmland, for example, converting it to housing developments in exurban regions. Contests for resources other than land have also impacted preservation of farmland, such as the competing needs of city and country for water. These contests are usually won by cities because of their greater political and economic power, as in Southern California, where the diversion of water to support cities as well as agriculture appears to be about to end in disaster for both. The role of politics in land use is exemplified in one of the few modern instances in which farming outweighed city interests: the increased value of rural land for producing corn for energy production in the United States.

In other places, such as in China and Brazil, damming rivers for energy has diminished rural lands. Civil strife in regions like central Africa and Southeast Asia has driven agriculturists from land. Droughts in central Asia as well as Sub-Saharan Africa have reduced arability. In other times, these pressures were opposed by agricultural interests and by civil society mindful of the importance of food production. With fewer persons employed in farming, the voice of agriculture is less politically powerful in many countries.

For all these reasons, farms in the United States and other affluent countries where the industrial model is supreme are being abandoned or bought by city dwellers as second homes or boutique enterprises producing highly priced and valued traditional commodities, such as goat cheese and heirloom vegetables, as in Vermont and the mid-Hudson region of New York. Rural areas in the United States have experienced population losses, higher poverty rates, wage disparities, and continuing impacts of the fiscal crisis of 2008, years after metropolitan areas have recovered. Poverty and underemployment in these regions helped influence the growth of industrial food animal production. The map of rural poverty in the United States coincides with that of the Broiler Belt in the Southeast, as noted by Steve Wing and evident in USDA maps. The small towns that were the center of rural life are being abandoned, and the list of farms and town dwellings on the realty market has grown exponentially. The website www.landandfarm.com, one of the largest databases of these properties in the United States, listed over ten million acres of country property on the market in mid-2014. The USDA likewise has thousands of farms listed on its property website. Farm purchases are now made mostly by persons not related to the owner, signifying a break in family ownership and, until the 2008 economic crash, often not for farming but for land development for commercial or residential use. Much of the farmland remaining in agricultural production is supported by off-farm employment, crop insurance programs, subsidies, and direct payments, indicating the problems in economic sustainability. Greater profits come from developing the land, and, not surprisingly, farm real estate values are heavily influenced by proximity to urban centers (within ten miles, according to the USDA, is the magic circle that makes farmland attractive for suburban development). Also not surprisingly, farm owners selling in the suburban regions of the richest US states (California and the Mid-Atlantic states) benefited the most. I count my grandfather among these beneficiaries, having sold his farm to the state of Massachusetts in the 1950s for the first ring road (now I-495) going through Marlborough, as well as my great-uncle, who sold his land in New Hampshire for recreational development at Lake Sunapee, and, more recently, my brother, who sold part of his land in Sonoma County for development (and vineyards). All of these values crashed in 2008, illustrating the fragility of growing housing developments, which, along with recent investments in biofuels, has driven some increase in the price of rural land in the United States. But the recent uptick in rural land value has not been associated with increased employment or wages for farmers and agricultural workers, as this shift in product use was accomplished at the expense of use in animal feeds.

Industrialized food animal production, including the end-stages of slaughter and processing, has additionally impacted rural communities through changes in the workforce on the farm and in the plants. The farms are now largely contract operations, increasingly owned by nonresident operators who, having contracted with the producers, in turn hire contract labor to manage their growing houses. Fewer workers are required to accomplish the same level of production, and these operations are not often connected to the other types of agriculture that a traditional farm would support— raising other animals for food and growing vegetable gardens for family or local consumption. Moreover, the profits made by contractors are relatively low and insufficient to support a robust local economy. The profits made by integrators, it goes without saying, do not stay in the locality of the farms.

Poultry and swine slaughter and processing plants are similar dead weights on local economies because of their low wages and high turnover of the workforce. There are also fewer of these operations as the industry has consolidated and operations have become more efficient. There are currently only fifty poultry processing plants operating in the United States, down from 360 in 1960. But production levels are substantially higher, such that the only real growth in the workforce in food animal production is in animal slaughter and processing. The nature of this workforce has stirred considerable local reaction. Workers in these industries are overwhelmingly drawn from poor minority populations, not only from the local population but also actively recruited by industry from other sectors.

These include recent emigrants to the United States, including refugees, undocumented immigrants, and the poor. Bill Satterfield, director of the Delmarva Poultry Industry Association, frankly acknowledged industry preference to hire Latinos on the basis that their "willingness to work and enthusiasm is better than others," omitting the important words "for less pay." In some regions, such as Delmarva, this politically unempowered and economically needy group includes prisoners on work-release programs. These demographic aspects have aggravated relations between long-standing residents and newcomers, with accusations of increased crime, burdens on social services, and other social problems.

Property values are a flashpoint in the social controversies over intensive agricultural operations. Most studies have found that property values decline in relation to the density and distance from a farm—up to an 88 percent decrease within a tenth of a mile from a large grow-out operation. Added to economic losses is the loss of quality of life associated with these operations. Slaughterhouses and farms or grow-out operations (particularly for swine) are called "LULUs"—locally unwanted land uses—by many communities because of their impacts on quality of life, such as odors from animal houses and waste holdings, discarded carcasses, and almost constant movement of heavy trucks. The impacts on property values and desirability offset, in economic terms, any community gains in terms of income for persons employed in the industry as a whole, and the low wages paid to workers also tend to decrease the overall socioeconomic values of a region.

These conflicts have revealed another loss of autonomy for rural communities. In addition to losing the class of traditional entrepreneurial farmers, these towns have lost any control over the siting of large production farms. In the absence of federal or state attention to public concerns, local jurisdictions have had to oppose the industry over locations of expanded growing operations and plants. The town of Carlisle, Pennsylvania, offers an example. The home of Dickinson College, Carlisle, is a pretty college town and destination for serious trout anglers. But it has found itself surrounded by the expanding swine industry in south central Pennsylvania. The town hired a lawyer to argue its case for regulating the development of new swine farms but was quickly slapped down by the state, which asserted its overriding authority when it came to agriculture. In North Carolina, from 2010 to 2012, a fight over the construction of a large poultry processing plant pitted two local interests against each other, Nash County and its interests in economic development and jobs against the more affluent Wilson County and its interests in protecting its environmental resources and tourism. Although Wilson did not prevail in its litigation against construction on the grounds of watershed protection, the poultry company withdrew in the context of continued public reaction. But the company has now opened its facilities with little opposition in Bladen County, a poorer county with much less political influence.

Many European Union countries have enacted regulations to limit density of intensive agricultural operations, often on the basis of ensuring that wastes can be managed successfully. The World Bank and the FAO have developed guidelines and methods to control density. No such steps have been implemented in the United States, where industrialized agriculture is still immunized from public criticism through the persistence of idealized, false images as well as legislation that prohibits public access to and criticism of industrial operations, including farms and slaughterhouses. In several states, the industry has acted to influence legislatures to pass laws protecting farms from political intrusions (all fifty states have so-called right-to-farm laws), limiting investigations of farming and food-processing practices (six states have so-called ag-gag laws) and even criminalizing statements about farming and food that are considered defamatory (thirteen states have so-called food libel laws), all of which have chilling effects on opposing industrialized agriculture from farm to fork. In Iowa, the state legislature passed a law explicitly prohibiting the state health department from any regulation of an agricultural operation. Not all states are complicit. In Washington, a federal court upheld a judgment holding a large pig producer liable for water pollution in 2015. In some states, legal victories have been followed by state laws prohibiting similar lawsuits, which act to discourage local responses to expansions in farms and processing plants.

Taken together, the demands of industrialized agriculture on resources and ecosystem services, its environmental inputs, and its stresses on local communities are among its most serious failings. Many of these problems could be reduced substantially, but the incentives for change are currently nonexistent. Regulation is minimal or nonexistent. The EPA's attempt to regulate water pollution from this industry in 2003 was overruled in the courts. Things are not much better at the state level; most of the major producing states—such as Delaware, Georgia, Arkansas, and the Carolinas—do not have agencies or offices dealing with the environmental impacts of intensive agriculture. To move forward, all of this must change. And, contrary to most opinion, evidence indicates that the costs of change will be the lowest for the largest operations.

9

HAVE A CUP OF COFFEE AND PRAY

A reviewer of one of our papers asked, "How big a town is Tar Heel anyway?" Tar Heel, North Carolina, is a spot on the map on Route 84, which runs southeast toward the Carolina coast. It is not on the map because of its population; according to the US Census, there may be a hundred people living there. I know the whereabouts of at least seven of them: the Hispanics running the luncheonette and general store, two women with an unpredictable flea market across the road from the union hall, and the inhabitants of two houses that appear to be occupied on the road between the flea market and the plant. Tar Heel is on my map because it is the location of the largest hog slaughter and processing plant in the world, through which over 32,000 hogs enter alive and leave as pork every day. It is where we conducted the first epidemiological study in the Unites States on pathogen exposures among workers in animal slaughter and processing.

Taking a lunch break in early afternoon during a pause in the flow of workers coming in for our health study, we were sitting in the back office of the union hall, sipping sweet Carolina iced tea and wiping juice off our fingers from *tacos al pastor* brought over from the luncheonette. It was a hot day, and the flies buzzed intrusively around the door every time it was opened. From years of research in the Amazon as well as most of a lifetime in Baltimore, I have learned how to be still in hot climates, such that the sweat does not even start to bead on my face. It is a stillness that lies between torpor and "riling up the humidity," as one of the chicken catchers in Maryland called moving around too much in August. I knew that all of us from Johns Hopkins University were thinking about the last worker to come into the union hall, an animated young woman named Olga. Olga was proud of her status as a shop steward and of her ability to earn enough money to provide for her young son and to purchase a pretty new SUV. Being a shop steward signifies leadership as a representative among workers in a unionized plant like Tar Heel. As part of our study, Olga answered our open-ended question about job satisfaction by pointing out that work at the plant was well paid in comparison to the available jobs at fast-food outlets and Wal-Mart, and that the union had won good family benefits. Being a shop steward, she knew a great deal about what brings people to work at the plant and the conditions that drive many of them to quit.

This day, she came straight from work on the cut / processing line, where freshly killed and quartered hog carcasses enter the highly ordered process of reduction into chops and roasts and the other products that we recognize on our plates. When I first met Olga during our preparative meetings prior to starting the study, she came dressed in her "street clothes," with fancy boots and obvious attention to her hair and makeup. This morning she was a transformed sight, wearing a blue quilted jumpsuit (the cut / processing room is kept at refrigeration temperature, so the workers usually have to buy their own work clothes—the company supplies only gloves, arm covers, and light aprons and in some cases workers have to pay for replacements of torn or punctured items). She was covered with animal blood, bits of flesh and guts, and, not to put too fine a word on it, shit. "You asked what it's like in there," she said matter-of-factly as she spread a newspaper carefully to protect the chair she was about to sit in. "This is it."

Seeing Olga and her coverall, which had started the day clean and neatly pressed but was now stained with blood and chunks of flesh, lit a mental spark that set me to thinking about the connections between worker and food safety in much more graphic terms than I had ever done before. Her clothing and boots were undeniable witness to what actually goes on in slaughter and processing plants and the connection between safety for workers and our food. These are the hands that touch our food, in the phrase of Father Jim Lewis, the Episcopal priest who cofounded the Delmarva Poultry Justice Alliance in Pocomoke City.

This chapter aims at the heart, to invoke Upton Sinclair's rueful comment about the silence that met publication of *The Jungle*. His searing story of the terrible conditions of worker health and safety in slaughter and processing plants was met with silence in a stark contrast to the public outcry over food safety that generated the rapid passage of legislation by the US Congress in 1905. That silence has continued to this day. Here I seek to connect heart and stomach, to end the almost total absence from current food debates of any consideration of the continuity between worker safety and food safety. Much attention is paid to immigrant workers and the callousness induced in workers toward the animals they handle by the conditions of work, but little to the experience of the workers themselves.

Say "food safety," and everyone has an opinion, a story to tell, a fear to discuss. Say "worker safety," and there's not much reaction from the public and not even from officials at OSHA. The silence is pretty complete. One of my goals in this book is to reestablish the connections between the safety of food and the health and safety of workers in food animal production. Both begin on the farm and eventually affect everyone whose hands touch our food and everyone who consumes these food products. When I started putting these parts back together in this book, like Bluebeard's wife, I opened a door that revealed the unacceptably dreadful state of the US system of food safety and worker protection. This chapter discusses worker safety; the next chapter examines the failed promise of food safety. But the two are inextricably entwined. What is unsafe for the worker is unsafe for our food, and what is unsafe for food is unsafe for the workers. It does not matter where we start; we can ignore this circle, as most of government regulation does, but we cannot escape.

As with all of agriculture, it is a matter of what we see. Most of us never see Olga, and we never think about her. One of the many blind spots in our vision of agriculture, she represents the continuity that unites our food with food animal production and those who work in it. We continue to envisage the life of animals and the work of raising them through a lens that shows us pictures that no longer exist, that have not existed for decades. In addition to our unwillingness to look at the life of animals, we even more rarely imagine the work and the workers whose job is to kill live animals and make them into our food. There are many organizations dedicated to animal welfare and to improving the conditions for animals in the industrial system; I have met with some of them to discuss this aspect of the food system. But, apart from a few labor unions, much less attention is paid to the workers. Even the United Farm Workers of America union mostly focuses on field workers, who harvest fruits and crops.

This is not new. For millennia, animal slaughter has been shrouded from our sight by powerful traditions and social taboos enshrined in religions and culture. Those whose work is slaughtering animals have often been drawn from outcast or very low-caste groups, such as the Burakumin in Japan and the Dalits and other butchering castes in India and Pakistan. Other traditions have endowed animal slaughter with special religious significance, as in Judaism and Islam. These extremes—degradation and exaltation— serve the same purpose: to draw a distance between flesh consumers and the unmentionable but necessary work of killing sentient life to make our food. Even at present, some of the practices of ritual slaughter with their own special peculiarities—such as kosher and halal methods—are exempted from most of the minimal requirements of humane killing and butchering. Those few laws related to these rituals that were passed recently in European countries to protect the welfare of animals at slaughter (to dignify death as it were) have, in most cases, been overturned on the grounds of religious freedom. History and custom separate us from the taking of animals' lives for our food, which continues in efforts by the industry to prevent the public gaze from penetrating its operations through state legislation that criminalizes criticism of agricultural practices, particularly those related to food animal production.

There is acknowledgment that food production starts off dangerously. Work on farms in the United States is notoriously dangerous. It is the only workplace where children are allowed to work, where few—if any—safety devices are required on large machinery with cutting edges, where grain silos and fertilizer storage tanks go uninspected and frequently explode, and where wastes go unregulated. But when we think about food safety at the level of the farm, we have a strange vision that blames the workers.

When workers in food animal production are noticed, they often get blamed for spreading disease. I have been told by the industry and by people attending my talks that the workers bring germs into the fields or the animal houses or the processing plants. When academics look at this issue, some of them write papers with titles like "Outbreaks Where Food Workers Have Been Implicated in the Spread of Foodborne Disease." In a publication by the University of Florida Institute of Food and Agricultural Sciences, the chapter on preventing food contamination includes a section on how food gets contaminated at the farm or during processing. The first six "causes" are all related to workers: sick employees, employees with unwashed hands or contaminated gloves, employees with open cuts and scrapes, employees who touch their faces and mouths with their hands, employees who improperly dispose of hygienic items (such as toilet paper and paper towels), and employees who do not wash their hands after using the restroom. The report goes on: "There is a direct correlation between poor personal hygiene and foodborne illness. For this reason, it is critical that produce handlers and other farm or packinghouse personnel understand and practice good basic hygiene habits, including proper handwashing, on a regular basis. The FDA has cited poor personal hygiene and improper handwashing as the third most important cause of foodborne illness. This report also cited that 93% of outbreaks related to food handlers involved sick workers. Problems associated with these outbreaks included poor personal hygiene, poor handwashing, open sores, improper glove use, and eating while on the job."

Even advocates for farmworkers seem to buy into this reverse causality (the assumption that workers cause contamination, rather than that work contaminates workers). In 2012, Melanie Forti, the coordinator of Health and Safety Programs for the Association for Farmworker Opportunity Programs, wrote, "If farmworkers wash their hands frequently, with potable water, soap, and paper towels, contamination could often be prevented." Once again, this assumes that the farmworkers are bringing the pathogens to the field or animal house, and not the other way around.

What is particularly galling about these extraordinary statements is the complete lack of recognition that, for most of these workers at the farm and in processing plants, there are few and often no facilities and very little time allocated for personal hygiene, especially handwashing, as I have repeatedly been informed by the workers themselves. Farther down the line from "farm to fork," as the USDA likes to say, there is little knowledge and less thought for the workers, and hence little pressure for change outside of organized labor. Episodically, when there is an event like the 1999 fatal fire in a North Carolina poultry processing plant, we are forced to acknowledge the horrific conditions in these plants, where, as in North Carolina, the doors are locked from the outside. Few of us know about the daily assaults on health and safety as well as dignity in workplaces where there are often no handwashing stations on the work floor, the bathrooms are off limits except for two visits per day, and (as at Tar Heel) the showers are turned off or (at Columbia Farms poultry plant, where we have also conducted a study of worker exposure to pathogens) nonexistent. I learned of a female worker in a South Carolina poultry plant who was denied permission to leave the cut floor for the toilet in order to deal with the unexpectedly early onset of her period; the supervisor later said, "Every woman knows when her period is going to happen, so she should have been prepared."

Where is OSHA? Largely absent. It is easier to blame the victim, to assert and assume that the workers are part of the problem, rather than acknowledging that this workforce faces some of the highest risks to health and safety in American industry. The goal of achieving the lowest costs of production is an unchallenged business practice, such that industry has successfully resisted intrusions related to environmental protection, animal welfare and health or even sanitation for workers solely in the name of profit without contesting the allegations of injury and illness.

Upton Sinclair tried to make the connection between work and food in *The Jungle*. This remarkable book forced the public to open its eyes and arguably had as immediate an effect on US public policy as did *Uncle Tom's Cabin* and *Silent Spring*. But public shock and sensation were quickly focused solely on food, and the workers—who were at the center of Sinclair's book—were just as quickly forgotten in the rush to protect the food supply. No matter that men fell into the machinery and were killed in the meatpacking plants of Chicago; the public concern was over the presence of rats and filth in the sausage. As Sinclair said, "I aimed at the public's heart and by accident hit its stomach."

Even after a place at the policy table for occupational safety and health was established in 1971 with the creation of OSHA, not much has changed. OSHA has never been responsive to its real constituency of American workers; rather, it has been almost completely captured by the industry. Killing a worker is literally cheaper by the dozen—the pathetic limit on OSHA fines for a death at work is only $20,000 for the first incident and $10,000 per death thereafter.

In the time since President Theodore Roosevelt and Congress reacted to Upton Sinclair's *The Jungle*, most of us have assumed that real improvements have been made, at least in food safety. As with much that I have subsequently learned from growers and workers, that would be wrong; this is the heart of this chapter and this book. Both food and worker safety are intertwined and, as we let the latter slip, the former has fallen.

The centerpiece of the current system that is claimed to be in place to protect our food and the workers who make our food is the Hazard Assessment and Critical Control Point (HACCP). Those who work in the industry have another definition for this ungainly acronym: Have a Cup of Coffee and Pray. HACCP is supposed to connect food safety and the health and safety of workers in food animal production. Although, on paper, OSHA has oversight over the end-stages of food production (that is, workers in slaughter and processing), its authority has always been limited in protecting workers in agriculture. At the end-stages of slaughter and processing, it is the USDA and the FDA that promulgate regulations and guidance that affect workers as much as our food. In this way, laws and institutions disrupt the continuities that should connect workers and food and impede our understanding of the common origins of problems in food safety and thereby our ability to develop preventive interventions for both problems.

This is not something that happened overnight. For decades, the industry and Congress have worked together to keep any regulation of agriculture within the industry-friendly purview of the USDA. Attempts by state and federal occupational health and safety agencies have been repeatedly and successfully beaten back. At one point, when OSHA announced an intention to issue regulations directed at the epidemic of ergonomic injury inevitable in jobs requiring repetitive motions for hours at a time—nowhere more prevalent than in food animal slaughter and processing—Congress defunded the agency until it came to its senses.

It took more than ten years for me to be forced to confront what really goes on in this opaque set of guidelines with the unpronounceable acronym. Figuring out HACCP is probably the most disturbing revelation that I have experienced in all my work on this topic. The inadequacy of HACCP is not a product of negligence or inactivity, but rather what can only be described as systematic and willful failure, built into the system from the start. When I came to understand the depth of the flaws in this system, I had to check my own realization by consulting colleagues in public health, infectious disease, labor, and the food industry. Only the latter were unsurprised. After my food industry expert confirmed everything I suspected, I said, "I guess this means our food safety system is a crock." He replied, "Just about." My labor expert only said, "You think?"

My enlightenment began with a proposal from the USDA to remove any limits on line speeds in poultry plants. The issue of line speed most clearly demonstrates the connections between worker and food safety. It is at the heart of the efficiency claimed for mass production, and it forces workers into compliance with the industrial model of lowering costs by speeding up the work, just as the integrators lowered costs of raising chickens by speeding up their growth through crowding them into houses and tinkering with their feeds. The line was a necessary introduction into slaughterhouse design and operations to handle the greatly increased volume of animal production. Thereafter, it generated its own feedback loop. Increased capacity for processing drove increased production of animals, which, in turn, necessitated further increases in processing capacity. With the integration of the industry by Arthur Perdue and others, the numbers of processing plants in the United States decreased markedly after 1950, while the volume of production at each new plant continued to increase.

This new proposal from the USDA became law in 2014. While it steps back from the original proposal that would have taken all controls off line speed in processing plants, at the same time it completely removes the requirement for on-site inspection by USDA personnel. This proposal was supported by the USDA with the astounding assertion that these changes would actually improve food safety with no adverse effects on worker safety. This hardly makes sense, and no information has ever been provided by the agency to support this claim. Even OSHA was alarmed, and in 2014 John Howard of the National Institute for Occupational Safety and Health at CDC sent a blistering letter to the USDA on their breezy and unfounded claims.

Prior to this, when I thought about HACCP, I assumed it concerned food safety alone and that its limits were mostly the usual problems of bureaucratic implementation: insufficient resources, increasing burden of work, resistance from the industry. As I unpacked the history of HACCP, I discovered that it has largely been destroyed from within by self-inflicted wounds, abetted by cynicism and exhaustion. The problems of HACCP are problems for the world. Like chickenization, the HACCP concept has spread globally. International organizations as well as regulatory agencies and industries throughout the world now rely upon HACCP, and its false promises have been propagated to worker and food safety programs worldwide. HACCP forms the backbone of resolving disputes in international trade in food, through its endorsement by the World Trade Organization in reference to the UN food safety system, Codex Alimentarius, known as CODEX.

The concept of hazard assessment and critical control point actions has its origins as a method to improve safety in engineering projects. It all sounds so technical and objective, free from bias and shielded from manipulation by its gleaming clarity. The core principle of HACCP is the critical control point, which means that all we have to do is identify these points or steps in a process and control them to eliminate all problems in the entire process. In engineering, this concept has real attraction, like building a bridge or designing the exit ramp of a highway. But applied to human workplaces, this is not so simple.

HACCP is a form of Taylorism, where controlling the process by requiring workers to comply with its demands takes precedence over learning from and empowering workers to accomplish what is humanely possible. Frederick Winslow Taylor was the man with the stopwatch on the production line, measuring the pace of work and production. In the last years of the nineteenth century, Taylor advocated the concept of *scientific management*, which was based on defining the methods of achieving efficiency in industrial production. His work was well timed to the dawning of the age of mass production, in which lowering costs through increasing worker efficiency was to be achieved above all. His dedication to the stopwatch was gently satirized in the movie *Cheaper by the Dozen*, about the marriage of two time and motion efficiency experts in the 1920s who tried to raise their twelve children with the same principles. The humor was lost on workers, who bore the adverse impacts of an increasingly dehumanized workplace and increased risks of injury from work that involved tending unstoppable production lines designed in accordance with Taylorism.

The dominance of Taylorism in industrial food animal production is dystopically appropriate. Just as chickens have had to be selectively bred to survive and flourish in intensive confinement and to survive on a finely ground artificial feed, workers have had to be shaped to endure the new factories and to bend their work to speed of the production line. Charlie Chaplin's "everyman" tightening bolts on the assembly line in *Modern Times* and Fritz Lang's clocklike workers in *Metropolis* depicted the change in work as a loss of the autonomy of the holistic craft model, which valued the expertise of workers who understood the entirety of the production process, to the supposed efficiency of highly delimited job duties, which today remains the defined structure of work in meat and poultry processing.

The central efficiency in both industrial agriculture and car production was the assembly or production line through which the employer could effectively regulate workers by controlling the speed of the line. By eliminating the variability, individuality, and emotionality of both workers and animals, it has freed corporations from the need to understand either workers or animals. Taylorism subordinates workers to machines, just as the methods of industrial food animal production subordinate animals to the conditions of their "job" to grow as quickly and as efficiently as possible. The match between Taylor's philosophy and food animal production was, as far as is known, as coincidental as it was for the early automotive industry. While Taylorism has faded into other modes of "scientific" management, it still influences theorists and practitioners of industrial management. US car manufacturers have adopted from Japan a more team-based approach to production, with a return to elements of craft production including more individual autonomy for workers, but animal slaughter and processing remains almost pure in its adherence to the original concept of Taylorism in both the animal confinement houses and processing plants.

This history has direct bearing on the failure of HACCP and of the new government agencies like OSHA to deliver so little in the way of reliability in either product or worker safety. This failure created space for the industry to erode what had existed in practice before 1971. Simply put, by eliminating the humanity of workers in food production and reducing food safety to an engineering principle, neither food safety nor worker safety was protected.

HACCP has a long history in government. It was adopted in the 1960s by the National Aeronautics and Space Administration (NASA) and was first applied to producing food for astronauts when the Pillsbury Company adopted the approach to ensure safe, high-quality food to astronauts in the US space program. Thereafter, its influence over food expanded. The FDA first adopted these early HACCP principles in 1969 and then more formally in 1997, about the same time that the USDA adopted HACCP by regulation.

From the beginning, it was rapidly accepted by both industry and government as the "standard of care." Why would industry and government unite in adopting requirements that could be expected to impose costs on both? This is the first hint that it is a rather peculiar form of regulation. Regulations generally take three forms: *legal mandates*, some of which are known as "command and control," in which numerical standards are stated (such as air pollution regulations that stipulate allowable concentrations of particles in air or lead in water), so that noncompliance is fairly obvious; *process* or *performance mandates*, in which specific processes or control technologies are required; and *voluntary compliance rules*, which usually mean very little. This mixture is characteristic of many regulatory agencies in the United States, notably the EPA. At the EPA, this mixture has often worked well as in the Toxics Release Inventory, under which industries voluntarily disclose their pollutant discharges because of the transparency of EPA processes and the unique opportunities in EPA statutes for public challenge and initiation of enforcement. At the FDA, an older agency founded before the reforms of the 1970s in administrative procedures of government, these operating conditions are absent, and the voluntary pathway is notoriously ineffective, as evident in industry programs related to nutrition and cigarette advertising as well as industry reporting on tests of drugs and adverse drug reactions in consumers. None of these programs by themselves achieved their goals: reductions in cigarette smoking followed on successful litigation that has funded state-level prevention, and the failures of industry reports on drug tests continue. The US system of postmarket reporting on adverse drug events is inadequate to support responsive oversight.

As a regulatory principle, HACCP is considered to be a mixture of the second and third type of regulation. I would call it something else, perhaps "aspirational," as it is critically lacking in the backstop of regulation and a strong enforcement culture, largely owing to a lack of clearly defined objectives against which industry performance can be determined. Or, as the workers say, "Have a cup of coffee and pray."

Even before the gutting of HACCP in the 1980s, it was never a well-designed policy concept. It was never based upon the goal of achieving a health-based level of safety or acceptable risk, including risks of consumer exposure to foodborne pathogens. This is in stark contrast to Clean Air Act regulations, which rest on clearly articulated and thereby enforceable standards for concentrations of toxic substances in air. Without this insurance, HACCP just sits there like Jabba the Hutt, without any challenge to its overall effectiveness; its success is evaluated within its own performance without any reference to external standards that have any relationship to food or worker safety.

This type of government policy making has been called "self-policing in the shadow of the regulator" rather than in the presence of enforceable regulation. Removing the regulatory instrument of legal enforcement and significant penalties tends to reduce incentives for appropriate behavior by the industry. This suggests that wise policy would adopt Teddy Roosevelt's axiom of speaking softly but carrying a big stick (appropriate, as he drove passage and implementation of the first food safety laws in 1906 after reading *The Jungle*).

The "new HACCP" of 1997 is a key example of this erosion of regulatory responsibility. The official histories of HACCP omit its sorry decline over the 1990s. Carol Tucker Foreman, who has had an influential career in all sectors of food policy—including government, consulting for tobacco and biotechnology industries producing GMOs (genetically modified organisms), as well as leadership in public interest groups—was among the first to make policy proposals to privatize enforcement of food safety regulation. Coming from Foreman, with her background in the consumer movement, these proposals were influential, and by 1999 the USDA had lost most of its authority to enter, inspect, and enforce basic fundamentals of sanitation and good practice.

HACCP is now a paper tiger. The responsibility—and opportunity—for ensuring HACCP is placed almost entirely on the industry, with government engagement focused on ensuring compliance through inspection of industry records and programs rather than any actual data. This approach is referred to as *management-based regulation* and is praised by policy analysts for shifting the burden of policy implementation from government and for permitting some degree of flexibility by the industry in meeting policy goals. But workers call it something else: checking up on paperwork rather than workers. Have a cup of coffee and pray.

Not surprisingly, the industry is enthusiastic about diminishing the presence of regulatory agencies to a shadow, and often refers to it as the welcome evolution of a relationship between regulators and regulated that is "beyond compliance." But beyond compliance can signify either less or more. It is not hard to see why industry likes this approach, and government officials express enthusiasm for the reduced burdens of inspection and constant litigation. The public is largely unaware how far this "evolution" has progressed or how little evidence exists to support the notion that a philosophy of "beyond compliance" actually improves performance in terms of worker health or food safety.

In an era of diminished government, the continued self-immolation of health and safety agencies will be hard to reverse. As of 2015, the safety net of HACCP had been almost completely shredded. In its final rule about line speeds and food inspection in poultry production, the USDA maintained an upper limit for line speed but acquiesced to industry demands to delegate responsibility for food safety management entirely to industry, and relegated government inspectors to inspecting industry records.

OSHA has been of little help to workers in industrial food animal production plants. OSHA has been limited from intervening too much in regulating work in agriculture, as in the case of ergonomic injury, and it has been extraordinarily passive in dealing with growing operations, which are clearly not farms and thus should never have received the traditional immunity of agriculture to regulation related to occupational health and safety. Moreover, in most of the states with large workforces in food animal slaughter and processing, OSHA has delegated responsibility for inspection and enforcement to state programs, which have largely distinguished themselves by inactivity and, in at least two cases, catastrophic failure. These are also the states of the Broiler Belt, among the most hostile to unionization and with high levels of surplus unskilled labor, particularly in the rural areas where farms and processing plants are, not surprisingly, located.

OSHA's problems began with its enabling legislation that promised a "safe workplace for all" within the constraints of "feasibility." Congress, stimulated by industry lobbying, has been vigilant in ensuring respect for the constraints rather than the obligations. OSHA has been caught between two definitions of feasibility, in its words, "a cost-benefit interpretation of economically feasible controls and a broader, plain-meaning definition of the term as 'capable of being done.'" In practice, feasibility at OSHA now mostly means protecting profitability, as distinct from a similar limitation on the EPA's power to regulate air pollution, where feasibility means what most people think it means, that there is a technical possibility of fixing the problem. OSHA's proposal for occupational standards for musculoskeletal injury, which would have been of considerable importance for protecting processing plant workers from injury and disability, was repealed by a hostile Congress in 2001 in response to heavy lobbying by industry litigation. This extraordinary intrusion ended one of OSHA's most ambitious attempts to protect worker health and safety, and sent a strong warning against similar activism by the agency on behalf of worker health. Since then, OSHA has fallen back on issuing nonbinding guidelines for workers in meatpacking and poultry processing. In OSHA's own words, these are "advisory in nature and informational in content"; that is, they do not include legal means of enforcement. Finally, OSHA, like every other occupational health and safety agency in the world, does not define diseases caused by pathogen exposures in slaughter and processing plant work as being work related. This means that no records are kept on infections among these workers, and they are not eligible for workers' compensation for any infections.

I had Olga in mind when I undertook my first real look at HACCP following the USDA's 2012 announcement that they were considering removing all oversight on line speeds within poultry slaughter and processing plants, as well as reducing the required frequency of USDA inspection of industry records on compliance with HACCP or any data collected from industry tests of pathogen contamination of poultry products.

Why is the USDA in charge of regulating line speed instead of OSHA, the agency with responsibility for occupational safety and health? This "regulatory perversion" (to quote Marc Linder, one of the fiercest critics of the industry and OSHA) has placed control of one of the most critical safety aspects of the work in food animal processing in the hands of the agency charged with enhancing productivity of US agriculture—acting "in collusion with the firms it is supposed to be regulating." Strong words, but no stronger than what is revealed by an examination of HACCP as it is today.

I kept Olga in my mind as I read the USDA proposals to deregulate line speed were justified not only as a means of saving money for the industry but also as a means of improving food safety. As far as the workers were concerned, the USDA used a Taylorist assessment of work on the production line with the express purpose of maximizing labor efficiencies by processing the maximum number of chickens possible, reducing time and thereby costs of production, with no attention to the burden on the workers' safety. This same goal had already been applied by the USDA and the FDA to food safety inspection, to achieve the maximum throughput—to use the industrial term of turning chickens into consumer products—rather than the maximum degree of food safety, an example of how food and worker safety have been sacrificed to the same production goals.

In its regulatory proposals, the USDA asserted that increased line speeds, allowable under deregulation, would have no impact on food safety. This assertion was based on the absence of evidence rather than evidence of absence, with the USDA blatantly asserting the negative: that there were no data to indicate that increased line speeds would adversely affect food safety. A later analysis by the Government Accountability Office (GAO)—an invaluable fact-checker on such claims—determined that their so-called research on the matter was too poorly conducted to yield any usable data.

The agency was silent on the subject of worker safety, but, as they could have said, to quote Fletcher's callous aristocrat in *The Jew of Malta*, "that was in another country. And, besides, the wench is dead." Worker and food safety died in this regulation because of the heavy hand of the USDA, which has claimed primary authority to regulate line speeds over interventions by OSHA for the past thirty years. OSHA's silence is not unexpected. Other attempts by OSHA to regulate line speeds have also been struck down by interference from other branches of government, in this case the judiciary, which has disallowed these regulations on the grounds that the agency neither has any data on the relationship between line speed and injury, nor can it set a maximum line speed that would *not* produce injuries. This is typical of the evasions by industry to evade regulation not only at OSHA but also at the EPA. First, you don't have the data, and second, you can't determine a safe level of working conditions or of exposure. Because line speed is considered confidential business information, neither the USDA nor OSHA has any real data. Industries do not disclose line speeds in their plants, and workers don't have the time to measure line speed on the work floor.

I began to think, could the line speed issue link worker and food safety? Thinking about this question opened the door to HACCP because the USDA claimed that data on any association between line speed and food safety came from HACCP monitoring. So I decided to look at HACCP more closely. I had already developed some skepticism about HACCP from the USDA's statements about food safety, always supported by references to HACCP information supplied by the industry and not disclosed to the public, to the effect that major strides had been made in reducing contamination of poultry by pathogens such as *Salmonella* and *Campylobacter* (two of the major causes of infectious gastrointestinal disease in the United States and thus important to public health, according to CDC). In 2010, the USDA and the industry jointly claimed that through application of HACCP the average prevalence of *Campylobacter* on poultry products had been lowered to less than 30 percent of products tested. Falling into line, the National Institute for Occupational Safety and Health, the research arm of OSHA and part of CDC, relied on these data to conclude that risks of worker exposures to these pathogens were also well controlled. But this did not make sense: at the same time as this pronouncement came out of the USDA, we were finding that between 60 and 90 percent of consumer poultry products were contaminated with *Campylobacter* when we conducted studies of consumer products, buying chicken breasts and thighs in packages sealed at processing plants by major producers such as Tyson and Perdue. And my lab wasn't the only one; shortly after our publication, FDA scientists reported similar findings, but without the freedom to name names. In 2010, Consumers Union reported that 62 percent of chickens tested by an outside laboratory were contaminated by *Campylobacter*. This is a global problem for the industry. In May 2015, a government survey in the United Kingdom reported that over 70 percent of poultry products purchased at retail stores were contaminated by this same pathogen. "Perhaps the producers are adding *Campylobacter* back in just before sealing the packages," I remarked to one colleague at the USDA. She was not amused. Neither was I. *Something* was wrong.

How could rates of pathogen contamination be so low in the processing plants and so much higher in consumer products that are packaged and sealed at the plants? What could this mean for those in the middle, the workers? This contradiction prompted me to rethink my assumptions that the failures of HACCP relate to limitations in implementation rather than a root and branch failure of the whole HACCP edifice. Many government and academic analysts (for example, the GAO study of HACCP in 2001) make the same assumptions, and that is the argument of Michael Taylor, currently director of food safety at the FDA, who called for "rationalizing regulatory oversight" without basic changes to the regulation. I could find only one dissenter. William Sperber, an industry scientist, has called HACCP the "black hole" of food safety regulation because of its nontransparency. According to Sperber, HACCP essentially swallows up whatever illumination exists on food safety in poultry and meat processing. But his solution focused not on changing what happens in the processing plant, but on adding more points of control before and after slaughter and processing, such as interventions at the farm level and improvements in commercial and consumer food storage and preparation. Like the USDA these days, he does not look inside the processing plant.

This is not a task for the faint at heart. No one wants to look for very long into processing plants, as Sinclair found out. Understandably, few people—even the most enthusiastic carnivores—really want to know what goes on between the farm and the fork. Donna Leon, the eminent mystery writer of Venice, has been possibly the boldest to do so since Upton Sinclair. In her mystery story "Beastly Things," a veterinarian is killed by venal slaughterhouse operators to prevent him from revealing the sick animals that are made into food as well as the terrible cruelties imposed on animals and humans alike in the name of increasing profits. But, like her hero, Inspector Brunetti, to solve the murder of the conscientious veterinarian, we have to go inside the processing plant in order to understand the locus of the problem with HACCP, just as we have to go inside a poultry house to understand what a misnomer "confined" is.

Failing firsthand experience, we have to talk to the workers, those who know the plants inside and out. Again, doing so is astoundingly rare. Once inside, literally or through the eyes of a worker avatar, we cannot avoid recognizing the basic failure and falsehood of HACCP to protect either food or worker safety. For example, who knows better than the cleanup and maintenance crew how often the decontamination water baths are changed or cleaned? Once a day, as we learned by talking with the cleanup crews.

To understand the fundamental flaw in HACCP, it is critical to understand that HACCP is not based on overall performance or evaluation of the end product, but on the engineering concept of a throughput system with no feedbacks, such that by accurately identifying the last critical point, the hazard can be completely controlled. Having been trained in engineering, I understand this mode of thinking. But this concept holds only if the last Critical Control Point (CCP) has been correctly identified, such that nothing else can go wrong after that point and the same problems do not recur after action at that CCP. This might be achievable in some systems, such as launching rockets or running trains on tracks in which the same problem, such as a bent track, that once fixed does not recur farther down the track. This does not hold for food animal slaughter and processing. Slaughter and processing, the things we don't really like to think about, are messy systems in which the same problems recur throughout the process. It is impossible to achieve perfect performance at any control point, in this case complete decontamination of chicken carcasses at an upstream control point. This is important for the problem of pathogens in the food supply because we are trying to eliminate the presence of microbes. Unlike chemical hazards, bacteria and other microbes are living organisms that can grow and grow back to the same levels or greater than before "control," just so long as a few remain unkilled. This is the hallmark of a recurring system. So if we do not control bacteria completely at the ultimate CCP, it makes no difference how much effort we place on that point. It is sort of like handwashing *before* using the toilet and assuming that this will protect you against subsequent contact with bacteria.

The HACCP system is illustrated in figure 9.1, and it deserves careful examination. As shown, the last CCP is set at the first stage after live hanging of the birds, slaughter, evisceration, and washing, the stage at which the freshly killed carcasses are disinfected. The two CCPs at the end are related to integrity of packaging, not to testing the poultry in the packages. Under the HACCP definition, this first CCP is the point at which an intervention will control the problem of microbial contamination once and for all. Just to be absolutely clear, the last intervention prescribed by HACCP is to disinfect animal carcasses and to test or observe the carcass after disinfection at the so-called rehang step, when the carcasses are removed from chilling and attached to the production line *before* they are moved into the subsequent stages of cutting. This assumes—and this is critical—that the carcasses have been so effectively disinfected at the last CCP that there will be no subsequent stage where pathogen contamination can reappear through regrowth. Everything depends upon these assumptions, because there is no second point of control for or testing of chicken products. It goes almost without saying that there is no testing of worker exposure at any point. It is important to observe that almost all of the workers in these plants do their work *after* the last CCP.

But as is so often the case, the assumptions of engineering are not always obeyed by biology, rather like the failure of people to behave like the
"rational economic beings" of classical economics. Although the CCPs in
figure 9.1 are important points for infection control, they are not the only
points, because actions at this point are never 100 percent effective at eradicating all pathogens on animal carcasses. Both the industry and the USDA
make this admission. A successful HACCP program, like the claims of the
industry to control *Campylobacter* in chicken, reportedly reduces the prevalence of pathogens (in terms of numbers of carcasses testing positive for
key pathogens) from 80 or 90 percent to at best 25 or 30 percent. This may
sound impressive, but it means in practice that every third or fourth carcass
will continue to carry bacteria, including pathogens such as *Campylobacter*,
Salmonella, and *Staphylococcus*. The USDA's own studies on different types of
control actions at the CCP, such as disinfection baths and chilling, admit as
much: in no case was complete pathogen control achieved. So what happens
next? The carcasses are rehung on a line and are moved on to the cut floor,
where the workers carry out their jobs on the line. One carcass out of three
or four will still be contaminated by bacteria. As the cutting process begins,
both contaminated and uncontaminated carcasses move on conveyor belts
to the workers, who carry out the subsequent steps of skinning, deboning,
trimming, and cutting. The conveyor belts, knives, instruments, and other
surfaces and equipment are quickly contaminated by those 30 percent of carcasses still carrying pathogens. This is what was found in a study conducted
by the French food safety authority that concluded that cross-contamination
increases over the workday at poultry slaughter plants due to contaminated
equipment, work surfaces, chillers, and process water.

In US plants, some wash-down may occur during the work shifts,
mainly to clean floors, but a full cleanup of all equipment as well as the
rooms usually takes place only once a day, usually after the first cycle of
animals enters the plant and ends up as packaged food. After that, the second cycle arrives. Then the first cycle of the next day starts. There is no
cleanup in between these two cycles. "I think I want to eat the food from the
second cycle," one of my students said after we learned about this from the
cleanup crew at a poultry processing plant in South Carolina. But nobody
pays attention or knows about the lack of proper cleanup. The USDA has
no idea what the pathogen exposure risks are for the workers on the cut

line or on the pathogen loads of finished products after they leave the cut floor for packaging.

There is also the problem of the decontamination and control steps themselves. The dipping tanks and the chillers are only cleaned once a day as well. Think of an elementary school, where children coming in from the playground are required to wash their hands in a common sink before going to eat lunch. Imagine that sink full of water, with no change during the school day. Now think of one hundred children dipping their hands in this sink. Suppose one out of three or four has dirty hands while the rest are clean. After twelve children have washed their hands, at least three or four have put dirty hands into the water. By the time the next child washes her hands, they will likely be dirtier than before she "washed" them. Moreover, unlike a sink that can be drained and refilled with clean water during the day, there is no cleanup of the tanks and processing work line during the work shifts.

We have evidence that this is happening from a comprehensive review of interventions to reduce *Salmonella* in processing plants that included studies of intervention trials conducted in the United States and other countries. Over time, the disinfection bath accumulates pathogens and other contaminants such that, relatively quickly, carcasses that go into the bath are just as or more contaminated coming out of the bath as they were prior to being put in it. As the workday goes on and the effectiveness of carcass cleaning at the ultimate CCP starts to fail, lines and equipment and surfaces become increasingly contaminated.

We do not actually have to go inside the processing plant to know that this contamination is occurring. Simple logic applied to the schematic of HACCP would tell you what is wrong, but somehow none of this logic has penetrated the HACCP community of industry and regulators.

Figure 9.1 comes from the agricultural extension service at the University of Georgia, which is supported (like all agricultural extension services) by the USDA. It is a schematic representation of the HACCP process in poultry slaughter and processing. Note that the last CCP inside the plant occurs *after* slaughter, gutting, and so-called disinfection, and *before* the carcass moves onto the cut floor. In fact, this figure is quite misleading, with multiple boxes denoting all the events between the arrival of live birds and the washing of the gutted carcass, which gives the impression that this is where most of the activity in a slaughter and processing plant takes place. This is

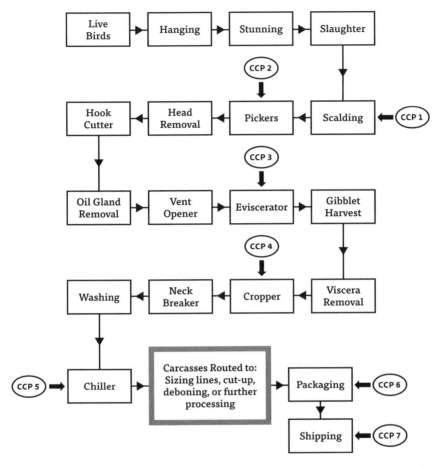

Figure 9.1. Schematic diagram of the role of HACCP in poultry slaughter and processing. The overall diagram is a misleading representation of the relative importance of various jobs within this industry, and the proportion of workers in each job category, by identifying the early stages in detail (from live hanging to carcass chilling) and lumping all the subsequent jobs involving carcass processing into a single box labeled "Carcasses routed to." Notably, these jobs and workers are after the last CCP and not covered by HACCP methods of assessing pathogen control. (From Northcutt and Russell 2010)

inaccurate. The majority of the work, the majority of the workers, and the key events in food processing in terms of both food and worker safety, all take place in one box at the bottom, where carcasses are routed. It is easily overlooked.

What this means is that it is *by design* that there is no effective control of foodborne pathogens or worker exposures in any system that is managed in this way by HACCP. What may have been clean ends up unclean. And the end is what counts. As a result, it is not surprising that up to 95 percent of poultry products purchased in stores end up testing positive for *Campylobacter* after they have been cut and packaged at the plant, despite the USDA's claims, on the basis of HACCP data, that *Campylobacter* contamination has been reduced to 30 percent or less at the CCP. This is why the USDA data based on HACCP do not relate to the USDA data on consumer product contamination.

There is only one thing that counts for us as consumers: the safety of food products when we buy and consume them. There is only one place to ensure that meat and poultry products are safe: at the end of the processing line. The USDA collects its data on food safety—or, more accurately, on carcass safety—at the beginning, at the early stages of the business of turning animals into food. Under the new HACCP management policy, this is the last place any information—let alone testing for pathogens—is required to be collected on pathogens in processing prior to food entering the marketplace and reaching our plates.

For this reason, the USDA can claim that line speed has nothing to do with food safety, because in the way they define food safety, it does not. The USDA defines the safety of food before it reaches the line, and as a result the USDA has no information on what is happening either to workers on the line or to the food as it moves through the line. All of us need to have a cup of coffee and pray.

The USDA has claimed repeatedly that there is no proven association between line speed and worker health and safety. They have no data on this topic, and, in fact, studies by the poultry industry refute this assertion. Because there are no data on actual line speeds, it is difficult to cite evidence one way or another. But absence of evidence is not evidence of absence, as I learned from a wise colleague at the Environmental Defense Fund. The speed of the line dictates the work. Workers now perform a set function as each carcass moves past; this is a strategy to create "interdependence" among workers (in contradistinction to the craft principle, in which the worker knows and performs all aspects of production of an object). The deboning line in poultry consists of hundreds of workers, each making one cut in sequence rather than trimming one carcass. These conditions, set to high speeds, generate a considerable burden of chronic and acute injury and disability. It is generally agreed that these injuries as well as chronic musculoskeletal diseases and disorders are underreported by the poultry slaughter and processing industry (as reviewed by a 1990 study sponsored by the National Broiler Council). Direct research on worker health supports the hazards of high line speeds: a study of poultry processing workers in North Carolina, conducted in 2009–10, reported that medically diagnosed carpal tunnel syndrome was 2.5 percent more likely than in other manual workers. Moreover, workers on the line were the most likely to be diagnosed with carpal tunnel syndrome as compared to workers in other jobs in these poultry plants. A 2007 study of women employed in poultry processing in North Carolina observed a 2.4-fold increase in rates of musculoskeletal disorders compared to women employed in other industries. These findings are similar to a larger study conducted in Sweden, in which workers involved in deboning processes had the highest rates of diagnosed carpal tunnel syndrome. Line speed has been also associated with increased reports of stress-associated outcomes, such as dysmenorrhea in female workers. Surprisingly, there are much less data on injuries on the line.

In the absence of data, it seemed to me that the burden of proof that such a change would not increase these risks should be on the USDA and industry, not for OSHA or workers to demonstrate that removing controls on line speed could only increase health and safety risks. But data are even better than presumptions. By sheer good fortune, we got access to a data set while we were thinking about this issue. Similar to the good fortune to come across the Perdue study that refuted claims of the efficacy of antimicrobials for promoting growth, this time I owed a debt of gratitude to the George W. Bush administration. During this time, OSHA conducted a project on injuries and infections in some of the largest hog and poultry slaughter and processing plants. Importantly, the data for this study came from reports filed by the industry, just as the information we used in analyzing the benefits of antimicrobials in feeds came from industry.

OSHA collected the reports but did nothing to analyze them, fortunately including not throwing them away. The boxes of reports were made available to the United Food and Commercial Workers Union (UFCW), which represents most of the meatpacking workers and some poultry processing workers in the United States and Canada. Jackie Nowell, the UFCW director of health and safety, called me to ask whether one of my students at Hopkins might be available to do some data analysis. Fortunately, Dr. Emmanuel Kyeremateng-Amoah, a highly motivated young doctor from Nigeria, trained in occupational medicine, was interested in taking on the job. He started commuting from Baltimore to Washington to transcribe thousands of OSHA reports into a database he could analyze. No one had ever had such a wealth of information before, and probably no one will ever have such information again.

These data came from reports by the industry to OSHA, and, although unions had always suspected that industry was systematically underreporting injuries and illness, we reasoned that no one—least of all the industry—could accuse us of overcounting these events. The reason for suspicion of underreporting lies in the process that has to take place at each plant before a report is recorded for submission to OSHA. At the plant, when a worker is injured, she (and most poultry processing workers are women) must ask permission from the industry supervisor to leave the floor in order to report to the health office at the plant. The health office then makes the decision as to whether the worker's report should be recorded. (Is it serious? Is it work related?) This person (who, in my experience and that of the union, is often not a qualified medical provider, such as a nurse) is an employee of the company. After passing this point, the medical office report is then reviewed by the plant medical office (a corporate position) to decide whether it should be officially entered as a reportable event. Most researchers, including those hired by industry to analyze injury problems, agree that all of these steps in reporting are likely to result in much lower rates of reported injuries than the actual rates. Often the most difficult stage is for the worker to get permission to leave the floor; leaving the floor without permission constitutes a demerit that counts toward dismissal. One of the many alarming facts I learned from workers at a major poultry plant in South Carolina was that the health office was closed for over eight working hours; there was a lively discussion as to what happened under those conditions, which were allowable so long as ambulance service was available within an acceptable distance from the plant. Without exception, the workers we interviewed stated that they would never take the time to go to a hospital for treatment "unless my hand was cut off or something like that." Having sat in the emergency department of my employer, Johns Hopkins, for over six hours waiting to be examined for a knee injury, I can understand the reticence to go there.

With Emmanuel's help, we were able to assemble and analyze all the boxes of OSHA reports. We found that the injury rates reported by the eighteen hog and poultry slaughter / processing plants from 2004 to 2009 were the highest in the private sector industry workforce, which is what other researchers had concluded with smaller studies as well as the study of four poultry processing plants sponsored by the National Broiler Council about fifteen years earlier. Most cuts and lacerations happened in areas where sharp tools such as knives and saws were used to kill and cut up animals. Most of them occurred in the cut and deboning areas, work areas after the last check by HACCP.

This brings us back to the connection between food safety and worker safety. Workers are at greatest risk for lacerations in the areas where pathogen exposures are not only uncontrolled but also unmonitored. This is probably our most important finding in terms of worker health. In the OSHA data, there was a strong link between lacerations and infections in the industry reports. We were not surprised: *Staphylococcus aureus* and its drug-resistant form MRSA can cause infection when they gain entry across the skin through a cut or laceration. Staph and MRSA are known to be present in industrial food animal operations at the farm and the slaughterhouse; they are also known to be contaminants of our consumer food supply.

One important signal of the connection between contaminated carcasses and sharp objects was that infections were often reported to be associated with lacerations caused by contact with the product (which I found out meant animal bones). These findings echo a much older description of sepsis, including infections by *S. aureus*, among workers in meat and poultry processing. Upton Sinclair intuited the risks of hellish infections on the work floor in meat packing over a hundred years ago in describing the work in each area of the plant: "Each one of these industries was a separate little inferno . . . the workers in each of them had their own peculiar diseases . . . Let a man so much as scrape his finger pushing a truck, and he might have a sore that would put him out of the world."

So the connection between unsafe food and unsafe work is clear. Yet no occupational safety and health agency in the world defines pathogen exposure as a work-related risk in livestock or poultry processing and slaughter, so the door is shut on collecting data related to infection. The OSHA reports we were able to review were an aberration, with recent OSHA 300 forms failing to record infections. Without data, there is not much traction in advocating for change; without information, it is hard to make a case for change, just as hard as it was for OSHA to take control of line speeds in the name of preventing musculoskeletal injuries.

Why is worker health and safety in the hands of agencies devoted to supporting production? Why was the fundamental flaw in HACCP not noticed earlier, either by the designers of HACCP, the drafters of regulations, the practitioners, industry, unions, or the public? Why was the obvious evidence of widespread bacterial contamination of the food supply—from USDA and FDA studies all along—not understood as proof of the failure of HACCP? There is so much obvious and avoidable harm within industrial food animal production that the good news is that small changes may result in major improvements. The widespread failure to recognize what HACCP is and is not resembles the failure of experts to recognize that intensive food animal production is not a contained process in terms of avian flu prevention, or the failure of the EPA to recognize that nothing is accomplished following USDA guidance on animal waste management. Like these neglected pits of danger, it is long past time to stop denying that there is a problem with food and worker safety in processing plants, to invoke our inner Upton Sinclair and admit that little has happened since 1904.

What Upton Sinclair did not say, this book must: we are all consumers and we are all victims. What *The Jungle* did not say clearly enough to be undeniable is as follows. If you don't care about workers, you need to care about the safety of your food. As Father Jim Lewis said in his motto for the Delmarva Poultry Justice Alliance, "these hands touch our food." We cannot separate the hands of the worker, lacerated and stiffened, literally dripping bacteria, from the state of our food. Even if the workers are wearing gloves, which the industry is wont to show in their rare photographs of workers on the line (not verified by the workers as common practice), the gloves are not adequate in preventing cuts and punctures, and sometimes their use actually increases injuries because of poor design for fine motor tasks. Gloves also quickly become modes of transfer from carcass to carcass, pork chop to pork chop.

We cannot separate food safety from our concerns for decent and dignified conditions of work. Instead of pulling against each other as the USDA proposal states, reducing food and worker safety to increase industry profits, these concerns are one and the same. As we prepare food, we touch the uncooked food as well. A CDC study in February 2013 included frequent reports of gastrointestinal illness by poultry workers at a Virginia poultry plant and confirmation of *Campylobacter* infection in 36 percent of fifty workers contacting live chickens. Most of these workers, incidentally, were prisoners on work-release programs. This situation is a perfect storm for triggering an outbreak. Place workers in an unprotected workplace so that they are contaminated or infected with zoonotic pathogens, then send them back, with their work clothing, without medical surveillance, to crowded living conditions to spread disease.

At the end of that hot day in Tar Heel, the quiet was broken by noise from the back of the building, where the union offices were located. Chairs scraped, a door slammed, and then shouts were heard from the local president, who had worked on the kill floor before his selection for office. "God *damn* it," he shouted, moving loudly to the reception area where we were sitting. "*Goddammit!*" he shouted in my face. He waved the copy of *The Jungle* I had given to him at our last meeting. "When was this book written?"

"In 1904," I answered quietly.

"Nineteen oh four? Nineteen fucking oh four?" He shouted back.

We all nodded. He shouted again, "Nothing has changed! Nothing has changed at all!" He wrenched at the book as if to tear it in half. "It's all the same." He sat down hard on a table, slapping *The Jungle* on it. "I never knew that this was all written down in 1904! You have to write another book."

10

FOOD SAFETY

Redesigning Products or Consumers?

Now, at last, we can go to the kitchen. Most books on our food system skip the workers and move directly to the kitchen. But this chapter on food safety deliberately follows the chapter on worker safety to emphasize the logical order that connects the workplace of slaughter and processing with the workplace of preparing our daily meals.

I am in my kitchen, cooking. I am pretty much an omnivore, yet I am more and more beset by moral and scientific qualms about eating meat, poultry, or fish. But this is not a cookbook or an evocation of food choices—like books by Michael Pollan, author of *The Omnivore's Dilemma*, or the great Julia Child, who together neatly bracket my attitudes toward cooking, including aspiration and caution—but rather this book is about how cooking has become a deadly serious mission to search and destroy. Or it should be. And if you are vegetarian or vegan, do not stop reading now. What you eat is unavoidably part of the same food system.

My kitchen looks very different from the first kitchen I ever had enough money to remodel. It had a lovely butcher-block countertop, something I had always wanted, and a sink big enough to defrost the turkey for Thanksgiving. I had a set of French hand-ground knives; I cleaned them carefully by wiping them with a soft cloth—no soap was allowed to touch their rustable blades.

That was a long time ago. Now I have two plastic cutting boards, not terribly attractive, but recommended for food safety. The French knives are no longer in use, replaced by much less attractive implements that can be washed with soap and hot water; they do not rust and they cannot be sharpened at home. The lamb for tonight's dinner was supposed to be defrosted in the refrigerator, but it is still rock hard because I misjudged how long it would take to thaw (it was purchased from the farm and slaughtered in a small operation where freezing was required). In the past, I would have put it in the kitchen sink in a bath of warm water, but today it must wait in the refrigerator or be defrosted in the microwave, which is too small for it. So I go back to the refrigerator and remove a fresh chicken. As I take it out, I notice that the package has leaked a few pinkish drops onto the bottom of the meat drawer. I put the chicken package into the sink and make a mental note to clean the drawer as soon as possible, although it is more likely that I, like many consumers, will forget in the press of preparing dinner. Turning the pages of the cookbook from lamb navarin to coq au vin, I open the chicken package and rinse the carcass in the sink with cold water, letting the water run freely to wash down the sink. The chicken goes on the large cutting board to be cut with the meat knife. The onions and garlic are on the small cutting board to be cut with the vegetable knife. I wash my hands before I pick up the vegetables to chop and then again after I put the chicken pieces into one bowl and before I put the vegetables in the other. Everything already used goes into the smaller sink, which is filled with hot, soapy water. As the chicken browns, I think about what to do with the semi-defrosted lamb; it cannot be refrozen and it cannot sit in the refrigerator for long after defrosting has started. I remember the pink droplets in the meat drawer and, armed with a sponge dipped in ammoniated water, I scrub the shelf; pulling out the drawer below, I see some drops there as well. Out comes the drawer and into the sink it goes. At the end of the meal, I will put the leftovers into a sealable container and then into the refrigerator as soon as I finish the dishes, possibly on the outside of the recommended time limit. I debate long and hard about that semi-defrosted lamb; I finally cut it up into pieces and cook it out of concern that my usual roast lamb with rosy meat might not be safe after its overlong thawing. I do not question myself about those droplets: Dr. Lance Price, when a student in my lab, once measured the numbers of bacteria in a droplet from a package of chicken thighs. You do not want to know what he found.

Dr. Meghan Davis, while a PhD student in my group, reported in a paper on her "search and destroy" mission to identify all the surfaces in the home where MRSA could be detected. A lot of these surfaces were in the kitchen, because food is an important source of human exposures to MRSA. Her paper was published in *The Lancet*, one of the world's most prestigious medical journals, and for it the editors provided an illustration on the cover depicting the kitchen as a planet invaded by foodborne pathogens resembling Dr. Seuss's oobleck. Unlike this illustration, however, we cannot actually see those pathogens. But they are there.

The situation of food safety in the United States is not good. In 2013, the FDA stated that there are an estimated 10 million cases of foodborne illness each year, affecting one in every six Americans, with 130,000 hospitalizations and 3,000 deaths. This hasn't changed much. And these are just the "known knowns," as Donald Rumsfeld famously once said. The real picture of foodborne illness is like the iceberg that hit the *Titanic*: most foodborne illness is unseen because it is unreported, and even for those that are reported, most causes are unknown. There is no dispute that the overall burden of foodborne disease in the United States is large and increasing. How large and how much it has increased is, like the available information on worker health and safety, limited by nonfunctional monitoring and reporting systems. Like injuries and infections in processing plants, we do not have much information on incidence and trends in food safety for the simplest reason: we do not collect it. We know that the industry has no reliable data on food safety, based on the false premise of HACCP. In addition to the failures of HACCP, there is another hole in the food safety net big enough to drive a convoy of tractor-trailers through. This is the failure to monitor what goes on in secondary processing, operations that buy raw meat from slaughterhouses for processing into retail products. Whatever safety net exists, which is pretty frayed, stops at the first stage. But much of the poultry and meat products we consume pass through these second-stage processors on their way to our tables, carried by those tractor-trailers often seen on highways. There is little or no inspection of these operations, and as meat and poultry move through secondary processing, as the packages or boxes are opened and the final product is repackaged, we lose the information trail that could connect the food we purchase with its point of origin. This information is critically important in tracking foodborne illness. In our study of pathogens in retail foods in Baltimore, we observed that none of the labels on food packages from these processors contained the required labeling information imposed on primary processors such as Tyson Foods, Smithfield Foods, or Perdue Farms. If anyone became ill from one of these products, it would be impossible to determine the likely source of the problem.

The government is in no better shape. Its response to outbreaks of foodborne illness is dysfunctional. Every outbreak is considered a new event with no connection to anything in the past. At every event, outbreak investigators roll out the same methods to initiate the search for cases of disease and then for causes. This process still governs response even when the same company is involved in repeated outbreaks, like Foster Farms poultry, which was responsible for two of the largest foodborne disease outbreaks that occurred in 2012 through 2014.

For drug-resistant pathogens in food, the situation is probably worse, despite the existence of a special interagency program called the National Antibiotic Resistance Monitoring System (NARMS). "National" is a false promise for this system, because monitoring for antimicrobial-resistant pathogens in food items is voluntary and only carried out by ten states that together cover about 15 percent of the US population (Connecticut, Georgia, Maryland, Minnesota, New Mexico, Oregon, Tennessee, and selected counties in California, Colorado, and New York). Surveillance of resistance in bacteria isolated from humans is also a voluntary program, and less than half of the states are currently participants. Even in many participating states (such as my state of Maryland, one of the major poultry producers in the country), only a few hospitals contribute information, mainly because most are not equipped to reliably isolate and identify bacteria in food or human samples. In its 2012 report on NARMS, the FDA claimed that its system had tested more than 56,000 clinical isolates from humans, 110,000 isolates from food-producing animals, and enteric bacteria isolated from over 40,000 retail meat samples. These numbers are considerably less impressive when it is revealed that they do not represent the total for one year, but rather the total over the past *fifteen years*. Animal surveillance is the responsibility of the USDA, and by digging into this report, at most 120 retail samples have been collected from each of the participating states every year. Considering that over 120 million hogs and 8 billion chickens are raised and slaughtered each year in the United States, and from each carcass multiple retail products are generated, this part of NARMS is also an inadequate program of surveillance. In its 2012 strategic plan for NARMS (released in 2015), the FDA admits that these efforts provide no real or timely information on the prevalence of food contamination and are clearly not national in scope.

Moreover, some dangerous and emerging foodborne pathogens—like MRSA and *Clostridium difficile*—are not reported at all, so we are largely in the dark as to the full range of identified pathogens in the food supply. The health effects are not limited to gastrointestinal (GI) problems, which are the most common health outcomes associated with foodborne exposures to pathogens. Some people may consider a stomachache or a limited bout of diarrhea to be of minor consequence, and many GI symptoms are treatable by over-the-counter medications. But some GI diseases can have serious consequences. One of these is the peripheral neuropathy that can follow on infections caused by the poultry-borne pathogen *Campylobacter jejuni*, or "campy," as it is known in microbiology labs. Campy infections increase the risk of contracting Guillain-Barré syndrome, one of the most severe diseases to follow bacterial infection, by over tenfold. The industry and government have both claimed that current methods of food safety monitoring have resulted in major decreases in transmission of campy by poultry through the hollow promise of HACCP, which does not actually test our food. As CDC notes more prudently, "reducing the incidence of foodborne infections will require commitment and action to implement measures known to reduce contamination of food and to develop new measures."

But let's get serious and consider a very serious infectious disease associated with foodborne pathogens: urinary tract infections (UTIs). UTIs are among the most common bacterial infections in the world, with 6–8 million cases a year in the United States and 130–175 million worldwide. In the United States, UTIs result in over one million office visits and 500,000 emergency room visits per year. The consequences of UTIs include kidney infections and bloodstream infections that can lead to death. Incidents of both are increasing in the United States, particularly in women and infants. UTIs were generally thought to be sporadic; that is, they seemed to occur unpredictably, in ways not clearly connected to each other or to any identifiable source of exposures. But since 2010, UTIs were recognized to occur in outbreaks, which are strong indicators that UTIs have common causes resulting in clusters of events within a specific area or time period. UTIs are caused by

E. coli, a group of bacteria that include many nonpathogenic strains but also some of the most dangerous pathogens in the food supply. The pathogenic strains, like the friendly commensals, are zoonotic—that is, they are resident in animals—and humans are exposed through the food supply. These pathogens provide some of the clearest evidence of the increased severity of infections by drug-resistant pathogens. Drug resistance in *E. coli* and other enteric bacteria delays the time to effective treatment by almost sixfold and increases the risks of death by almost twofold.

In 2013, a major outbreak of a highly pathogenic foodborne *E. coli* strain caused multiple illnesses and hospitalizations in the United States. The source was identified as the Rich Products Corporation, a company that has repeatedly made the FDA list of food recalls. Rich Products demonstrates how "too big to fail" plays out in the world of today's food industry. This one company had to recall 10 million pounds of its products, all produced at a single plant, between July 2011 and April 2013, including a substantial number of pizzas sold to schools for lunches. Also among the top ten, in 2011, National Beef Packing Company recalled over 60,000 pounds of ground beef because of *E. coli* contamination, and, in 2012, Trader Joe's recalled more than two tons of chicken salad because of *Listeria* contamination.

I could go on and on, but the reality is that, in the twenty-first century, food safety remains far from certain. Over the past hundred years there have been important improvements in food safety, mostly owing to improvements in transportation and storage. The introduction of refrigeration during transport as well as in our homes is widely considered to be one of the major advances in food safety, which among other things has contributed to reductions in gastrointestinal cancers in the United States. In contrast, industrializing food animal production has done very little to promote food safety. Arguably, industrialization has made it worse.

The industry and government alike proclaim that our food is safer than ever. This is often the trump card played by proponents of industrial food animal production in the debate over its impacts: *There may be some things you do not like about our methods, but our food is safer.* I used to believe them. The simple and brutal answer is, it is not.

Go back to the kitchen, this time with the eyes of the US government. The FDA website on food safety paints a scarily accurate picture of foodborne hazards for the consumer, with key points of danger identified, that resembles *The Lancet*'s illustration accompanying Meghan Davis's paper. Number one is washing your hands, number two is using two cutting boards to prevent transfer of bacteria from one product (such as meat) to another (such as a tomato), number three is cleaning the meat-cutting surface with hot water and soap, number four is ensuring thorough cooking, number five is reheating leftovers to a temperature sufficient to kill bacteria, number six is safe defrosting, number seven is maintaining low temperatures in your refrigerator, and number eight is putting leftovers into a refrigerator within two hours or less. In my kitchen, I try to act responsibly with regard to all these dangers.

Now go out to the backyard. The government food safety program (www.foodsafety.gov) has a terrifying video called "Recipes for Disaster: Bacteria BBQ." Public service announcements like this one force us to face the truth that our food is dangerous. There is no clearer admission of the lack of control in our present food system. But the message of the website is correct: we must protect ourselves and as consumers we should heed all of these warnings.

This is not a food safety policy that protects the public and improves food safety. This is a food safety policy that protects the industry and accepts unsafe food, shifting responsibility to the victim without attention to the origin of repeated exposures to the hazard. The government has opted for a role that does not ensure a safe food supply but rather tells us what to do because they are not taking effective actions to make our food safer.

The FDA has its websites, and the USDA requires that all packaged meat and poultry products carry labels on safe storage and preparation. Do these measures work? CDC and the FDA conducted a national survey on how well this information campaign works, which requires that consumers actually follow their recommendations. They discovered (as most of us would confess) that the answer is, not very well and not very consistently. Maybe people are not paying attention to messages on packaging or on the Internet. In the government survey, less than half of the people in the study recalled seeing information on safe food handling, preparation, and storage. That may be because labels are not always there, as we found in a study of urban retail food stores.

Labeling can be used as a complement for more definitive forms of government intervention, and it has a role in communicating risks of regulated products that have both benefits and risks, such as drugs and pesticides. But labeling as a substitute for stronger actions and enforceable requirements related to food safety does not reduce actual exposures so long as the entire burden is placed on consumers, with no change in practice required by producers or government. Moreover, labeling about safe food preparation and storage practices will not influence the industry to reduce hazards, as argued by those who assume that markets will work effectively to reduce risk in response to consumer pressures over food safety. But information is essential to empowering us to choose. In the absence of government action and producer responsibility, our only power as consumers is the power of choice. But in order to make choices based on safety, we need information on *comparative food safety*, so that we can use the power of our pocketbooks to preferentially buy food products on the basis of their safety. In a recent example, because it was available, the public was able to respond to information about Alar (daminozide), a ripening agent used in apple production, by making a clear choice between products made of apples grown with and without this chemical. The public quickly reacted by refusing to buy the former, and almost as quickly, major producers of apple juice—notably the Heinz Company—responded by buying their apples from growers who did not use Alar. Unfortunately, in the case of food safety, however, the public is limited in making informed choices because there is no information. Under FDA rules, companies cannot advertise their products based on claims of comparative safety. It is not clear that the major food producers could even make such claims, because they do not test their products at the final critical point, before the package leaves the plant. Without an economic advantage for a producer to improve product safety, relying on the market to resolve the problem of food safety is not possible.

We conducted possibly the only transparent study on *Campylobacter* contamination of poultry products in which we named the names of the producers, including Tyson and Perdue. The government is not permitted to conduct studies like ours, and the industry was angry that we did so. They pressured the George W. Bush administration to request that the FDA replicate our study, but without naming names. The FDA replication confirmed our results, which may be why it was not widely publicized.

If labels and infomercials, government websites and educational programs do not work, how well do recalls of unsafe food—that is, action after the fact—function at least to limit exposure to foodborne pathogens? Amazingly, only in 2012 did the FDA receive legislative authority to enforce recalls; before that time, they could only announce a problem and advise corporations to take their products out of the food supply. Even with the power to issue recalls, they do not move very fast—two major foodborne outbreaks that were first detected in 2012 were finally closed in 2014, and there was no recall.

Information is limited on the effectiveness of food recalls. In 2004, the GAO found that less than 40 percent of recalled food items were actually recovered, according to data they were able to obtain from the FDA and the USDA. In some cases, recalls were not done within a year after the notice of hazard. Because the food agencies (the FDA and the USDA) do not monitor or maintain records on what happens after recalls are issued, we have no information on compliance, and we are once more in the familiar landscape of self-imposed ignorance. In the case of drugs, the FDA has recognized the flaws in relying on this type of system in order to inform actions on postmarket drug recalls, but even there its system is still passive, that is, responding to information rather than eliciting it. If a watched pot never boils, an unwatched pot often boils over and sometimes causes fires.

In the United States, these problems are not unique to food safety. There comes a time when labels and warnings are not sufficient to protect public health and safety. "Redesigning people versus redesigning products" is how Robert Adler neatly phrased the policy interplay between consumer education and product regulation. In other words, sensible public policy recognizes the limitations of preventing injuries by placing the burden on consumers, and at that point the burden must shift to the producer. As Adler notes, "this is a wise approach, for it is much easier to re-design products than to re-design consumers." This approach has been adopted in auto safety, children's toys, and many consumer products. But we have not made similar changes with respect to improving food safety; here we continue to rely on scaring consumers.

Why is food unsafe today—possibly more unsafe today—with all the advances in food production, all the economies of scale with large operations, all the advantages of modern knowledge, methods, equipment, and oversight? Claiming "modernization" in terms of food safety tends to dissolve upon closer examination, and, in fact, with the recent revisions in regulation and failures of implementation, the safety net for food, as for workers, no longer exists.

We are at the same point in ensuring food safety as we were at the moment of the revolution in agricultural production in the early nineteenth century. In short, we have squandered many of the advantages that could have resulted from a highly integrated system of production. In addition, we have disconnected the information network that could facilitate linking outbreaks of foodborne illness with their origins at processing plants and farms because of resistance to requiring trace-back and tracking systems from farm to fork. With this failure, we lost the key element in both animal health and food safety policies and programs.

We do not have an agency dedicated to food safety whose authority extends back to the farm. Agencies dedicated to food safety were set up in France, the United Kingdom, and elsewhere in the EU during a brief moment of activism following outbreaks of zoonotic diseases, such as avian and swine influenzas and mad cow disease, that greatly damaged farmers as well as public confidence in the last two decades of the twentieth century. Despite several efforts at similar legislation, the United States has no agency that centralizes all aspects of food safety.

From a historical perspective, we have not reached the magic year of 1875, when both England and the United States recognized that national food safety programs needed to be established (or reestablished). Most of our programs in food safety are voluntary and nontransparent. These voluntary programs are run by the industry with little public access, and the stated goal of most of these programs is not to protect consumers but to ensure the productivity of the industrial sector. But ignoring the farm as part of food safety can affect productivity, as evident in the massive losses in the Chinese and Thai poultry industries and the European beef industry following epidemics of animal diseases, including highly pathogenic avian influenza and mad cow disease. In the United States, the pork industry was in full damage control during the pandemic swine flu outbreak of 2009, and the National Pork Board and American Meat Institute succeeded in persuading both Secretary of Agriculture Tom Vilsack and President Barack Obama to cease and desist from using the words "swine flu," instead using the less informative nomenclature of H1N5.

There is reason to be concerned about the efficacy of the voluntary programs now prevalent in USDA regulations in terms of their effectiveness to achieve public health goals. Moreover, handing over the role of messaging in public health has additional dangers, given the demonstrated ability of the tobacco industry to manipulate campaigns to reduce childhood smoking or the fast-food lobby's ability to twist messages about unhealthy diets. An inevitable conflict exists between public and private interests; consumers, authorities, and even retail food marketers often wish to know more than producers wish to disclose.

The public sector receives inadequate information, and what information exists is difficult to access. Just as in Goya's etching *The Sleep of Reason Produces Monsters*, depicting all evils freed at night, the impenetrable darkness that shrouds current food safety programs run by industry succeeds in turning off the stimulus for full disclosure and the cleansing power of sunshine. Only with mandatory, transparent, independent monitoring and surveillance of the food production system is it possible to stimulate and ensure improvements in food safety. But we do not have that. No one has that, as it would be much more expensive and burdensome than trying to access to information when we need it, in the midst of an outbreak of foodborne illness.

We have a national food system, but are the risks of foodborne illness equal across our population? This is an unexplored issue. What if the food sold in poorer neighborhoods, those with less access to the abundance of our national supermarket chains, is actually less safe? Such a disparity would put the debate in another light; it would be like segregating the supply of drinking water by neighborhood. We may accept the harsh dominance of income in terms of food access, but we should be unwilling to let income determine risks of infection, if only out of self-interest. The nagging problem about infectious disease, as we know in the age of Ebola and SARS, is that even if exposure can be segregated, disease cannot be easily contained. The nobles sequestered in their castle in Edgar Allen Poe's "The Masque of the Red Death" eventually died by the epidemic ravaging the poor inhabitants outside their walls.

Ask a question; find no answer; do the research. We did the study with the help of the food access map that two students had developed by walking the streets of Baltimore along with reading the census data. We picked stores within neighborhoods with high and low food access, according to the map. From the start, we noticed a problem. In the low-access neighborhoods, there were no large supermarkets and no stores operated by national corporations like Giant Food or Safeway. This was a big issue in Reservoir Hill, the first neighborhood in which I lived after moving to Baltimore. Long before urban homesteading and gentrification, my family had been stakeholders in the urban experiment of inner city living, an experiment for "rich white folks," as my neighbor Reggie White reminded me forcefully. Reggie and I later worked together on another gritty urban problem, lead poisoning, and much of what I know about the social context of public health comes from late-night discussions with him. The task was to get a large supermarket to locate in Reservoir Hill, a crazy dream for a neighborhood where we could not get a mortgage to purchase our house. (This was during the days when the home loan industry would not issue mortgages in certain neighborhoods.) I enjoyed being back on the streets of Baltimore as we selected stores from the food access map. Our study design was not perfect, given the lack of similar markets in the two groups of neighborhoods, but we were able to find smaller national chains that had opened stores in the low-access areas, even if Whole Foods and Giant had not done so. We bought chicken parts and ground beef from each store and took them back to the lab to analyze for pathogens. But even before we got the packages out of the stores, we could see differences. There were no "organic" products available in the low-access stores, so we did not buy those in the high-access stores. Ground beef in low-access stores was more likely to be poorly wrapped in lightweight plastic; in high-access stores, ground beef was more securely wrapped in heavier-weight plastic that was heat-sealed. The microbiology results were also different. Products purchased at stores in low-access neighborhoods were more likely to carry pathogens and drug-resistant pathogens as compared to the same products purchased in high-access neighborhoods. How could this be? For the chicken parts, it was particularly puzzling because all the packages we bought had been sealed before they reached the store. I talked to one of my few advisers inside the food industry, who taught me about the mysteries of poultry processing. Most of the poultry products sold in the United States go through several steps after the slaughterhouse to become consumer products. So-called secondary processors buy chicken carcasses from the big companies like Perdue and Tyson, and they make the final consumer products, such as boneless chicken breasts and chicken nuggets. We do not know much about these secondary processors, including how many times packages are opened and reopened, how products are manipulated, and how the packages are resealed. Each of these events represents another opportunity for contamination. We don't know how often these plants are inspected, and we have little data on contamination issues in these plants. This is important in terms of the potential for differential risks related to food safety. We did not find any Perdue or Tyson products in the low-access stores.

These stores in low-access neighborhoods probably represented the bottom of the food system, in the words of my industry adviser; that is, products that have gone through several stages of reprocessing and repackaging at each stage done by small plants are less likely to have much food safety oversight. I also learned from my guide that it would be impossible to figure any of this out.

Ground beef was another story. Much of it is prepared at the store or immediate supplier, particularly in the case of small stores. Consistent with this fact, we found the highest rates of pathogen contamination in ground beef purchased at small stores regardless of neighborhood.

How did we get to this state? What are we to demand? HACCP will not protect us, and neither will any other part of the food safety system. Having delegated responsibility for HACCP to the industry, the FDA is now proposing to withdraw itself and the USDA from any responsibility for inspecting imported foods. History, once again, can advise us. We are in the midst of one of the recurring cyclic patterns in food systems, where food safety concerns have waxed and waned. These cycles reflect the historical pattern of changes in agricultural production responding to consumer demand. The long view of the history of agriculture informs us that as human populations increased or settled in more concentrated locations, demand for food increased, which then drove increased production. As soon as stable markets, however small, were established, some kind of system to reduce risks was developed. Then a new round of increased demand stimulated increases in production as well as the changes needed to supply food to larger populations living farther away from farms. This rising demand soon strained and exceeded the methods of reducing food safety risks that had been sufficient for a smaller or simpler food system.

We are now living within one of those cycles, which began with industrialization of food animal production and took off with the post–World War II increase in consumer demand and population growth. This is not the first time that we have had to live through the seemingly inevitable time lag in developing new structures and rules for ensuring food safety to meet the challenges of newly expanded food production systems.

The history of food safety in England, which is among the most completely documented, reveals these rising and falling tides of attention to food safety, in response to changes in population, demand, and agricultural production. By the end of the Napoleonic Wars in the early nineteenth century, the British economy was growing, its *imperium* unchallenged, and its cities recovered from the last visitations of the plague. Demand for food grew and expanded in scope. Sidney Mintz, a sociologist of food at Johns Hopkins University, equates this expansion with profound social change, stating that "the first sweetened cup of tea to be drunk by an English worker was a significant historical event." Taking a cup of tea with sugar signified improvements in both agriculture and the economy, which had brought about social circumstances such that elegant novelties that elevated food beyond sustenance had become available to more than the privileged classes.

The new economy of food in the nineteenth century placed stress on existing systems of production and delivery. The first political responses were characteristic of many stressed systems in the modern world: reduce the "heavy hand" of regulation in order to expand supply. In 1815, the English Parliament repealed the ancient judicial rulings that provided some consumer protection, limited to the safety and purity of bread. The stresses of the ensuing catch-up period were well recognized in nineteenth-century England, in the horrors of orphanage food as described by Charles Dickens and the comment that bread was less the staff of life and more "a crutch to help us onwards to the grave." The demand for vastly increased amounts of foodstuffs overwhelmed traditional market structures in cities, structures that had hardly changed from the days when most of the population lived in small villages proximate to farms. The need to distribute this food to cities revealed further inadequacies, which, in an age before refrigeration, led to increased product spoilage and rotted crops. The response of food distributors and sellers was to employ extensive adulteration to mask the smells and discoloration of bad food by using the new products of organic chemistry, such as artificial colors to mask the evidence of poor quality of both food and beverages. There were often acutely toxic results, also noticed at the time with the 1820 publication in both London and Philadelphia of Accum's "Treatise on Adulterations of Food and Methods of Detecting Them."

Forty years later, the first food safety laboratory was established in the United States in the new Department of Agriculture, but it was not until 1875 that new national food safety laws were adopted in England and the United States. Not coincidentally, by this time, agricultural productivity in both countries had caught up with population expansion, urbanization, and changing demand. Tariffs on food imports were relaxed or abolished. These developments reduced the price of food and, along with increases in the real wages of the urban working class in the late nineteenth century, created a climate for regulation that was acceptable to both producers and consumers by creating political and economic "space" for the cost of regulations of producing and buying food. Those pillars of capitalism—the FAO and the OECD—would welcome the observation that the English food supply was significantly expanded by the abolition of tariffs and expansion of free trade, while Friedrich Engels (if not Karl Marx) would approve of the increasing power in wage negotiation attained by skilled industrial workers.

The expanded and more reliable food production system, including imports, in turn led to market consolidation, with larger firms driving out smaller ones, and the resulting efficiencies of scale supposedly also supported improvements in quality and reliability, an assumption I held until writing this book. As a Quaker, I am compelled to insert the view that the presence of Quakers like Sir Adrian Cadbury—now most famous for the chocolate company bearing his name—in the business of retail food marketing in England may have had an elevating influence on the modern British food system dating from that time.

The United States followed a similar history, of largely local regulation starting in the English and Dutch colonies, which lasted until the first era of postcolonial agricultural expansion and the growth of cities in the nineteenth century. The same process of degrading existing food safety protection took place, with the removal of earlier colonial-era codes and the accretion of common law protections related to preventing food adulteration, defined as the addition of nonfood materials to food, during a similar expansionist phase of national agriculture. Reminiscent of Dickens, dire warnings about American food were issued by visitors such as Fanny Trollope in 1827, the indefatigable traveler and mother of the novelist Anthony Trollope, and Alexis de Tocqueville, who both noted our propensity to bad manners, overeating, and frequent snacking. Mrs. Trollope, in her *Letters from America*, said that "we are still baffled by the sheer quantity of food that people somehow stuff down their gullets. Besides breakfast, dinner, and tea, with which Americans eat ham, they have very copious suppers and often a snack." Self-deprived of historical authorities through common law traditions and unequipped to respond to changes in production, it took years for both countries to reconstruct a food safety system that empowered national authorities to intervene to protect consumers. In 1875, the same year in which the British Parliament passed the first national food safety act, the US Congress passed the Safe Foods and Drugs Act. Some thirty years later, in a second burst of activity in the economic and political climate of progressivism in the United States, Theodore Roosevelt was able to achieve rapid enactment of a new food safety system under the Pure Food and Drugs Act of 1904, stimulated by the publication of Upton Sinclair's *The Jungle*.

In both countries, these laws established a structure of food safety regulation that was anchored by direct access to and oversight of food production by government inspectors, free from the supervision of industry. The public also had access to this system through the publication of annual reports by these analysts. Both the English and American food safety systems encompassed the whole process of turning animals into food. Their inspectors had lawful access to farms and slaughterhouses as well as to markets and commercial eating-places. Although these innovations are often ascribed to the influence of advances in public health and food science, it is also the case that economic factors supported these improvements, just as they had driven deteriorations.

This was the food safety system that was more or less in place in Europe and North America until the mid-twentieth century. More or less, because the system once again had by then become unable to keep pace with changes in the scale and organization of both production and consumer demand consequent to industrialization and the economic expansion of consumerism in the United States after the Second World War. The complexity of food hazards also increased with the adoption of chemical methods in crop production, additives to animal feeds, and extensive use of synthetic chemicals for flavor, color, and preservation. More fundamentally, implementation of new laws and authorizations frequently fell short of what was required, leading to the general assumption—that I once shared—that failures of implementation are the root of our current problems. In actuality, the cause was related to the combination of changes in the food system accompanied by willful destruction of critical elements of the system in place beginning in the 1980s, once more repeating the cycle of food expansion and food safety.

The increased complexity of food safety issues in the twentieth century challenged the assumption on which the nineteenth-century system was based, that visual and tactile inspection by trained officials could detect problems in the food supply. The newly recognized microbial risks and the novel uses of chemicals in growing and processing foods made such inspection impossible. Nevertheless, organoleptic methods (touch, sight, and smell) are still the basis for food safety inspection to this day. The continued expansion of production with industrialization, such that the magnitude of processing—tens of thousands of pigs and poultry handled each day in the largest plants—exceeded the most comprehensive system of real-time checking, and mirrored the expansion of food transfers into nineteenth-century cities that exceeded the traditional modes of market management. Once again, the system needed to be reinvented, this time by adopting HACCP.

For all the reasons described in chapter 9, this system has also failed, a victim of its own poor design and often at the hands of its agents. We are now at or close to the nadir in terms of having in place effective systems to manage food safety, and this situation is aggravated by the design failures of HACCP in its current form. Moreover, with the globalization of the food supply, the capacity of national systems can no longer meet the need to monitor and control food safety issues arising from sources outside national jurisdictions. A recent analysis by the US Congress found that the US consumer's market basket is increasingly filled with imported food, a total of over 16 percent overall and more than 85 percent of fish and shellfish. Poor as food safety inspection is in the United States, vigilance over imported food quality and safety is even more limited. In China, for example, the FDA inspected only ten facilities out of an estimated one million processors. When the United States determined that poultry produced in China (often by companies affiliated with US integrators) was unacceptable in terms of safety, the World Trade Organization overruled the US ban as an illegal barrier to trade.

As before in history, these challenges were aggravated by willful destruction of the system in place. This deliberate destruction has been little noticed by many of those concerned about food safety as well as by the public. Government and industry claim that no reform is needed. But now that HACCP has been largely destroyed, our food safety system needs to be reinvented again.

The industrial model can claim to provide solutions to some risk factors: a general level of better practice and efficient transportation within food networks to wholesale and retail outlets. But because the problem of food safety is not solved before food leaves slaughter and processing, the problem of food safety is not solved. Moreover, as we found for Baltimore, having a plentitude of large food systems and highly integrated and efficient supply chains does not result in equal access to food or to safe food in every neighborhood. The industry claims that industrialization and concentration have reduced food safety risks. We might be persuaded that industrial methods are better by contrasting them with images of backyard slaughter or of Asian wet markets (where live animals are butchered on site). That might be arguable if the same industry had not succeeding in eroding food safety systems within their large operations.

But is it possible that they have increased risks of food safety? The WHO has expressed concerns that the industrialization of agriculture and food production through integration and consolidation has created an environment in which foodborne diseases can emerge and spread rapidly through farms and food processing, increasing the likelihood of larger, even if fewer, outbreaks of foodborne illness. There are several factors involved: one related to increasing scale and concentration of production; one related to industry stances on food safety; and the final and most important factor, one related to the methods of production. The problem of scale involves the problem of "too big to fail"—when large operations crash, they cause more damage than smaller operations, whether they are banks, jumbo jets, or processing plants. The size of slaughter and processing plants in the United States, like banks, has steadily increased with industrialization and integration. Just five hog slaughterhouses in the United States account for 55 million, or 50 percent, of the hogs consumed in the United States; the

Smithfield hog slaughter and processing plant in Tar Heel, North Carolina, kills over about 10 percent of this total, or 32,000 pigs a day. Perdue processes about 2 billion pounds of broiler poultry per year, or over 20 percent of the US total.

The density and concentration of food animal production mean that problems can spread quickly, and the same problem can affect millions of animals through common practices of feeding and housing, and the concentration of animal slaughter means that failure to control pathogen contamination at this stage can result in millions of pounds of unsafe consumer products entering the market. Feed production is as concentrated as animals. Only a few companies, dominated by US corporations, account for the feeds for most industrially produced animals in the world. Problems associated with animal feeds, such as *Salmonella* or contamination by biotoxins such as aflatoxin, which is produced by a fungus commonly found in grains, thus have the potential to affect the world market.

Industry opposition to food safety inspection and related regulation has created a second set of problems, which have greatly diminished the effectiveness of the food safety net. In addition to turning a system of hands-on inspection into paper checking, the industry (including trade associations for producers) has opposed antimicrobial drug use bans and restrictions in animal feed, the collection of data on antimicrobial use in feeds, improvements in animal welfare, updated risk assessments of methyl mercury and bisphenol A in food, release of nutritional information to consumers, product labeling, and traceability. All of these positions contribute to the shredding of the food safety net. The "dance of regulation" has always involved vigorous debate among stakeholders, but it is something new for the industry to succeed in blocking almost all opportunities for government and consumers to know what is going on in our food.

Small producers are not immune to exerting this type of pressure. Organic and agroecology trade groups have lobbied successfully for relaxation of the modest improvements in food safety under the Food Security Modernization Act (FSMA). They have argued that although episodes of exposures to pathogens produced in their sector have occurred, the relative contribution of this sector to the nation's food supply is so much smaller than industrial production that the overall burden of disease is considerably lower. That does not mean that their food is safer, just that fewer people will be exposed to it. Some agroecological producers even deliberately flout food safety regulations. Michael Pollan greatly admires the "rogue" producer Joel Salatin, self-described as a "Christian, libertarian, environmentalist, capitalist lunatic," who slaughters his chickens without regard to any of the safeguards required of industrial scale producers. Is his way less safe? We have no way of knowing because he does not test his products.

Others argue that nonindustrial organic production may actually increase risks of food safety. Because organic farmers use animal manures, the risks of being exposed to drug-resistant pathogens may be higher than from conventionally grown crops. This is not always the case: industrial-scale crop production can become contaminated from irrigation water taken from sources contaminated by runoff from areas where animal wastes have been disposed. In April 2014, three of the seven food items listed by the FDA on the recall list were from natural or organic food sources. The debate is further inflamed when an agroecology website denounces the FDA for urging them to forgo the use of animal wastes as manures, a practice that is strongly supported in this type of agriculture. No one should be using untreated animal wastes to produce crops that people eat.

THE SCORE IS: INDUSTRIAL FAR OUTWEIGHS TRADITIONAL

The overall conclusion as to whether industrial food animal production has increased or decreased food safety risks is overwhelming for one reason: industrialized food animal production has introduced a new food safety risk through using antimicrobials as feed additives. Back in 1998, when I learned for the first time that food was a major source of drug-resistant infections, I was surprised, not about food being contaminated by *Salmonella* and other infectious pathogens (practically everyone knows that, and my mother, like most other mothers, was vigilant about keeping the potato salad refrigerated for a family picnic), but to learn that food also carried risks of exposure to drug-resistant pathogens. Importantly, whatever headway has been made in controlling foodborne pathogens and disease risks in the twentieth century through the industrialization of food animal production has been totally decimated by the contribution of these methods to antimicrobial resistance. And these effects spread far beyond food in terms of contributing to the emergence and environmental dissemination of multidrug resistance.

WHAT ABOUT NUTRITION?

Nutrition is another important aspect of food quality, where fault has often been assigned to the food industry. We live in a period of perverse incentives and burden shifting when it comes to food safety and nutrition. Incentivization in agriculture is wholly directed toward the support of agricultural production and not to food value, except to remind us how cheap our food is. As soon as industry claims that a reform will inhibit profitability, that reform becomes less likely to prevail. Even the antitrust laws are bent in deference to profit. Although early litigation against integrators failed, certain aspects of older legislation still remained in effect to constrain the economic power of the industry. That is, until 2004, when a US Court of Appeals overruled a federal jury that had found Tyson in violation of the Packers and Stockyards Act of 1921 through its use of contractual agreements to artificially lower cattle prices. However, a higher court threw out this verdict on the grounds that Tyson had a legitimate business justification to manipulate prices. The USDA proposed regulations that would stanch this wound to some extent, under the Grain Inspection, Packers and Stockyards Administration (GIPSA). Predictably, the American Meat Institute, National Cattlemen's Beef Association, National Pork Producers Council, National Chicken Council, and National Turkey Federation are all opposed to any limit on their ability to conduct business as usual. In 2015, the USDA bowed to their pressure and ended all activities on this topic. In the absence of active steps by the USDA, the clock has been effectively turned back to the period before Roosevelt and William Howard Taft took on the trusts to level the playing field between the industry and the public.

The contradictions between production and profit also spill over into debates over nutrition and public health, to the extent that some charge that the two goals are irreconcilable within the market and therefore require intervention to address these priorities. This topic includes what advice should be given by government about food and nutrition and the importance of examining the role of the current food system in the childhood obesity epidemic.

There are a range of stakeholders vying for control and even the very definition of nutritious food: medicine (of all types), public health, industry, religion. Like food safety, nutrition involves the USDA and the FDA, agriculture and public health, along with extensive participation by industry through the USDA, in this as elsewhere its enabling ally in government. The result is an uneasy relationship, with nutritional experts proposing guidelines and recommendations with the goal of optimizing health and preventing disease, but only up to the point that sectors of the food industry do not perceive that their economic interests are threatened. Historically, the USDA has had the lead role in giving nutritional advice through the 1862 legislation establishing the agency decades before the creation of the FDA. Over a hundred years later, the USDA was required to share this role with the Department of Health and Human Services after the passage of the Nutrition Education and Labeling Act in 1978. Within this partnership, the USDA started work on its first "Food Pyramid" concept. The Food Pyramid was intended to guide consumers through the complex process of making nutritious choices in a landscape filled with messaging from food producers, health purveyors, and others. But as soon as the USDA published the first Food Pyramid in 1991, trade associations representing meat producers objected to their placement on this structure and the federal dietary advice to limit meat consumption. They successfully lobbied to change this advice from "decrease your consumption of meat" to "have one or two servings of meat a day." This was not enough for the meat industry and the USDA withdrew the first version. A new Food Pyramid was published in 1992.

The visual of a pyramid was effective at conveying both qualitative and quantitative advice, placing the less nutritional elements at the top in the smallest space, indicating smaller amounts of recommended intake, and placement lower down in spaces of increasing size, indicating recommendations for increased intake. In this way, going down the pyramid signifies wise choices of more nutritional food components. The 1992 Food Pyramid was a compromise version, bumping meat and poultry down one level, just below fats and oils but still less preferred—that is above—fruits, vegetables, breads, and grains. Not everyone was satisfied. Walter Willett and his colleagues at Harvard offered an alternative pyramid, in which meat was placed at the highest level of the pyramid, symbolizing the advisability of least frequent consumption. The controversies from other stakeholders—including industry, vegans, and popular health advisers—continued.

In 2005, after years of dissatisfaction with the Food Pyramid on the part of almost everyone, the USDA did away with the pyramid altogether and replaced it with a plate. But doing away with the pyramid has resulted in a loss of clarity and a retreat from general advice to encouragement for individuals to develop their own decisions on diet. MyPlate, finalized in 2012, completely obscures the goal of providing a pictographic statement of nutritional advice that includes anything either quantitative or qualitative. Its image is a plate, an even, flat space with four more or less equally sized compartments for fruits, grains, vegetables, and a category called "protein," which could indicate a range of sources and in the supporting text includes meat. MyPlate could be considered a deliberate maneuver to avoid criticism from both industry and nutritionists.

The MyPlate program has a lot of endorsements from industry, including the Alliance for Potato Research and Education, the beef industry, the frozen and canned food industries, Boston Chicken, the Beef Cattle Institute, Frito-Lay, the National Dairy Council, General Mills, the Food Marketing Institute, and Sodexo—keeping company with the American Medical Association, the Center for Science in the Public Interest, and the American Cancer Society. But it's easy to understand why nutrition experts like Marion Nestle and Walter Willett still consider that the USDA advice dilutes science with the influence of agribusiness. You can get a replica of MyPlate, complete with children's games, interactive sites, and other programs associated with this cheerful icon. Everyone is happy; or at least, no one is publicly upset anymore. As a consumer, I find MyPlate to be unhelpful. But clarity in nutritional advice is a minefield too dangerous to enter, apparently. It's too early to assess MyPlate's effectiveness, as there was only a proposal by the USDA in 2013 to undertake an evaluation, which has not been done.

In addition to the decades of fighting over pyramids and plates, there are other tensions between health-based nutritional goals and the production goals of industrial agriculture. Some consider that there is a fundamental "incompatibility between a system based on private ownership and profit and the production of sustainable, healthy food." Given that nonprofit and collectivized agriculture have no record of success in feeding much of anything for too many people, the resolution of these tensions requires discourse within the system we have.

We can examine two "poster children" in this debate: high fructose corn syrup and its association with subsidies for corn production, and the chicken nugget as a driver of increased reliance on fast-food outlets for family meals.

HIGH FRUCTOSE CORN SYRUP

Many opponents of the current US food system point to high fructose corn syrup (HFCS) as being among the "most wanted" for its contribution to obesity in the United States, especially among children. Undeniably, its presence has increased to an extraordinary degree in the US diet—by 1,000 percent from 1970 to 2000. HFCS rapidly displaced refined sugar, which was disadvantaged by high tariffs, as well as other sources of sucrose.

Proponents have argued that the subsidies given to corn producers, which reduce the cost of HFCS, have been an important factor in the displacement of cane and beet sugar. But the extent to which subsidies drive consumer choice and contribute to outcomes such as obesity is not at all clear. The argument that subsidies for corn production are driving consumer exposures to HFCS and increased risks of obesity has somewhat subsided in the context of fierce competition for corn between the biofuels industry and food animal producers.

A closer look indicates that HFCS may be inappropriately singled out for blame in contributing to obesity, a claim first advanced on the basis of timing. HFCS is not markedly different from refined sugars or honey in terms of its fructose content, although there is continuing debate on possible differences in metabolism. Whether that warrants comments such as this one, by the medical blogger Mark Hyman, is worth considering: "The last reason to avoid products that contain HFCS is that they are a marker for poor-quality, nutritionally-depleted, processed industrial food full of empty calories and artificial ingredients. If you find 'high fructose corn syrup' on the label you can be sure it is not a whole, real, fresh food full of fiber, vitamins, minerals, phytonutrients, and antioxidants. Stay away if you want to stay healthy."

A more obvious contributor to obesity in America is increased caloric intake. The introduction of HFCS has only slightly increased total intake of fructose in the United States, as HFCS has largely displaced refined sugar. Over this same period, what *has* increased is the total caloric intake of Americans.

Consuming more calories, along with lifestyle changes of reduced activity, is a likely culprit. And it leads to the next question, about the involvement of industrial agriculture in health as well as the obesity epidemic.

THE CHICKEN NUGGET

Another charge laid at industrial food production is the claim that fast-food companies have contributed to obesity through introducing new products and increasing portion sizes. Over time, portion sizes at many fast-food outlets have increased two to five times as compared to their first introduction.

Are larger portions associated with agricultural policy? There is no direct evidence that supports for industrial food animal production have in any way driven increased portion size, as this trend is observed across food products. Does industrial agriculture share some of the blame for consumers switching to fast-food sources for meals of lower nutritional quality? Although not as tightly organized as the tobacco or lead industries, these industries are nonetheless in contact, such that producers and retailers shake hands across many issues. Industry also exerts its influence through benignly named organizations such as the Alliance for a Healthier Generation, an organization established to confront the challenge of obesity, which includes among its supporters ConAgra, the National Turkey Federation, Tyson Foods, Rich Products, and Kraft Foods. The foxes are in the henhouse, and the result is a misleading strategy for guiding consumers toward healthy food choices (such as the Food Pyramid and MyPlate).

In terms of innovations in food products that are particularly attractive to children, there is more to connect agriculture and the fast-food industry. An example is the invention of the "McNugget" and the accompanying spike in industrial poultry production and consumption of chicken-based meals at fast-food outlets. It has been suggested that the introduction of the nugget, or poultry strip, was responsible for increasing poultry consumption in the United States from 34 lbs. per year in 1965 to 84 lbs. per year in 2011. The nugget may have been invented some twenty years earlier, but it did not enter the market until the early 1980s. Ironically, according to McDonald's official history, the instigation for the McNugget was based on nutrition: McDonald's sought to reduce controversy over its meat menu by introducing a chicken-based product in response to the USDA's 1977 guidelines recommending reduced red meat consumption. The new project was quickly seized upon by the poultry industry as an important stimulus for broiler production. Following the introduction of the McNugget and similar products at other outlets, broiler production in the United States more than doubled, from 4.13 billion in 1982 to 8.54 billion in 2011. In addition to supplying "further processed" poultry meat for the fast-food industry, the companies have begun marketing their own similar products for home preparation, such as Tyson and Perdue chicken nuggets.

Over the same time as these developments and innovations, the numbers of Americans eating at fast-food outlets have greatly increased. This is unlikely to be due solely to the invention of the chicken nugget, although some charge the fast-food industry with being an aider and abettor with toy promotions and other enticements. Marion Nestle, a nutrition expert at New York University, has stated that "the toys are the only reason kids want Happy Meals and the only reason parents buy them. It's not about the food."

Many factors inform how people (usually adults but often pressured by children) choose where and how to purchase meals, including time and convenience as well as cost and nutrition. Demographics influences choice, and the continuing erosion of the traditional two-parent family with children to a population with many children living with one parent or households made up of adults without children has much to do with increasing reliance on outside sources for meals.

There is an ongoing debate as to whether, for cost, buying foods with lower nutrition but higher energy content (carbohydrates and sugars) is not unwise, and for that reason fast food may well be an economically sound option for populations with no sure access to more nutritional foods that are also affordable. Most of the debate on this topic is meaningless—for example, claiming that a home-cooked meal is cheaper and more nutritious overlooks the time and resources needed to cook at home—as are claims made by tourists in poverty, that the federal food assistance program of $5 per day is enough to support home cooking. Also ignored is the problem of access to the uncooked ingredients, a subset of the problem of food insecurity. The intellectual class can brush off the problem of access by stating that because most poor people have access to cars, they could drive to supermarkets outside their neighborhood. But if they had ever stood in the parking lot of an inner city large market (as I did during our food safety and food access study), they would note the number of shoppers utilizing gypsy cabs and jitneys for transportation. Having a car in a household does not equate to access to that car or money for gasoline. In terms of the time required to make healthy food choices, Mark Bittman, an influential food writer and op-ed columnist for the *New York Times*, responded by essentially saying, let them stop watching so much television. This is cruel stuff to read and not reflective of the conditions of urban life in poverty. A reader's response to this commentary says it all: "The problems lower income adults have are not their food choices—their limited life choices and incomes are the problems."

Shifting the burden is where this chapter began, away from me in my kitchen, preparing a chicken for dinner while abiding by the lists of dos and don'ts and scary maps of kitchens from the FDA. It does not have to be so dangerous. We have established guards and gatekeepers to regulate pesticides and food additives; we may disagree with the standards imposed by the Environmental Protection Agency and the FDA for these foodborne risks, but there is a systematic way to change the standards and, most importantly, to enforce them. When it comes to pathogens, we live by the rule of redesigning people, not products.

What does a twenty-first-century system of food safety demand? Most of all it needs us, especially the readers of this book. From the nineteenth century to the present, the impetus for change has come from outside federal agencies and industry. We have forgotten the first leaders in the movement for food safety, but this book pays homage to them all.

Especially deserving are Mrs. Walter McNab Miller, president of the General Federation of Women's Clubs; Dr. Edward F. Wiley, food and drug safety official of North Dakota; and Miss Alice Lakey of the National Consumers League. Historians and Dr. Wiley himself credit the "clubwomen" of the country—women who led neighborhood and city civic associations, garden clubs, and school support programs—who turned the tide of public opinion in favor of the "pure food" bill. If, as the FDA website says, food safety is a women's issue, then let's roll up our sleeves and get to work.

11

CAN WE FEED THE WORLD?

How this question is asked and answered establishes some of the most contested divisions among proponents of different agricultures. This chapter approaches the question of whether we can feed the world by asking three additional questions. First, what do we mean by "feeding"? Second, what is the "world" that we commit to feeding? And third, "what" are we to feed the world? These questions are not verbal tricks, like President Bill Clinton's infamous "It depends on what the meaning of the word 'is' is." Each of these questions, unpacked, reveals layers of enough complexity to ensure an endless debate that never actually intersects if we insist that there can be only one answer to each of these questions. Unpacking them may get us to a common ground for discussing solutions.

WHAT DO WE MEAN BY "FEEDING"?

Feeding the world means several different things, from ensuring survival to improving nutrition and providing food security. Each of these issues is urgent for at least 900 million of the world's population, a number that is likely increasing with reduced resources of water and arable land, armed conflict and failed states, internal and external migration, urbanization, and changes in demand and supply. But they do not mean the same thing, and responses to one meaning of "feeding" may not solve all the challenges important to a significant part of the problem, so we must consider all these meanings in order to understand the challenges before us.

Survival is about the minimal sustenance required for life, *nutrition* is about quantities and qualities of food required to support good health for all and especially for the growth of children, and *food security* is about ensuring reliable access to food. Lack of sustenance is famine and starvation, represented by the dreadful poster child with the distended belly of kwashiorkor and the matchstick limbs of sickness before death. Undernutrition is the more complex and sometimes less overt state of populations that may appear "fed," but without adequate diets and ravaged by diseases that can be prevented by supplying nutrients like vitamin A, as Al Sommer, former dean of the Johns Hopkins School of Public Health, demonstrated in his pioneering studies of vitamins and essential trace elements among children in South Asia. Food security is the final battleground in feeding the world; it creates the uncertainty of not being able to obtain food, even in places with all the advantages of the developed world. As many as two billion people, including an estimated 10 percent of the population of the United States, are at risk of food insecurity. Without food security, we only offer an intermittent, usually crisis-driven solution to feeding the world. Sustenance is a necessary and immediate response that does not last, and nutrition is undermined if it is not reliably available on a daily basis. Food insecurity is the wolf outside the door, waiting until hunger and malnutrition return after the aid workers leave on the day after the last meal.

Food insecurity can coexist cheek by jowl with food security in the same societies. This is true in my city of Baltimore, where thousands are hungry while at the same time dumpsters sit behind supermarkets, filled with food thrown away after its sell date, and the array of politically correct recycling bins at my university are filled with partly eaten sandwiches, salads, hamburgers, and pizza slices. But just like providing free turkeys on Thanksgiving, one day of bounty among a year of need does little to reduce food insecurity in Baltimore, just as periodic transfers of food from the overfed fraction of the world's population to the poorest of the poor do not feed the world. As Chinua Achebe wrote in his great novel *Anthills of the Savannah*, "While we do our good works let us not forget that the real solution lies in a world in which charity will have become unnecessary."

So why can't we feed the world? We need to start by agreeing that we have never really fed the world. In fact, we have never succeeded in feeding all the people in relatively small social groupings, such as in cities like mine. Talking about feeding the world paradoxically seems to distract us from solving local issues of access, poverty, education, and polity. Feeding the world is often framed in a simple manner: growing sufficient food and delivering sufficient food. That is a necessary prerequisite, but only a prerequisite. Because the problem is not so simple, most debates focus on part of the answer, and not always on the same issues. For example, in the argument over feeding the world, many argue chiefly about means of production, with some asserting that only the modern production model makes it possible to feed the world, and others asserting that alternative methods can meet these needs.

But both viewpoints presume that production is the most significant barrier to feeding the world. Although sufficiency of food is essential, feeding the world is not simply a matter of increasing production, and the simplest of the dry approaches, calling for more technological innovation to enhance production in Africa, as advocated by Jeffrey Sachs, is not enough. Production without solving the challenges of delivering food is no solution. Feeding the world, like feeding Baltimore, is neither just a matter of matching supply to demand, nor is it supporting agriculture only in areas of greatest need. Likewise, there are at least two definitions of *sustainability* in developing solutions to feeding the world: one that is invoked by those concerned about avoiding or reducing the externalities of food production in terms of ecological impacts, and the other invoked by economists referring to the importance of developing solutions that are fiscally sustainable and not dependent, as Achebe wrote, on continued influx of donor support or other subsidization.

There are distractions in our debate about productivity and feeding the world. One is the ethical value given by some to food sovereignty, which is defined as the ability of a nation or a culture to choose its own food and to provide sufficient food for itself. But food sovereignty is not the same as food security, although the two are often commingled. Food sovereignty by itself is a political and social construct that has in itself little to do with actually feeding a culture or a nation. Having secure access to food is independent of its provenance, and insisting upon national or cultural provenance can work to reduce food security. A reduction in food security can be sentimentally supported in developed countries, as seen in the public reaction in Sweden over the government's decision in 1989 to end most supports and protection for dairy production. It can be difficult to ensure food security in the hungry world, much of whose population lives in countries that are unlikely to be able to fully support sufficient production to feed their populations, even with every possible investment in agricultural technology. India, for example, still promotes agricultural policies to ensure self-sufficiency of poultry and egg production, excluding imports of more efficient and hardy breeds.

The consequences of prioritizing sovereignty over security can be serious. As Jared Diamond, the ecological historian, has written, over human history, empires have fallen when their sovereign food production systems failed, or—as Robert Thomas Malthus, the English economist, argued earlier—when their populations outgrew the resources they controlled. In both instances, populations either perished or migrated. Our own history has been marked and enriched by what has been called the great exodus from hunger, the emigration of Irish, Germans, Norwegians, Italians, and Russians, among others, from countries when national agricultures failed.

But we now live in a world of walls and dangerous seas, a world that does not encourage mass movement of peoples often fleeing from insufficient food resources for any reason, including civil conflict or insufficient natural resources. For these reasons, the argument for open markets for food through reducing tariffs and other barriers to agricultural imports often has more ethical validity than calling for investments in national or local food sovereignty. It is difficult to make the case for propping up local agricultural systems in regions with no demonstration that these efforts could actually feed any community beyond the most local populations (including sustenance, nutrition, and food security) or for any sustained period of time. There are too often political justifications, but never any ethical justification for policies that result in starvation.

WHAT IS THE "WORLD" THAT WE COMMIT TO FEEDING?

The world is a complicated place. We need to start by agreeing that the problem of feeding the world has to be solved in the world as it is and in the contexts in which hunger persists. Hunger is an immediate, pressing concern; waiting for long-term solutions that rest on complicated social and behavioral change is not acceptable. Something of a disconnect exists between "the world as I found it" (to quote Wittgenstein) and the world that appears to be assumed by many who advocate against the industrial model of increasing food production in lesser developed countries.

The world is now urbanized: whatever people wish to eat, they now wish to eat it in cities. Making the jump from Neolithic communities to rural villages happened about ten thousand years ago, and for the past six thousand years, people have increasingly chosen to live in what we would recognize today as cities in Asia, Mesoamerica, and the Middle East. As of 2008, according to the United Nations, most of the world lives in cities, and, since 1975, most of the population in developing countries has lived in cities.

More importantly, most of the world's hungry and poor people live in cities. In the Horn of Africa, there are 20 million poor residents of cities. For better or worse, time and human migration are on the side of urbanization. Those societies that have attempted to combat urbanization with programs of forced resettlement in the twentieth century have done so with drastic and tragic consequences, as in China and Cambodia.

This point deserves emphasis because there are food policy and agricultural experts who insist upon a "global consensus" that solving food issues should focus on rural communities in the poorest countries of Africa and Asia, where problems can be solved by aid to smallholder farmers with a nod to urban and periurban agriculturalists. This position has a stake at the Food and Agriculture Organization of the United Nations and has influenced major donors, such as the Bill and Melinda Gates and Rockefeller Foundations, that together have given millions of dollars in grants to support smallholder agriculture in Africa.

This next sentence may be controversial, but I will state it anyway. These projects may meet some social goals, but they are not likely to feed most of the hungry and malnourished populations living in the growing cities of most Asian and African countries. There is something almost creepily imperialistic, in fact, about the language on the websites of these foundations, featuring personal stories (often of admirable women) succeeding in generating both income and food at the local scale. It is as if they are willfully ignoring what the demographers tell us, that Africa, like most of the world, is urbanizing and is already mostly urbanized. Their insistence on seeing Africa as a rural paradise is not so different from the Utopian visions of countries like the United States shared by Wendell Berry and Wes Jackson. If you think this reads like an angry screed, I refer you to Jonathan Crush, director of the Southern African Research Centre at Queen's University in Canada, who reacted to rural-centered proposals for feeding the region he knows better than most this way: "Why do governments, international agencies, and foreign donors insist that increasing agricultural production by small farmers will solve food insecurity in Africa, even in countries like South Africa where two thirds of the population is already urbanized?"

Like Crush, other experts in world hunger have argued for greater attention to urban populations in the poorest countries of the world, but they are not often heard in the discourse at development agencies and foundations in the developed world. This may be because there are those—the UN Population Fund, or UNFPA, for example—who see urbanization as the problem, insofar as they explain the movement of peoples to cities only in negative terms, as a flight from the hardships of the countryside.

Cities are not just refuges of last resort for rural people; more often, they represent opportunities both for simple survival as well as economic and cultural development. Movement to cities is not only driven but also often freely sought. There are national literatures describing the motivations for moving from country to city in the literary canon of almost every European and North American country. Such motivations are most pithily summarized by Dr. Samuel Johnson, that "to be tired of London is to be tired of life." The unwillingness to ascribe motivations to rural populations in other countries similar to those we recognize (and celebrate) in our own history of urbanization represents another type of cultural imperialism. As in the history of rural migration to cities in Europe and the Americas, in Africa it is the more educated and ambitious and young who leave the limits of rural life for the anticipated opportunities offered, if not always fulfilled, by cities.

Dr. Chimedsuren Ochir, dean of the School of Public Health in Mongolia (a rapidly urbanizing country), interviewed internal migrants from traditional rural life to the capital city of Ulaanbaatar. She found that they had both negative and positive reasons for relocating. The main negative driver was the difficulty in transcending the poverty and uncertainty of rural life in a nomadic herder economy; the positive drivers were many and included access to education for children, healthcare, and "a better life." Here I must admit being the child of an internal migrant (my mother), who, with financial support from her father to attend Wellesley, left the countryside for the city. My son left our small city of Baltimore for the big city of New York. Like generations before them, they acted on an optimistic if apprehensive view of cities.

Cities, like most things in human society, are what we make them. Poorly managed, they are disastrous places to live. But cities are also essential for the social and cultural development of human societies; just as they have served this purpose in the developed world, they are now serving this purpose in the developing world. In the words of Barney Cohen, a demographer at the US National Academy of Sciences,

> If well managed, cities offer important opportunities for economic and social development. Cities have always been focal points for economic growth, innovation, and employment. Indeed, many cities grew historically out of some natural advantage in transport or raw material supply. Cities, particularly capital cities, are where the vast majority of modern productive activities are concentrated in the developing world and where the vast majority of paid employment opportunities are located. Cities are also centers of modern living, where female labor force participation is greatest and where indicators of general health and wellbeing, literacy, women's status, and social mobility are typically highest. Finally, cities are also important social and cultural centers that house museums, art galleries, film industries, theaters, fashion houses, and other important cultural centers.

Cohen goes on to note another aspect of urbanization, which will arise again in considering the ecological footprint of industrial agriculture: "High population density may also be good for minimizing the effect of man on local ecosystems. High population density typically implies lower per capita cost of providing infrastructure and basic services. And despite the high rates of urban poverty that are found in many cities, urban residents, on average, enjoy better access to education and health care, as well as other basic public services such as electricity, water, and sanitation than people in rural areas."

The fact that urban populations are the most likely to experience hunger must influence our discourse on solutions. The needs of urban dwellers cannot be fully met by urban food production, although this can be a contributing sector in some periurban situations. But megacities like São Paulo, Mumbai, and Shenzhen are expanding primarily by unplanned and unregulated internal migration into these same periurban areas. Such expansion drives opportunities for agriculture farther and farther away from the population center. As a consequence, the *regional* food system, rather than the *local*, is of prime importance in terms of responding to hunger for most of the world.

Embedded in many agrarian visions is antagonism to cities and the cosmopolitan excitement and expense of city diets, such that living in cities is one of those choices that can be predicted to bring hardship and evil upon individuals and populations. The solution is therefore to move back to the land, away from the city. For recognizing and respecting the legitimacy of forces that attract rural workers to cities, Karl Marx is a better guide to human desires and needs than Wendell Berry. But this is not an issue to argue ideologically in comfortable living rooms at First World universities. Like dietary choices, human populations are making their own decisions to move to cities in the context of many drivers.

"WHAT" ARE WE TO FEED THE WORLD?

Accepting the world in all its complexity is also to understand what people want to eat. Some argue that this understanding involves preserving traditional diets and food cultures, another "right" asserted by Olivier de Schutter, the former UN representative for food, and others. Preserving food traditions is more of a concern for the very developed world, particularly Europe, than it is for the hungry world. It takes surplus income to worry about protecting the integrity of heritage foods such as prosciutto di Parma and champagne from Reims.

How consumers perceive reliable access to food includes a considerable amount of preference, which is at least as important as the assumptions and calculations of government agencies, nutritionists, and advocates for specific food choices. Recognition of consumer preferences in food consumption is important for sustainable feeding in every definition. Once beyond sustenance, people seek food that they want to eat. Perhaps we are immature and irrational in demanding access to the foods of our choice, but ignoring this reality is not so different from arguing that if people had only made better lifestyle choices, the war on AIDS would be more manageable.

Of course, what people want to eat is not simply the exercise of individual choice. Over the twentieth century, the influence of manufactured desire has played a major role in what people choose to consume, not only in food but also for the entire world of consumption. Sigmund Freud's nephew Edward Bernays deployed the tools of *engineering consent* (his term) to create or manufacture consumer desires through public relations and advertising. Interestingly related to the topic of this book, his undergraduate education was in agriculture at Cornell. Bernays wrote, "if we understand the mechanism and motives of the group mind, is it not possible to control and regiment the masses according to our will without their knowing about it?" While Joseph Goebbels exploited this insight to genocidal ends, Bernays, who understood the potential of these techniques for evil, utilized these methods in the marketplace on behalf of food industries as well as politics.

We can argue about the responsibility of corporate advertising for driving dietary change, and limits have been proposed on food advertising for this reason by Michael Bloomberg, Marion Nestle, and others, with relatively little impact on consumption patterns. It does little to blame consumers for greed and ignorance. These approaches come across as scolding, one more castigation by the developed world of the protean aspirations of the developing world. A case in point is the emphasis on preventing developing countries from adopting the "Western" diet, as described by B. Bajželj. Campaigns for dietary change in affluent societies, such as "meatless Mondays," are not doing all that much for reducing meat consumption and are unlikely to gain widespread adherence in societies newly able to access the animal protein diets of the more affluent.

Where and what we want to eat are connected. Urbanized consumers in particular demand the diets of affluent societies. Trends in urbanization are strongly associated with changes in diet, as noted by the USDA, the OECD, and the FAO. These trends complicate and often defeat attempts to utilize traditional diets to ameliorate hunger. Preventing these changes in the age of the Internet would also require drastic interventions and constraints on individual choices, regardless of the external forces influencing choice in the modern world.

Some lament the changes in where we want to live and what we want to eat, but in the meantime people go hungry in places that some consider they should not live and for food they should not desire. In the absence of economic pressures, constraints on food choice have never been imposed successfully in other countries. The Romans experimented with sumptuary laws (as always, more lightly enforced on the more sumptuous of consumers), and the movie *Babette's Feast* is one of the best depictions of the pathologies of repressing material desires, including food, among a strict religious sect in nineteenth-century Denmark. Recognizing the foolish and risky choices of the public is a useful principle in public health, where our allegiance is to reduce harm rather than to insist upon lifestyle conversion, such as equipping cars with seatbelts instead of limiting car speeds. A cardinal principle in public health is to provide even for those who may contribute to their own hardships, such as persons with sexually transmitted diseases and addictions. As my uncle used to say, "while we wait for the Messiah, doing acts of justice can't hurt."

HOW ARE WE TO FEED THE WORLD?

Now that we understand better the many definitions of "world" and "feeding," let us examine the arguments about *how* we are to feed the world. There are two sides: the productionist side and the sustainability side, to use shorthand for what is more appropriately conceived as an interacting complexity.

Productionism emphasizes technologies as well as policies that increase the amounts of food that can be produced. Because feeding the world is not just a matter of providing masses of edible food, production by itself is not enough, although it is a necessary element. Production has been doing quite well; increases in agricultural production have mostly exceeded the rate of global population growth (over fivefold since 1940 for corn and wheat production, fivefold for meat and poultry production, and threefold for the human population). But these figures do not reveal the unevenness of gains in productivity. The OECD countries (roughly, the developed world) and the rest of the Americas continue to produce more than 75 percent of these productivity totals, while Africa and west Asia produce less than 3 percent, far out of balance with their populations. The continued lag of these regions has rightly focused attention on improving their agricultural production, but what kind of agriculture is the source of contentious debate.

Critics of productionism are correct to point out that production in terms of the amount of raw materials that make our food must include the amount of food products available to hungry populations. Focusing only on production at the national or regional scale tends to downplay the importance of the dual problems of friction, or loss, during movement along the way from producer to consumer as well as the barriers to consumer access to food when it gets to where they live. One of the achievements of integration in industrialized food animal production is the reduction of much of the friction between farm and fork through technological innovations in food processing (including chemical stabilizers and other agents that prevent spoilage and increase shelf life) as well as efficient transportation and refrigeration. The industrial model has functioned well to reduce friction and waste at several stages of food animal production through employing a mix of advanced technology and economies of scale in terms of management, or to reduce unit costs as the total size of production increases. This is one of the general benefits of industrialization, and why it tends to result in lower prices to consumers.

The sustainable agriculture or agroecology position argues that further increases in production in general should not be the highest priority because currently available land and less intensive methods can produce sufficient quantities of food and reduce friction-associated losses by enhancing systems of local production and local markets. But there is a real question about reducing the scale of food systems in terms of feasibly producing enough food even for most local populations and markets (if we include cities). It is also not clear how much loss we will reduce by acting on this concept.

Reducing losses at every stage is important in agriculture. Transporting produce and animals from farm to market is not the only source of losses. And friction and wastage in transportation are not solely functions of distance but also involve the presence or absence of technological advantages and economies of scale. Through integration, the supply flow that moves crops from fields and animals from houses to harvest and processing is highly efficient even when distance is increased. At the beginning on the farm, the industrial model has greatly increased the efficiency of feed consumption—that is, the conversion of grains into animal protein—and thus reduced losses related to the production of crops. Industrial food animal processing has greatly increased takedown, or the yield of consumable meat from an animal carcass. This may be thought of as advantaging producers, but FAO has estimated that increasing takedown in lesser developed countries could increase the food supply by as much as 35 percent. The efficiency of this system is hard to match without integration of functions, if not of ownership, and it is almost impossible to match on a deliberately reduced scale. In addition to efficiency, it is hard to match the integrated system for reliability, which relates to food security.

Production is important, and it may still require expansion. Is it feasible to produce enough food to feed the world, where people live (urban) and what people want to eat (increasingly, Western diets), without industrialized organization and methods of production? Agroecology advocates—from academics to international organizations and NGOs—have broadly claimed that their methods will actually increase agricultural production sufficient to supply the unmet food needs of the world. Some advocates of this position have gone further to argue that *only* by adopting its principles will it be possible to feed the world, making compelling references to the increasing degradation of arable lands, rising costs and eventual scarcity of fossil fuel–based energy, and climate change impacts.

The meritorious contribution of agroecology is its emphasis on social values. These values have been stressed by its proponents, particularly for those regions where food production currently falls well below that needed to support livelihoods of smallholder producers as well as to reduce hunger for the poorest of poor countries in Africa. In these settings, proponents argue that agroecology not only supplies food but also has the additional social value of maintaining smallholder farming, which is an important means of empowerment and income generation for women and for regions where much of the potentially arable land is marginally productive. Sustaining and increasing smallholder farming have been two of the rationales for government policy in India.

Agroecological positions have obtained support from some sectors of international organizations. To quote the disapproving words of Nikos Alexandratos, former director of the FAO Agricultural Development Economics Division, "It follows that in the debate on world food issues, the traditional productionist paradigm [how to promote further growth in production and the associated focus on agricultural research and technology] will continue to reign supreme in a significant part of the world." Alexandratos goes on to argue for a shift in paradigms and perspectives to those "that emphasize food quality, food safety, health and environmental impacts of food production, consumption, and trade, while giving lower value to the traditional emphasis on agricultural research and policies aimed at increasing productivity and production. Additionally, this perspective moves from the global to the local, a point not sufficiently emphasized in the literature on the population–food–environment nexus."

But these statements, while challenging the productionist position, are silent on the questions of whether this new "paradigm" can actually produce enough food to replace in whole or in part the now-dominant industrial methods in terms of ensuring adequate, affordable, and reliable food production where it is most needed. In many of the regions with the most critical food needs, increasing yields are essential if we are to end the need for periodic shipments of food to these places and populations, and the never-ending need for international donors, as Achebe warned. Increasing these regional yields is a complex problem and likely to be most appropriately and effectively dealt with through nuanced and complex interventions, including understanding technologies that are appropriate to scale, markets, and needs, in order to support and sustain the adoption of solutions at all levels of social organization, including but not limited to local growers for local consumers.

There is a need for conversation among these perspectives. Alone, they have not fed and will not feed the world. For the proponents of industrial agriculture, failure to acknowledge the adverse impacts of intensive farming will interfere with achieving the goals of feeding the world without destroying its resources, and avoiding debates on the limits of market-based systems to end hunger continues dysfunctional systems of production and distribution. For proponents of agroecology, it would be regrettable if they were to repeat the hubris of the Green Revolution (the archetype of productionist solutions through plant breeding and biotechnology) in claiming that its methods can solve all problems everywhere.

So let us try to focus on the evidence. Can nonindustrial methods feed the world? At what scale? What changes would be necessary for these methods to supplant or even compete with the industrial model to a significant extent? Some of the best-documented studies have been conducted by Jules Pretty of the University of Sussex and his team of international researchers:

> It is in developing countries that some of the most significant progress toward sustainable agroecosystems has been made in the past decade. The largest study comprised the analysis of 286 projects in 57 countries. In all, some 12.6 million farmers on 37 million hectares were engaged in transitions toward agricultural sustainability in these 286 projects. This is just over 3% of the total cultivated area (1.136 M ha) in developing countries. In the 68 randomly re-sampled projects from the original study, the number of farmers increased 54% and the number of hectares increased 45% over the study's 4 years. These re-surveyed projects comprised 60% of the farmers and 44% of the hectares in the original sample of 208 projects. For the 360 reliable yield comparisons from 198 projects, the mean relative yield increase was 79% across the very wide variety of systems and crop types. However, there was a wide spread in results. Although 25% of projects reported more than two-fold increases in half of all the projects had yield much lower increases of between 18% and 100%.

These are impressive numbers, but only in part. The proportion of cultivated land studied in this large set of data amounts to less than 4 percent of the total cultivated area in the countries studied. The number of farmers enrolled in the study is less than that. The share of total agricultural production is much less than that. These facts raise questions as to the problems of scaling up to levels of production sufficient for larger populations. As an engineer, I know that is where the world can be lost.

Most of the research on agroecology does not inform us as to its capacity to feed cities in addition to the rural areas of southern Africa, southern Asia, and Latin America. In the analysis of recent agroecological research by Pretty, for example, there is no information on whether these projects were predominantly in rural areas serving local markets or on the extent to which they contributed to the food supply of broader regional and especially urban populations. In his 2011 compilation of papers on the topic, most concerned rural farmers. In one study of periurban agriculture in Nigeria, it was noted that the efforts to develop larger markets did not succeed.

This does not mean it is impossible to increase the productivity of agro-ecology, but it does raise legitimate questions as to whether feasible increases are sufficient to meet the projections of global urbanization, which are highest in the poorer half of the world. This is one of the most serious, and most ethical, challenges to those who hold to the superiority of agro-ecological and other alternatives: can they provide sufficient food for the world, for the urban centers that are significant foci of hunger within poor countries? But proponents of agroecology do not deal with this issue, focusing rather on the primacy of feeding rural populations.

BEYOND PRODUCTION TO FOOD SECURITY

We know even in the richest countries of the world, which have the most productive agriculture in human history, that food security—ensuring reliable access to food—remains an unsolved problem. Cities have always faced challenges related to food insecurity, linked to problems in food access. Cities are where the bread riots of history, feared by politicians, have always occurred, from the Roman consul Sulla through the bread riots preceding the October Revolution in Russia in 1918 to uprisings that presaged the first wave of the Arab Spring in Tunisia in 2012. Food insecurity is strongly related to food access, as exemplified in my city of Baltimore. Baltimore is a mid-sized conurbation distinguished not so much by its size as by its proximity to an enormous engine of economics and innovation (Washington, DC). Together, the joint population of these two cities is nearly 10 million. Baltimore is home to many institutions of higher learning (including my own, Johns Hopkins University), such that nearly 20 percent of the city's population is made up of college students. But Baltimore, like many similar cities around the world, is really two cities, a bimodal distribution of income, education, and opportunity that continues to divide along race. Nowhere is this so clear as in the division between high and low food access, which is a characteristic of the city's neighborhoods. Food access in Baltimore is delineated by neighborhood, by distance to the nearest supermarket, and lack of availability of other food outlets providing healthy food (such as convenience and corner stores), as well as by socioeconomic variables including poverty.

As is the case generally in the United States, in Baltimore, the risk factors for low food access are lacks: lack of income, lack of quality food outlets, lack of affordable and nutritionally superior food products, lack of adequate transportation, and lack of neighborhood safety. These lacks reinforce each other. Lack of income at the neighborhood level discourages higher-quality food outlets from locating in these neighborhoods; lack of these outlets, in turn, increases the price and availability of better products; and lack of transportation and lack of safety reduce the ability and willingness of residents to travel to better stores in other neighborhoods. Transportation is also a barrier. Some of Baltimore's food deserts were created by transportation policies, evident in the abrupt divisions in the center of the map. These divisions follow major traffic arteries that, when they were built to advantage suburban workers entering the city, resulted in disrupted neighborhoods. In Baltimore, construction of multilane expressways in and out of the city impeded the informal method of food delivery known as "Arabbing," a traditional practice of selling fresh and wholesome food from horse-drawn carts. Low food access and food insecurity can contribute to a range of health problems, including diabetes, obesity, early child mortality, childhood asthma, diabetes, and heart disease. And then a cycle emerges, where differentials in food access become differentials in health that then contribute to lack of income and exacerbate problems in food security.

The most effective policy attempt to reduce food insecurity and improve access within affluent societies has been to subsidize food purchases. The United States has implemented subsidies to support the Food Stamp Program and Supplemental Food Assistance Program, which were cut for the first time in a climate of political discord in 2014 and again in 2016. While other countries have implemented broader centralized policies to enhance access to social needs, the United States utilizes a method that directly transfers food to lower-income groups with a special emphasis on those with special needs—specifically women, infants, and children—known as the WIC program (formally known as the Special Supplemental Nutrition Program for Women, Infants, and Children). WIC has had several interesting effects, one on the ability of the poor to afford food; another on the decision of food outlets to locate in areas that serve the poor; and another, most importantly, on forming a critical political link between public and private goals through the use of subsidies to support agriculture and reduce costs of food. But it has not ended inequalities in food access or the conditions associated with food insecurity, and political support for this program has eroded despite the common interests of agribusiness and advocates for the poor.

The obesity epidemic underscores the importance of access. Obesity is increasing in many populations, while food scarcity, or the actual lack of food in addition to access problems, continues in the same countries (as in China, India, and Mexico). Is this a market failure or a social failure? Inadequate incomes continue to be the lot of billions in a world of rotting food, and poverty, particularly in urban populations, is the major driver of food insecurity. Poverty is a topic that has filled many books. It has been noted that although increasing incomes has been a driver of opening agricultural markets, it has not worked as well as had been expected in terms of reducing hunger. This may be because of the complicated policies of donor agencies and banks, which require poor countries, as a condition for receiving aid, to balance their budgets in the name of "structural readjustment." Structural readjustment is a complicated and controversial policy, but there is general agreement that its impacts on social welfare systems have counteracted much of the progress associated with international food aid programs.

The linked challenges of food access and food security demand more consideration, particularly by advocates of alternative methods. The industrial model can claim to provide solutions to three of the main risk factors related to access and food security: reliable availability of agricultural products, a level of generally acceptable affordability, and efficient transportation within food networks. If food insecurity and access still persist, as they do in the United States, this persistence reflects factors other than the mode of production. In fact, they are best considered separately, because if sufficient food is not available, then access and security are choked in the cradle. As is evident from the prevalence of food insecurity, the problem of access cannot be solved by increased production alone.

In many developing countries, food insecurity is aggravated by food scarcity, not only arising from limitations in agricultural productivity but also from other factors related to food production, including food losses before reaching the consumer. Here, even some of the advocates of smallholder agriculture recognize the importance of integrating these farmers to larger networks of product dissemination in order to improve their role in the national food supply as well as increasing their economic returns. This is not "local production and local consumption" as advocated by some strict proponents of agroecology, but it is realistic.

CAN WE FEED OURSELVES WITHOUT INDUSTRIAL AGRICULTURE?

Equally intense scrutiny needs to be applied to the feasibility of nonindustrial methods for supporting populations in the developed world. Some argue that we in the developed world can and therefore should lead the way to the reforms that will support new global paths in agriculture. But we ought to examine whether these methods are sustainable and economically viable within our comparatively rich societies before we propose them as solutions for regions with greater challenges related to components of food systems, such as transportation, storage, and technical expertise. We must examine the extent to which these alternative paths are consistent with meeting the demands for food within highly developed countries.

There is not a large amount of data on this topic, and comparisons across studies are limited by different methods of measuring production. The economic sustainability, or profitability, of alternative agriculture is less clear because these farms tend to utilize family labor, thus reducing or avoiding the variable costs of hired labor needed during the cycle of small-scale agricultural production. Separating agricultural sectors is also less clear in the developed world. The agroecology movement, as advocated, is small scale, almost always family run, and usually linked specifically to local or nearby markets. In the United States, the organic sector can be quite large and industrialized in many respects of production (including contract growers and integrated management), and this sector sells over 80 percent of its products through the wholesale market rather than locally. Nonetheless, as of 2015, the organic sector accounts for less than 5 percent of US food purchases.

For smaller producers, such as those supplying farmers' markets and CSAs, profitability is debatable and largely dependent upon the existence of consumers willing and able to pay premium prices for the same product, differentiable on the basis of perceived quality. The peak of the CSA model was probably attained in the United States when a luxury boutique poultry farm was opened to supply heirloom breeds to very upscale consumers, with its animals fed on table scraps from Daniel, Per Se, and Gramercy Tavern, among other top restaurants in New York City (where a dinner can cost $400 without wine). This may be a self-limiting phenomenon, like Trimalchio's outlandish dinner in *Satyricon*, but it is not part of a realistic food system.

Apart from this bagatelle of boutique farming for high-end urban restaurants, it is not clear whether small-scale, independent operations that use nonindustrial methods (usually including organic methods) are providing a livelihood—that is, profits that exceed costs sufficient to support living expenses, housing, and all those things we have to buy from medicines to gas—in the United States for farmers, marketers, and others who participate in these systems. Some of these farmers have even made this point. Ben Smith, a farmer on Long Island, New York, titled his essay on this topic "Don't Let Your Children Grow Up to Be Farmers." He wrote:

> The dirty secret of the food movement is that the much-celebrated small-scale farmer isn't making a living. After the tools are put away, we head out to second and third jobs to keep our farms afloat. Ninety-one percent of all farm households rely on multiple sources of income. Health care, paying for our kids' college, preparing for retirement? Not happening. With the overwhelming majority of American farmers operating at a loss—the median farm income was negative $1,453 in 2014—farmers can barely keep the chickens fed and the lights on.
>
> Others of us rely almost entirely on Department of Agriculture or foundation grants, not retail sales, to generate farm income. And young farmers, unable to afford land, are increasingly forced into neo-feudal relationships, working the fields of wealthy landowners.

Even Wes Jackson, one of the progenitors of the agroecological movement, has expressed doubts as to the economic sustainability of the movement, as recounted by Dan Barber, a leading chef and director of the Stone Barns Center for Food and Agriculture:

> Of all the insights and observations I've gained from farmers, breeders and chefs doing the research for [my] book, I can't help dialing back, again and again, to the one that sits with me most heavily. It was after I told Wes Jackson about Klaas' [a friend's] farm, arguing that it was a good example of sustainability. Wes didn't buy it. "It won't last," he said. And just like that, he rejected not only Klaas' work but also a generation

of farmers looking to transition their farms in similar ways . . . A truly
sustainable food system is not simple . . . and [won't] last without a permanent food system to sustain them.

There are small studies on CSAs, the micromarkets in which farmers and
consumers are linked. In principle, such linkages should encourage profitability, as there is only one step between producers and consumers, such that
farmers should be able to directly pass on costs and reduce risks of losses—
much as the simplification of the food chain by the integrated system of
industrial food animal production has had economic benefits in reducing
risks for consumers and farmers. But, as described by Michael Pollan and
experienced by those of us who have tried or know of those who have tried
it, alternative farming is a return to many of the more onerous aspects of
preindustrial modes of production. By eschewing much of modern agricultural technology, it requires considerable contributions of human labor and
other resources to support the relatively small levels of production of these
farms. In other words, it is not efficient. "But," my agroecologist colleagues
say, "this is not the point." But money must be made for the necessary items
that farm families cannot grow (medicines, salt, coffee, clothing) as well
as for hiring labor, gasoline for machinery, and energy costs for light and
heat. In CSA systems, consumers contribute some of the labor by helping
with the harvest and transportation of goods. At some point, though, the
commitment to the cause wears thin. This has happened before in our social
history, from Brook Farm to the intentional communes of the 1960s; there
have been many "back to the land" movements and adoptions of "simple
life," but none have lasted much beyond a few decades of the first generation. It is hard to convince most consumers—as opposed to theorists—to
go backward in time. It is also the reason why these sectors are unlikely to
significantly displace industrial food systems in the national food basket.

In 2014, according to the USDA, about eight thousand farms participate in farmers' markets in the United States. They fall far short of meeting
consumer demands. Take USDA data that eight billion broiler chickens are
consumed each year in the United States—or about thirty chickens per person per year. In comparison, total US production of organic chickens in 2012
reached a peak of six million, or about 0.001 percent of the total. Even without economic and locational barriers, the current levels of nonindustrial,

small-scale production would only yield enough product to feed a very small number of consumers.

A national food system must be able to meet national demands. For developed countries as well as the rest of the world, the challenge is the same: to feed large numbers of people mostly living in cities. And industrial agriculture is currently the best means of providing food to the most amount of consumers.

In addition to economics, there is also an ethical dimension to this discussion, which some consider to be a separate way of thinking. But the relatively high price of food produced by nonindustrial methods, including CSA products, excludes most consumers even in affluent countries from participation. Some advocates and practitioners of alternative methods have begun to notice how large segments of society are excluded from accessing their products.

Critics claim that industrialized agriculture's ability to feed so many is a mirage created by subsidies and giveaways, as well as by the exclusions from the balance sheet of its high externalized costs to environment, health, and society. Subsidies and externalities are ways of hiding costs or shifting them away from the enterprise to society at large. Many argue that agricultural accounting should consider both unvalued and undervalued costs. They advance the position that the true value of industrialized agriculture should include the costs of adverse impacts on health, dangers in the workplace, environmental degradation, reduced biodiversity, animal welfare, water use, and reliance on fossil fuels.

Subsidies remain controversial for their effects on global food supplies. For a range of purposes, countries use both subsidies and tariffs to raise the bar for entry of goods in order to protect domestic markets. Japan famously blocked importation of rice grown in the United States, and the European Union blocked importation of bananas from the Americas (in this case to protect former colonies). We may be contesting the wrong issue to argue about subsidies when tariffs are more influential on a global scale.

WHAT IS THE POINT?

Is the debate about means of production a sideshow to the larger topic of feeding the world? Can it contain openings to a different future? Is it a road forward or a road back? After a rather exhausting immersion into agricultural productivity and economics, I have found it puzzling as to why intelligent commentators like Jules Henry insist that nonindustrial methods can feed the world, including those subsets of the world like our own.

Talking about agriculture without the mists of a romantic past is one factor. Wendell Berry and others advocate a vision of agriculture that is similar to the traditional crafts sector, where a higher value is assigned to endeavors that apparently override or ignore the mundane nature of profit and loss. We must acknowledge that this is not a food system, and largely irrelevant to the serious questions of present-day agriculture.

So what is the point of alternative agriculture? One analysis found relatively specific socioeconomic characteristics of CSAs in terms of the supporting community, including political liberalism, high education, and commitment to environmental and other communitarian goals. Also, most farmers in CSAs were not from farm families and in fact had little experience in farming prior to setting up relatively small operations in the CSA networks. These findings do not disqualify alternative agriculture, but they may raise concerns as to the longevity of the movement.

These are all topics worth discussing. But, like so much else related to agriculture, we must be realistic about the benefits and limitations of all models of production. It will not be easy to feed the world.

12

A PATH FORWARD, NOT BACKWARD

We are at the end of this story, which has traveled through history, politics, and science. History offered a path back from the present to the past, based on the assumption that there was discernible and useful information from presumptions that were reasonable earlier in time to the problems revealed over time and increasingly important in the present. In the course of writing this book, I have been amazed by how few historians of agriculture have examined the transformation of food animal production, so my historical work was more challenging than anticipated. As the start date, I looked to 1920, with the first expansion in broiler poultry production in that peninsular patchwork of Delmarva. There was a reason why industrialization—intensive, confined, and integrated—began there and in the Deep South. A history of indentured and inefficient agriculture, isolation from other industries and economic opportunities, hostility to organized labor, and lack of political power of their rural populations all led to the conditions that eased the transformation of traditional agriculture into an industrialized mode of production, first in poultry and then in growing other livestock.

At the beginning of this book, I promised readers that I would not end with outrage or without proposing ways forward from the problems of the present. I made this commitment before I undertook much of the research and listening that has informed this book along with my own primary research in the field. And I added on some additional pledges to those I made at the outset, to promote public health and to feed the world. That last pledge was more complicated than I had first assumed. In fact, it raised many questions I had not anticipated, about what we mean by "feeding," the "world," and even "what" are the foods that people want to eat. Our diets have been flattened by cyberspace through advertising and social media, both of which give almost universal windows to view what is on dinner plates around the world.

I did not make any pledge to the concept of sustainability. The multiplicity of stated and unstated definitions of this term makes me cautious because, at some deep level, humans have altered forever the meaning of sustainability through our ability to invent new technologies that have stretched the boundaries of natural limits without a balancing consideration of anticipated and unanticipated impacts. As my thinking and writing progressed, two definitions of sustainability emerged. First is an *ecological* concept of sustainability in terms of the conservation of nature and natural resources, and the second is an *economic* concept in terms of assuring adequate remuneration of the human effort of producing food and ensuring affordable food. In practice as well as theory, I observed deep conflicts among proponents of these two definitions. Clearly, both are essential. We cannot produce anything that will eventually prevent future production, and we cannot produce anything that does not support a fair marketplace for the whole chain of workers and producers as well as products that consumers can afford and want to eat. I found little in the way of productive conversation between proponents of these two definitions. And as I began to write this book, similar problems of communication seemed to stand in the way of meaningful conversations about agriculture, so I began with that topic.

As implied by the title of this final chapter, what I offer is a path forward, not a road back. This is not the most comfortable place to be in the disputed landscape of current opinions and much of the writing about agriculture and the food system. There are relatively few friends in the middle ground to assist in proposing a path forward between the adamantine cliffs—to quote Shelley—of industry and agroecologists. But to industry I advise: if you do not accept reform, you will continue to face increasing controversies and a growing body of evidence of the harms caused by your current practices. And eventually reforms will come. To the agroecologists I advise: if you insist upon a thoroughgoing renunciation of current agricultural technology, you will be challenged by the likelihood of failure to provide sufficient and affordable food for more than a limited elite unless you can demonstrate that your solutions of small farms, local markets, and inefficient systems are more than one of the many "Fortress America" solutions that we have applied to too many social ills, whereby we too often and sometimes literally barricade ourselves against them, creating refuges for the privileged (such as private schools, gated communities, hired guards, corporate bus services) and ignoring the despair of those who cannot enter the castle of privilege.

So here are six conclusions, with which I propose a way forward for the short term to the midterm. For the longer term, there are major changes required for creating a more rational, equitable, and reliable food system that extends beyond the production of some of our food from animals. There are cogent writings on these topics; here I choose to start the journey along a path that may eventually lead us to such foundational changes.

Conclusion 1: Sustainability is about human society as well as the natural world

Agriculture involves humans as well as the natural world. To achieve its stated purpose, to feed us, agriculture must be feasible within the constraints of the natural world, understanding the limits of resources and ensuring those resources' continued availability. But, equally, agriculture is a human activity, and the humans who perform the work of feeding us all must themselves be able to survive in both simple and complex systems. One sustainability cannot sacrifice the other; we have to seek ways that optimize both.

Conclusion 2: Agriculture is technology; from the Neolithic Age to the present, it is the response of an inventive species to the challenge of surviving in the real world

Early in this book I asked, "Can we talk about agriculture?" Problems in communication run throughout conversations and policies on agriculture. Much of the fog of this particular theater of conflict, I found, arose from deep cultural memes and themes. Agriculture and farming are deeply freighted concepts going back to creation stories in several religions, some of the earliest human writings, and ensuing centuries of art and poetry. In the West, there is a long cultural tradition, reinforced in the Romantic Age, about nature and the place of humans within a benign and nourishing natural world.

But contrasting with Eden and Arcadia is the equally fundamental view of agriculture as a punishing hardship of the human condition. Some of the earliest writings in our history define agriculture as a curse by the gods for human presumption to knowledge. "For the gods keep hidden from men the means of life. For now truly is a race of iron, and men never rest from labor and sorrow by day, and from perishing by night; and the gods shall lay sore trouble upon them . . . Else you would easily do work enough in a day to supply you for a full year even without working; soon would you put away your rudder over the smoke, and the fields worked by ox and sturdy mule would run to waste," wrote Hesiod, identifying agriculture as a life of toil and punishment to humans for accepting the Promethean gift of fire, certainly a form of knowledge and technology. In the Book of Genesis, upon the expulsion from Eden for a similar crime of wanting knowledge, Adam and Eve are condemned to a life of hardship: "Because you have listened to the voice of your wife, and have eaten from the tree about which I commanded you, saying, 'You shall not eat from it'; cursed is the ground because of you; In toil you will eat of it all the days of your life" (3:17).

These themes about agriculture are more than just literary tropes from ancient sources. Our unwillingness to acknowledge the hard reality of agriculture depicted in the narrative in both stories—Hesiod's Golden Age and the Judeo-Christian Eden—makes us easy victims of advertising and policies that tempt and persuade us through invocations of an agriculture long lost (if indeed it ever existed). We must see agriculture for what it is and not seek solutions in an imaginary past. Seek to change the present, not to re-create the past.

To simply state, as this book does, that agriculture is technology, is to stir up some strong reactions. To go on, as this book does, to state that "industrialization" is not a pejorative term is to lose close friends. This experience drew me, unexpectedly, back to my own personal history with agriculture as a young child at my relatives' farms, where even intermittent experience revealed the unromantic work of farming, which has made me more likely to appreciate the views of Stella Gibbons, author of *Cold Comfort Farm*, than those of Rousseau or Michael Pollan. Nothing more than that, nothing in the way of special knowledge, but that early experience, I have learned, is not a little thing in a country where few of us still have a direct connection to the vanishing world of traditional agriculture.

Conclusion 3: Industrial food animal production is porous, not confined

Food animal production is intense and dense, but it is not actually confined, the use by government and industry of terms like "confinement houses." In that failure to recognize reality and to substitute misleading words lies much of the impact of these methods on public health and the environment. The porosity of industrial food animal production is overlooked by those who should know better. All it takes is a simple consideration of the need to ventilate tens of thousands of animals held in dense herds and flocks. Pathogens, like avian and swine influenzas, can enter these buildings, and these pathogens can leave by the same route of ventilation. Sadly, the global response to outbreaks of zoonotic influenzas has accelerated the shift away from the backyards of smallholder production on the assumption, without evidence, that both humans and animals are better protected by confinement. This is a false promise, as the current outbreaks of highly pathogenic avian influenza and porcine epidemic diarrheal disease indicate.

The largest hole in the concept of confinement is the overlooked product of industrialization. Animal wastes are the largest product in terms of mass, but their true impact is masked by euphemistic terms such as "lagoon" for the reality of open cesspits. Agricultural wastes are not subject to the elemental regulations most countries require for handling and treating human wastes. Even slaughterhouse wastes are not adequately regulated, with requirements focusing solely on the simplest parameters of water quality.

Conclusion 4: Industrial food animal production does not necessarily produce safe food

Put simply, there is currently little left intact of a system that would require the actions needed to ensure food safety in modern agriculture. Over the past seventy years, industrialized food production has brought plentiful, reliable, and affordable food for hundreds of millions of people in developed countries. But its proponents overreach when they claim that industrialization has also brought the benefit of safer food. At the beginning of writing this book, I was willing to believe this claim based on the regulations I thought were in place in animal slaughter and processing plants. It also seemed plausible, as industry representatives have argued, that the increased scale of production brought greater resources to improve food safety and inspection. Throughout this book, you have followed my discovery of the hollowness to these claims. Operations in large slaughter and processing plants are in many cases haphazard and dangerous (this work has the highest rates of injury in any industrial sector in the United States), and the industry has used its economic power to overturn the food and worker safety inspection systems put in place by Theodore Roosevelt's early twentieth-century reforms. As well, the use of antimicrobial drugs—an unnecessary use as far as the current evidence goes—has added a new dimension to food safety, the emergence and spread of drug-resistant pathogens around the world.

Conclusion 5: Worker safety is food safety

Among the agricultural matters we do not want to talk about are the people who make our food on farms and in animal slaughter and processing plants. "I aimed at the public's heart and by accident hit its stomach," Upton Sinclair said in dissatisfaction over the enormous but incomplete response to *The Jungle*. The public and President Theodore Roosevelt together propelled legislation establishing the food safety powers of the FDA, but left out of those reforms was the safety of the worker. This omission continues to this day. Just as the heart and the stomach are inextricably connected, there is no food safety without worker safety. And by food safety I don't mean preventing workers from contaminating food, as some contend, but rather improving the conditions of work that do not protect either workers or our food.

We avert our eyes from much of agriculture, and doing so has empowered the industry to demand an end to intrusive regulation and an acquiescence of government in these demands. It takes gyrations of thinking and inversions of logic to maintain this blindness. A court determined that because occupational safety and health regulators could not determine a line speed in poultry processing that would prevent worker injuries, then no limits on line speed could be imposed; another court recently determined that practices by integrators to control prices, such that independent producers were shut out of the market, was nothing more than the industry's right to act in the interests of its own profits.

This extreme laissez-faire approach has dismantled food safety regulation as well. The primary rationale has been based on preserving the profits of the industry rather than consumer or worker health and safety. On July 30, 2014, the USDA ceded to industry much of what remained of its authority to carry out food safety inspections on-site in slaughter and processing plants. As I feared when I submitted comments on this proposed regulation, the regulations remove most required actions by industry or government to verify the effectiveness of their actions, requiring only for industry to keep records of having undertaken these actions.

By looking the other way, we allow other problems with agriculture to continue. CDC and other agencies do not collect comprehensive data on foodborne diseases or on the extent to which antimicrobial drugs are used in animal feeds. Participation in these programs is voluntary, and as a result monitoring for foodborne illness or infections by drug-resistant bacteria covers less than half of the US population. Public health officials from CDC as well as medical organizations join with the food industry, wringing their hands over the tidal wave of antimicrobial resistance, almost always without mentioning the enormity of drug use in animal feeds. This has not changed with the formation of new committees and "wars" against antimicrobial resistance. OSHA does not even recognize exposure to pathogens as a work-related health risk for food production workers. OSHA undertook a pilot study of injuries and infections among slaughter and processing plant workers from 2005 to 2009, and then threw the data into a box until we rescued it. OSHA turns a blind eye to the exploitation of vulnerable populations, including illegal immigrants and prison inmates, in slaughter and processing. The industry has intentionally located its operations in regions of the United States where these populations are available and where the political climate is hostile to unionization and workers' rights to a safe workplace and decent wages. Delegating responsibility to some states that are leading producers of poultry and hogs has led to abuses and even fatal fires in processing plants—in the twenty-first century.

When I first started working on poultry production in Delmarva, studying the workers in poultry houses, I was told by the industry that cats brought pathogenic bacteria into the workplace. I looked up all the studies I could on these workers and others in pork production, but I found nothing about cats. I did find many reports by academics and even union representatives blaming workers for food contamination. I found few academic studies blaming the industry for contaminating workers with pathogens in workplaces little changed from Upton Sinclair's descriptions of dull and deadly labor.

Put simply, there is no structure to ensure food or worker safety in this industry in the United States at present. The whole system is premised on the flawed concept of HACCP—what workers call "have a cup of coffee and pray." For what it is worth—which is not much, as it is based on what is called "organoleptic inspection," or what you can see, smell, or touch—HACCP leaves off just before processing meat and poultry begins and long before meat and poultry products leave the processing plants for our tables. Unsafe food passes through lines of workers, and workers cut and snip lines of unsafe food. The FDA and CDC rightly warn us about the dangers of our food, but they push the burden of protecting public health onto us, the consumers, and they give us little useful information with which to defend ourselves. Any attempt to tighten the links between food and disease—going forward to prevent illness or working backward to find out the sources of disease—is met with fierce resistance by the industry. Organic and alternative producers similarly object to any directives related to increasing food safety in their operations. Actions after the fact—such as recalling contaminated food products—are always late and sometimes impossible to detect.

Conclusion 6: Industrial food animal production endangers global health, beyond food

Using antimicrobial drugs in animal feeds undermines whatever gains in food safety could have been achieved by advances in industrial agriculture for the benefit of public health. This single event in industrial food animal production has eroded not only food safety but also the entire safety net of antimicrobial therapy that has saved billions of lives since the discovery of penicillin in the 1940s.

How did this happen—how could this have happened? Unraveling that history has been one of the finest chases that I have experienced. At the very end of it, how unnecessary it all has been. I hope I have restored Dr. Lucy Wills to the position of eminence she deserves in medicine and nutrition; if her work on the role of yeast extracts had won the day over the pharmaceutical industry, we would never have started down the sorry road of throwing one precious drug after another into animal foods. The evidence proffered by industry in support of their applications was paltry even by the standards of the day. No full examination of the claims of growth promotion was undertaken until 1984, when Perdue—not government—ran an extraordinary experiment. A Perdue scientist alerted me to the study, and I thank him for it.

With a team that included my extraordinary graduate student Dr. Jay Graham (who came to public health with an MBA) and my wise colleague Dr. John Boland (a resource economist), we looked to the Perdue study to find out exactly what the benefits of growth-promoting antimicrobials were. To our surprise, these benefits were vanishingly small—likely nonexistent—and the costs of using drugs were not offset by the small profits of slight increases in weight gain and even slighter decreases in feed consumption. Very importantly, the Perdue researchers reported no increases in deaths, disease, or other losses in flocks receiving drug-free feeds.

In the face of the new industry line on antimicrobial feed additives, this lesson bears repeating: antimicrobials are not being used for growth promotion, but ostensibly for disease prevention. In this new world, the industry is once again aided and abetted by the FDA, just as it was in the 1940s, when industry applications to the FDA for permission to use drugs in feeds were approved on the basis of inadequate evidence for efficacy and no consideration of risk. Recently, a court ruled that, even today, the FDA is not required to undertake evaluations for the health impacts of antimicrobial use in animal feeds. The FDA issued recommendations for more "judicious use," rather like suggesting to an arsonist that she burn only a small building rather than taking away her matches. The industry responded by renaming the same uses of antimicrobials in feeds as "prevention" of disease, a move much like putting a toad in a new dress. These uses of antimicrobial drugs were approved as feed additives by the FDA at subtherapeutic doses, *which by definition means they cannot be effective for treating or preventing disease*. Unfortunately, the FDA advances this subterfuge with new voluntary programs that passively permit continued use of drugs in feeds for the purported goal of preventing disease. They know better. A 2014 investigation by Reuters found that many companies are continuing to use antimicrobials in feeds even while claiming to produce chicken without the use of drugs.

The WHO, CDC, and most experts in infectious disease consider the use of antibiotics as feed additives to be inappropriate. The Danish government reacted quickly to a similar end run by its pork industry and stipulated that their regulations were meant to ban all use of antimicrobial drugs administered as feed additives.

Antimicrobials in animal feeds have seriously compromised the defenses against many infectious diseases that we have enjoyed since the discovery of antimicrobials in the 1940s. According to both the WHO and CDC, as well as health agencies in many other countries, such as the United Kingdom and Germany, we now face the imminent end of the antibiotic era. This end will be disastrous for health while interesting for science, as much of what we know about bacterial evolution in response to antimicrobials has come from the long, uncontrolled experiment of drug use in agriculture. "Really exciting research findings, but terrible for public health" is a common expression in my experience as a public health researcher.

From that experience, we should conduct our relations with the microbial world with much more respect and circumspection. "Who are we?" asked Martin Blaser, one of the world's experts on the microbial systems that live within and on us and our planet. The answer: mostly bacteria, by ten to one. We live through the presence of bacteria, and, as a species, we have evolved with our own bacterial ecosystems, or microbiomes. Our discovery of the usefulness of antimicrobial drugs is very recent, and we have based our knowledge on the natural toxins produced by microbes for billions of years in the preservation of their communities. We have nothing new to show them, and so they quickly respond—as highly efficient communities—to our use and misuse of what we think of as "wonder drugs." We think that understanding antimicrobial resistance is restricted to the emergence of highly pathogenic bacteria resistant to increasingly powerful drugs. That is how we phrase the problem and how we monitor. But this view is too anthropocentric. We will never regain our foothold in combating infectious disease unless we shed those glasses. Antimicrobial resistance is a conversation among bacteria—pathogenic and commensal, or bad and good—in which they share experiences and tools to persist in the face of toxic stress; they use highly sophisticated methods of conversation, including what I have called "cloud computing" to form social networks, like cliques, in which they converse using the language of genes.

THE WAY FORWARD

So much for conclusions. Now for my promise to find a way out.

Step 1: Abandon illusions about agriculture

This first step has been reiterated throughout this book. Agriculture is and always has been a technology. Like other human activities, agriculture can and has been industrialized in terms of its organization, economics, and technologies. We are all guilty of holding on to illusions of Arcadian rurality: the industry for enticing consumers, governments for continuing outdated policies that exempt agriculture from modern regulatory requirements, and many of us for our attraction to a return to past practices. But the way forward is not the way back. The mythical paradise of traditional agriculture no longer exists and probably never existed for those who farmed for a living. We humans have voted with our feet for millennia, leaving the depths of rural life and agrarian work for the vastly greater opportunities—and perils—of cosmopolitan life. Our towns have grown into cities, and our cities need food, more food than can be produced by traditional or alternative methods. So accept that agriculture is an industry, and treat it as such.

Step 2: Accept the ethical challenge to feed the world, and accept the ethical obligation to respect the aspirations and choices of others

Until we can produce as much food as needed and more without modern agriculture, we should not urge alternative agricultures on developing societies, such as in Africa, that are themselves rapidly urbanizing. Too many solutions depend upon persuading affluent societies to make radical changes in their current diets, and developing societies to maintain traditional diets. No solution to a public health problem has ever been accomplished by requiring individuals or societies to make major changes in lifestyle or to limit personal choice, particularly individuals and societies whose scope of choice is finally widening with the trickle down of affluence that characterizes the modern world. Requiring radical change is to abandon the concept of a partnership.

Step 3: Create a "Bill of Rights and Obligations" for industrialized agriculture

Agriculture is an industry. Let it be an industry, accepted as an industry by critics and industrialists alike. If industry has a right to be industrial, we have a right to treat it accordingly, and to expect it to comply with the rules and regulations that constrain the operations of other industries, including restraint on economic concentration and legal responsibility for currently externalized costs. Industries must submit to local and state zoning authorities and, when large enough, submit documentation of their potential impacts on the environment (the so-called Environmental Impact Statement, a policy initiated in 1969, even before the creation of the EPA). We have a right to expect government to carry out the actions necessary to create a level playing field, such that all industrial enterprises must meet the same conditions. This has been the fulcrum of environmental regulation from the beginning, as typified by the pesticide industry, which grudgingly supported the federal regulatory system in order to avoid patchwork variations in state regulation and that all producers had to bear the same costs.

First and foremost under this new Bill of Rights and Obligations, no party shall continue to enjoy special treatment for industrialized food production on the grounds of any existing exemptions or conditions specific to "agriculture." In other words, agriculture is an industry, and as such it carries certain obligations, including:

- Industries must abide by laws that prevent monopolization, price fixing, and overconcentration. Industries cannot utilize contracts to restrain trade or the freedom of workers to organize.
- Industries must not be exempted from the constitutional guarantees of freedom of speech, such that legislation that attempts to hinder public discourse and access cannot stand. If antiabortion demonstrators have the right to protest those practicing and seeking abortion, then your opponents have the same rights related to speech as well as access to public activities, within bounds that respect the rights of others.
- Industries must disclose the presence and use of hazardous materials in their operations.
- Industries must provide evidence, on the public record, of the safety of all materials used in production.
- Industries must bear full liability for unsafe products and the burden of guaranteeing safety of their products.
- Industries must be responsible for the entire lifecycle of production, including their external impacts, especially regulation and reduction of waste streams. As with chemical wastes, delegation of waste management to other parties does not absolve producer responsibility under the waste management laws of the United States.
- Industries must comply with local and state regulations on zoning in terms of location and concentration, including documentation

of anticipated health and environmental impacts as well as submission of environmental impact statements and participation in open hearings.

- Industries must obey the labor laws of the country, including providing a safe workplace for all, not employing children, permitting the lawful organization of workers into unions, and ensuring a minimum wage.
- Industries must be subject to workers' compensation laws, including state regulations on contributing to workers' insurance, as well as all other conditions governing safe and equitable workplaces. Industries must justify the legal classification of any workers as contractors.
- Industries must permit on-site inspection by authorized personnel of local, state, and national agencies; if state agencies are unable or unwilling to perform these duties, responsibility for inspection and enforcement is delegated to the federal government.

Governments at all levels also have obligations in ensuring the conduct of the industry, including:

- Governments must institute and maintain adequate programs of oversight and inspection to assure worker and food safety within the industry. Data collection within these programs shall be made public.
- State and federal governments must comply with statutory requirements to devise and implement adequate and transparent systems of inspection and regulation. If states are unable or unwilling to do perform this role, the responsibility falls on the federal government.
- Governments must approve any proposed change by any industrial enterprise in its operations, including feed formulation, that could affect worker safety, food safety, and the environment.
- Governments have zoning authority over the siting and operation of any proposed or operating industrial operation. Governments must provide for citizen comment on such proposals prior to approval.
- Governments must respond to petitions by workers and citizens alleging malfeasance by industry in terms of worker safety, discharge of pollutants, and other matters.

- Governments must collect and publish data on industrial operations in terms of hazardous materials, waste disposal, worker health and safety, and violations of food safety standards.
- Governments must promulgate binding regulations on industrial processes that ensure protection of human health, the food supply, animal welfare, and the environment.

All of these rights and obligations already exist within the environmental, occupational, and consumer safety laws of the United States. They have withstood extensive pushback from industry, including a lawsuit brought by the Dow Chemical Company in an attempt to block EPA inspectors from flying over its Midland, Michigan, headquarters to monitor air pollution releases.

So our problems with industrialized agriculture are not impossible to solve within this country. Nor is change only possible by turning away from the industrial model. The harder—but necessary—road is the road of reform, which does not require deep thinking or innovative structures of governance. We do not need to invent new bureaucracies but rather to require existing structures of government and industry to accept the reality of agriculture as an industry. It may be more efficient to integrate mandates from some of the existing agencies—such as the FDA and the USDA—into a new and independent organization. Similar integration happened in 1970, when Congress transferred authority for regulating pesticides from the USDA to the new EPA in order to prioritize the importance of ensuring safety, empowering a new agency authorized to consider more than efficacy. In fact, it is why the EPA was founded. Charlie Wurster, a chemistry professor at Stony Brook University and one of the founders of the Environmental Defense Fund, told me how he had asked officials at the USDA why they permitted DDT to be used in the face of compelling evidence for its adverse effects on songbirds. "We don't do birds," they told him. So Wurster and other pioneers in US environmental organizations knew that a new agency was needed.

We know how to reform agriculture, having developed a portfolio of policy tools to constrain other industries to our social norms and expectations over the past forty years. In some instances, enforceable standards are appropriate (such as air and water quality standards); in other instances, technology-based standards are more appropriate (such as waste

management); and in others, economic instruments have been highly effective (especially requiring transparency in reporting). Governments can
raise funds for much of these activities through charging for reviewing and
approving new substances or processes and for licenses to operate industrial
production, including waste management.

This way forward bears analogies to the problem of producing enough
energy for all. There are many voices clamoring for the microphone and,
as in agriculture, groups advocating alternative methods such as the "soft
energy path." This alternative, like agroecology, gives priority to natural
sources of wind, sun, geothermal vents, and tides over current technology.
But without a (as yet undetermined) technological breakthrough, even a
portfolio of these alternative methods will be insufficient to meet present
and projected demands for energy where and when people want. Like the
challenges with feeding the world, people live in cities, where needs for
energy are concentrated. And people want energy for a range of reasons
beyond survival: to power private transportation, entertainment devices,
and air-conditioning, for example. The technological road down which we
started in the 1950s was nuclear power, now receiving some new respect
for its zero carbon footprint. But, like industrial agriculture, nuclear power
disadvantaged itself by gaining exemption from most environmental and
economic regulations as well as by hiding its problems from the public eye.
Moreover, like agriculture, the nuclear power industry (with government
complicity) was never held responsible for its waste stream. If it is to regain
any momentum as part of national and global energy strategies, the nuclear
power industry must also accept its position in the world of industry, subject to the requirements and expectations that we have all acquired over the
intervening decades.

The current problems of industrial agriculture are not inevitable. Going
back is not the way forward. There are no insoluble obstacles to reforming
industrialized food animal production—not the health of the environment,
workers and animals, or food and communities. All of these are being damaged by two forces: the current practices of industrialized food animal production and the extreme political forces that prevent adequate responses.
The result is such that I understand why critics call for an end to this type
of agriculture on the grounds that its impacts are too great to be allowed to
continue, that there is no way that the industrial model can be reformed into

something that does less harm to humans, animals, and the natural world. And industry and government are complicit in driving this argument by resisting almost every change.

But the answer is not a return to past practice. There is no real going back, to options with limited capacity to feed communities larger than self-forming networks, with no proven capacity to provide food at costs bearable to most of the world, and no demonstrable sustainability in terms of providing livelihoods to those who work in food production, particularly on the farm. I found many of the alternative proposals and solutions unsatisfactory as I examined them more closely. Most of them—local production and consumption, agroecology, organic production, expanding traditional methods of animal husbandry—failed the tests of feeding cities, to say nothing of the world. I became increasingly uncomfortable with much of the recent writing on food systems and feeding the world because it seems to be directed at a privileged elite, whose income and location enable them to exit the existing food system and to afford the expensive products of alternative agriculture. I cannot advocate this type of solution, available only for a few and inflexible in its requirements. This book is about the existing world and food systems and the challenges they present; turning away from reality does nothing to deal with these problems. Unfortunately, we have a lot of this kind of thinking in books about some of our most challenging social problems—education, urban environments, public safety, and ecological living. Such "fortress thinking" encourages those of us who are truly concerned to drop out of the public market; to send our kids to private school; to live in exclusive neighborhoods; to hire private guards; and to invest in "green" products such as cars, toilets, and energy sources.

For agriculture, if we choose this path as a solution, we do nothing about the problems of food production, food access, or food security. We remove ourselves from engagement with social and economic change. We buy ourselves out of the society in which most of us live, a plot familiar to many dystopic sci-fi novels like Chang-rae Lee's *On Such a Full Sea* or a kind of nightmarish extension of São Paulo, where those that can are helicoptered over the misery of those that can't. We cut ourselves off from thinking about those who cannot afford to exit unpleasant systems, in this case, to purchase garishly expensive food. Garish, that is, to most of our fellow citizens and the rest of the world. Most of all, by turning away from the present agricultural system, we discard any consideration of those who cannot escape: the farmers turned into contractors, the rural communities sapped of their economic blood, the workers in slaughter and processing, the ecosystems affected by intensive food animal production, the animals themselves.

When we disengage, we are not part of the solution. We are enabling the problem. I began this book by saying, "This book is not about food," because I do not believe that by eating correctly we are changing much of anything. Neither are we exempt from the collateral damage created by intensive agriculture by opting out by dietary choice. This is perhaps clearest in terms of the industry's dominant role in driving the emergence of antimicrobial drug resistance. I used the image of the nobility barricaded in their castle to avoid the plague in Poe's "The Masque of the Red Death." We can buy our way out of the market of mass-produced food, but we cannot insulate ourselves from the global exchange of drug-resistant infections. Vegetarians and others who choose not to consume meat are not immune to the malfeasance of food animal production, because crops have been contaminated by runoff from land disposal of animal wastes. Organic food is no solution either, because the use of animal manure is a mainstay in organic production of crops.

All of us must work together on finding the way forward, because reform is essential for all of us. Reform—feasible and sustainable reform for an agriculture that feeds the world—needs the participation and stamina of all of us to achieve the changes necessary for health, nutrition, animal welfare, social dignity, and sustainability. The power of ordinary people eventually becomes the power of change. Ordinary people led the response to Upton Sinclair's *The Jungle*, with strong leadership from women's clubs around the country. The food industry is remarkably responsive when it comes to consumer disfavor. "Pink slime"—a meat-based food additive—disappeared within weeks after it was outed by the media. These are things we can do, and we must do them together—with our wallets, of course, but with other actions, too, as solutions based on money alone do little to save us all and can do much to divide us.

What I have proposed is both short term and midterm, embedded in options and opportunities within the US system of government and regulations. As the originator of the transformation of food animal production, the United States should lead the way toward reform. But over the longer term, the way forward must be global. Like climate change, what I called the "collateral damage" of industrial practices—on the environment, society, and health—is not constrained by national boundaries. Like carbon, as Tom O'Brien said, the use of antimicrobials anywhere increases the risks of resistance everywhere. Food moves internationally, as do animals and people. Microbes—viruses and bacteria—are the most efficient travelers, moving with animals and people and by other means as well. Bacteria and their genes have been tracked on the dusts blown from Africa to North America and in the bilge water of cargo ships. And bacteria have long memories.

This book has documented how we got the agriculture we now have and how those same drivers are now operating globally to replace traditional methods in developed and developing countries alike. Solutions that do not accept the conditions of what it means to feed the world today—the world that exists, the food people want to eat in the cities they want to live in—are not realistic. Aspirational programs are not to be discarded, but the reality of hunger must be fed. Feeding the world safe and affordable food without degrading humans who produce our food, the environments in which we produce food, and the animals that are produced for our food were the premises I accepted in writing this book. The way forward arose effortlessly from this examination, and the signposts for that road can be discerned in this history. We can take them up again.

Notes

CHAPTER 1. CAN WE TALK ABOUT AGRICULTURE?

p. 7: M. Mazoyer and L. Roudart's *A History of World Agriculture: From the Neolithic Age to the Current Crisis* (London: Earthscan, 2006) has informed my thinking about the history of agriculture and human societies, but I did not fully appreciate how early the divisions in language appeared before reading Douglas Anthony's extraordinary book *The Horse, the Wheel, and Language* (Princeton, NJ: Princeton University Press, 2007), which illuminates the interplay between early advances in agricultural technology and the evolution of proto-Indo-European languages. The very words we use to this day in talking about agriculture are formed by our history of rural life.

The literature of talking farm animals goes back to Aesop; I cite E. B. White's *Charlotte's Web* (New York: Harper, 1952), George Orwell's *Animal Farm* (London: Secker and Warburg, 1945), and the movies *Babe* (released 1995) and *Chicken Run* (released 2000).

p. 8: Some of the conversation that opens this chapter is based on many hours in the Hopkins coffee shop as well as a special issue of the Johns Hopkins School of Public Health magazine on food (*The Food Issue*, Spring 2014) and *Food Tank*, the always provocative food blog by Danielle Nierenberg (http://foodtank.com/danielle-nierenberg).

pp. 9–11: I was reminded of Chang-rae Lee's novel *On Such a Full Sea* (New York: Penguin, 2014) about dystopian agriculture because of its setting in B-Mor, a fictional future city that had once been my hometown of Baltimore. For aquaponics, see work by the Center for a Livable Future at Johns Hopkins: http://www.livablefutureblog.com/2013/11/raft-plate-aquaponics-harvest.

Many writers, notably Percival Bidwell, "The Agricultural Revolution in New England," *American Historical Review* 26 (1921): 683–702, have provided the context for the short history of my family's leaving their New England farms. I recognized common threads in the stories of my friends as well as Isabel Wilkerson's study of the migration of Southern blacks from sharecropping to the factories of the North in *The Warmth of Other Suns* (New York: Random House, 2010). For the periodic social waves of going "back to the land," my parents were motivated by Scott and Helen Nearing's *The Good Life: Helen and Scott Nearing's Sixty Years of Self-Sufficient Living* (New York: Schocken, 1954), but this tradition can be traced in the United States at least to Brook Farm. See Sterling Delano, *Brook Farm: The Dark Side of Utopia* (Cambridge, MA: Harvard University Press, 2004).

I testified in Harrisburg, Pennsylvania, before the Pennsylvania House Majority Committee on antibiotic use in livestock on August 10, 2010, where I had the experience of talking to the state's secretary of agriculture before the hearing started. The first Environmental Protection Agency meeting on industrial food animal production, which I attended as an invited speaker, was held in Washington, DC, in 2001.

Campylobacter jejuni is the leading bacterial cause of foodborne gastroenteritis, as detailed by the US Centers for Disease Control and Prevention in *Antibiotic Resistance Threats in the United States* (Atlanta, GA: US Department of Health and Human Services, 2013). Cats can carry this pathogen, but most human exposures are through contact with poultry because it is an avian commensal; that is, birds normally carry the bacteria without harm to their health. See J. I. Keller and W. G. Shriver, "Prevalence of Three *Campylobacter* Species, *C. jejuni*, *C. coli*, and *C. lari*, Using Multilocus Sequence Typing in Wild Birds of the Mid-Atlantic Region, USA," *Journal of Wildlife Diseases* 50 (2014): 31–41.

pp. 11–12: David Grande has written on the influence of the pharmaceutical industry on medical education in "Limiting the Influence of Pharmaceutical Industry Gifts on Physicians: Self-Regulation or Government Intervention?," *Journal of General Internal Medicine* 25, no. 1 (2009): 79–83. The structure of agricultural research funding was elucidated by M. Peterson in "As Beef Cows Become Behemoths, Who Are Animal Scientists Serving?," *Chronicle of Higher Education*, April 15, 2012. I know firsthand about the challenges of conducting research at state universities on the health and environmental impacts of broiler and swine production from the experiences of my colleagues in North Carolina, Dr. Steve Wing of the University of North Carolina and Dr. Joanne Burkholder of North Carolina State.

Industry comments on arsenic include the assertion "It's not like there's arsenic in [chicken]," which was made by Toby Moore, a spokesman for the USA Poultry and Egg Export Council, on February 26, 2004, in response to our first publication. Alpharma, one of the companies manufacturing arsenicals for poultry feeds, topped Moore's remarks with a press release stating that "arsenic is natural," which is factually correct—just as lead, mercury, and anthrax are natural, too. An amazing article followed, by Professor F. T. Jones on behalf of the poultry industry, titled "A Broad View of Arsenic," *Poultry Science* 86 (2007): 2–14, in which Jones lamented, "In the mind of the general public, the words 'arsenic' and 'poison' have become almost synonymous." Similar usage can be found in many medical dictionaries.

My own experience with the disdain for science rife in Washington came when I testified before the Subcommittee on the Environment of the US House of Representatives Committee on Science, Space, and Technology on February 11, 2014. A transcript of that event is available online from https://science.house.gov/legislation/hearings/environment -subcommittee-jhearing-ensuring-open-science-epa.

In 2011, when the FDA finally acted to ban arsenicals in poultry feeds, the industry objected again. My colleague Dr. Keeve Nachman is a leader in developing the science that finally forced the FDA to act; see E. K. Silbergeld and K. Nachman, "The Environmental and Public Health Risks Associated with Arsenical Use in Animal Feeds," *Annals of the New York Academy of Sciences* 1140 (2008): 346–57. With my students, I summarized the literature from Denmark and other Nordic countries in 1994: E. K. Silbergeld, M. Davis, J. H. Leibler, and A. E. Peterson, "One Reservoir: Redefining the Community Origins of Antimicrobial-Resistant Infections," *Medical Clinics of North America* 92, no. 6 (2008): 1391–407.

Dr. Joshua Lederberg won the Nobel Prize in 1958 "for his discoveries concerning genetic recombination and the organization of the genetic material of bacteria" (http://www.nobelprize.org/nobel_prizes/medicine /laureates/1958/lederberg-speech.html). He was an early supporter of my research, for which I remain grateful.

pp. 14–16: I deliberately invoke John Stuart Mill and David Ricardo among the English School of classical economists for their assertion that economics is a part of moral philosophy. See Ricardo's *On the Principles of Political Economy and Taxation* (London: Dover, 2004; first published 1821) and Mill's *Principles of Political Economy* (Oxford: Oxford University Press, 1994; first published 1848, the same year as the *Communist Manifesto*).

Mark Tauger's quote on how agriculture is unique from other industries can be found in his *Agriculture in World History* (New York: Routledge, 2011), 162. For the tragic view of industrialization in agriculture, I refer to Leo Marx, *The Machine in the Garden* (Oxford: Oxford University Press, 1964). See also Peter Laslett, *The World We Have Lost* (London: Methuen, 1965), and Peter Jackson, Neil Ward, and Polly Russell, "Moral Economies of Food and Geographies of Responsibility," *Transactions of the Institute of British Geographers*, n.s., 34 (2008): 12–24. The strange refusal to accept industrialization as the latest stage in technological change in agriculture is sometimes evident by omission, as in Mazoyer and Roudart, and sometimes by absolute denial, as in Tauger's more concise history of world agriculture. The writings of Karl Marx and Friedrich Engels will be discussed further in chapter 2.

My adoption of Lady Thatcher's nomenclature of "wets" and "dries" seemed to be useful; I borrowed the terms and their explanation from contemporary newspapers and other sources, including her autobiography. Her reputation and achievements are still contended in the United Kingdom, so it is wise not to recommend any specific source.

For more about agroecology as it is defined here, see at http://www .agroecology.org/. There are numerous organizations, websites, and publications arguing for the space to define agroecology; I cite just one and also suggest consulting writings by Wes Jackson and Jon Piper, "The Necessary Marriage between Ecology and Agriculture," *Ecology* 70 (1989): 1591–93, and Olivier de Schutter, until recently the United Nations (UN) special rapporteur on the right to food, who penned reports to the UN General Assembly in 2010 and 2013; see http://www.srfood.org/images/stories/pdf /officialreports/20131218_Malaysia_en.pdf. For a provocative analysis of the cultural context of agroecology, Cone and Myhre's comparisons to other communitarian movements were useful and matched my childhood experience of intentional communities built around agriculture. See Cynthia Abbott Cone and Andrea Myhre, "Community Supported Agriculture: A Sustainable Alternative to Industrial Agriculture?," *Human Organization* 59 (2000): 187–97.

Parma is the home of the new European Food Safety Agency as well as some of most loved heritage foods of Italian cuisine, so it is a fitting location for thinking about food and agriculture.

pp. 17–21: Wendell Berry is among the most eloquent advocates of the wets, and I respectfully cite his book *Another Turn of the Crank* (Washington, DC: Counterpoint, 1995). Jeffrey Sachs, "Government, Geography, and Growth: The True Drivers of Economic Development," *Foreign Affairs* (September/October 2012), provides a worthy counterpoint for the dries. The quote from Secretary Butz comes from C. E. Beus and Dunlap, "Conventional versus Alternative Agriculture: The Paradigmatic Roots of the Debate," *Rural Sociology* 55 [1990]: 590–616. Wes Jackson made the comment about human cleverness and the nature's wisdom people in the context of agriculture in an essay on natural systems agriculture: "Natural Systems Agriculture," *Agriculture, Ecosystems and Environment* 88 (2002): 111–17.

In addition to those studies by the USDA, analyses of CSAs have been published by friends and foes alike; among the former is a fair analysis published by the Center for Agroecology and Sustainable Food Systems at the University of California, Santa Cruz (Research Brief 4, 2004). Skeptics are represented by Steve Schnell's "Food with a Farmer's Face: Community-Supported Agriculture in the United States," *Geographical Review* 97 (2007): 550–64.

I cite Michael Pollan's *The Omnivore's Dilemma* (New York: Penguin, 2006) and Stella Gibbons's *Cold Comfort Farm* (London: Longmans, 1932) as two polarities of the rewards and tribulations of attempting to re-create traditional agriculture; of the two, Gibbons has the greater sense of humor. Laura DeLind updates this literature in "Close Encounters with a CSA: The Reflections of a Bruised and Somewhat Wiser Anthropologist," *Agriculture and Human Values* 16 (1999): 3, an account of her own experience in CSA farming. DeLind has also written thoughtfully on the limits and contradictions of these alternative operations in "Are Local Food and the Local Food Movement Taking Us Where We Want to Go? Or Are We Hitching Our Wagons to the Wrong Stars?," *Agriculture and Human Values* 27 (2010).

For attitudes about the uplifting effects of agriculture among the early Zionists, I was deeply informed by Ari Shavit's *My Promised Land: The Triumph and Tragedy of Israel* (New York: Random House, 2013). On the Red Guards and the purification of urban elites through resettlement on farms, I read Robert Elegant's *Mao's Great Revolution* (New York: World Publishing, 1971). Of course, there is an older tradition in Western literature on the moral nature of agricultural work, for example, in Hesiod's *Works and Days: The Homeric Hymns and Homerica*, translated by H. G. Evelyn-White (Cambridge, MA: Harvard University Press, 1914; London: William Heinemann, 1914; originally written around 700 BCE). Hesiod, like later writers on this topic, was not a farmer himself. I briefly ventured into the Chinese tradition, through a thoughtful article by Yiqun Zhou, "Honglou Meng and Agrarian Values," *Late Imperial China* 34, no. 1 (June 2013): 28–66, only because I had read *Honglou Meng* by Cao Xueqin, translated into English as *The Dream of the Red Chamber or The Story of the Stone* (Bloomington: Indiana University Press, 1980).

p. 22: World Watch data are available at http://www.worldwatch.org /node/5443.

p. 23: Prince Charles's lecture on returning to traditional agriculture has been published as *On the Future of Food* (New York: Rodale Books, 2012). On the closing of his farm store, see Kristene Quan, "Prince Charles' Pricey Organic Produce Shop Shutters," *Time*, May 9, 2013.

pp. 24–26: Tackling the challenging issues of economics, sustainability, subsidies, and the goals of national agricultural policies, I was fortunate to have Michael Plummer, professor of economics and now dean of the Johns Hopkins School of Advanced International Studies in Bologna, as my neighbor at the Bologna Institute for Policy Research. He was an invaluable guide through the thick literature on subsidies, including the OECD report of 2011. Other main sources for facts about agriculture—including the USDA, the Food and Agriculture Organization of the UN, the World Bank, and the OECD—were important, particularly *Agricultural Policy Monitoring and Evaluation* (Paris: OECD, 2011) and L. A. Winters's "The So-Called 'Non-Economic' Objectives of Agricultural Support," OECD Economic Studies, OECD, Paris, 1990. I also consulted publications from the World Bank, specifically a paper by B. Hoekman, M. Olarreaga, and F. Ng, "Reducing Agricultural Tariffs versus Domestic Support: What's More Important for Developing Countries?," Policy Research Working Paper 2918, World Bank, Washington, DC, 2002, available at www.papers.ssrn.com. I also consulted critics such as World Watch, the Pew Foundation, and other nongovernmental organizations, as well as specific studies on CSA and other alternative systems. The quotation about the vast series of subsidies is from Tony Weis, "The Accelerating Biophysical Contradictions of Industrial Capitalist Agriculture," *Journal of Agrarian Change* 10 (2010): 315–41. A country-specific analysis of Sweden by L. Lohr and L. Salomonsson was also informative: "Conversion Subsidies for Organic Production: Results from Sweden and Lessons for the United States," *Agricultural Economics* 22 (2000): 133–46. Information on the connections between US farm subsidies and domestic as well as international programs of food aid can be found from the Foreign Agricultural Service of the USDA (www.fas.usda.gov) and US AID (https://www.usaid.gov /what-we-do/agriculture-and-food-security/food-assistance/quick-facts/).

p. 27: With respect to the effect of economic downturns on consumer priorities in food choice, Randy Schnell authored a report for the US Congressional Research Service: "Consumers and Food Price Inflation," CRS 7-5700, 2013, available at www.crs.gov.

For more on Daniel Summer's comments, see http://www.freakonom ics.com/2008/07/24/the-illogic-of-farm-subsidies-and-other-agricultural -truths/.

CHAPTER 2. CONFINEMENT, CONCENTRATION, AND INTEGRATION

p. 29: This chapter takes the position that industrialization is a process by which technological innovation, reorganization of capital, and internal migrations from land to cities have greatly altered the landscape of human society and the world. I draw a good deal on the work of Immanuel Wallerstein, Marx and Engels, and David Harvey in *The Condition of Postmodernity* (Oxford: Blackwell, 1989). The arguments about industrialization include Frank Lloyd Wright's views in the plangent essay "The Art and Craft of the Machine," *Brush and Pencil* 8, no. 2 (May 1901): 77–90, which can stand for the position of the artist and craftsman. Again, I lean heavily on the magisterial history of global agriculture from the Neolithic to the late twentieth century by Mazoyer and Roudart (see chap. 1), and the dense but beautifully organized repositories of information available from the USDA and the Food and Agriculture Organization of the United Nations (FAO), particularly its reports on world agriculture.

I went to Solesmes myself to hear the purest Gregorian chant. Industrialization coming to the Amish is analyzed by Marc Olshan, who views the opening of formerly closed markets as the intrusion of modern models of production. See his "The Opening of Amish Society: Cottage Industry as Trojan Horse Human Organization," *Human Organization* 50, no. 4 (1991): 378–89. For more on how modern food animal production has become industrialized, see chapter 8.

pp. 30–31: For more on the transformation of agriculture to include the raising of animals, see P. K. Thornton, "Livestock Production: Recent Trends, Future Prospects," *Philosophical Transactions of the Royal Society B* 365 (2010): 2853–57. Agriculture was the last great productive endeavor of human societies to be "industrialized," which is not separate from developments, starting in the Neolithic, by which an interplay between growing sizes of human settlements required increased agricultural production, which in turn supported larger populations needing still more food. What we generally think of as industrialization—reorganization of work and capital, the capture of energy beyond the capacity of humans and animals—started in the eighteenth century and accelerated in the twentieth century, according to Mazoyer and Roudart. For more details, see P. K. O'Brien's especially helpful "Agriculture and the Industrial Revolution," *Economic History Review*, n.s., 30, no. 1 (February 1977): 166–81. Remarkably, this transformation remains invisible to many historians. That some have argued as late as 2010 that it is inherently impossible to industrialize agriculture is baffling, but that claim is made by Sigfried Giedion and I. Wallerstein to Michael Tauger. See Sigfried Giedion, *Mechanization Takes Command: A Contribution to Anonymous History* (Oxford: Oxford University Press, 1948); I. Wallerstein, *The Modern World-System I: Capitalist Agriculture and the Origins of the European World-Economy in the Sixteenth Century*, new ed. (Berkeley: University of California Press, 2011); and M. Tauger, *Agriculture in World History* (New York: Routledge, 2010).

pp. 31–35: I equate regret over the loss of preindustrial agriculture with the romantic fog that obscures our ability to talk about agriculture, as recognized by Peter Laslett as well as Peter Jackson, Neil Ward, and Polly Russell and discussed at greater length in chapter 1. That preindustrial agriculture still persists is notable but not noteworthy. José Saramago and Carlo Levi provide some of the more vivid pictures of the real desperation of landless laborers in preindustrial agriculture. See José Saramago, *Raised from the Ground* (New York: Houghton Mifflin, 2012), which was written in 1980 but published recently, and Carlo Levi, *Christ Stopped at Eboli* (New York: Farrar, Strauss, 1945).

My comparison to the history of the industrialization of the textile industry is drawn from, among others, Eric Hobsbawm, *The Age of Capital, 1848–1875* (London: Weidenfeld and Nicolson, 1988). I draw parallels to Michel Foucault, *Discipline and Punish* (New York: Vintage, 1977), in discussing aspects of industrialized food animal production in terms of the concept of confinement and control through physical design. The connections between confinement of animals and workers and penal confinement are very real in this industry (Prison Industries Enhancement Act of 1979), and the separation between agricultural work and the public gaze is also codified by ag-gag laws. My comments about concentration and integration draw on definitions from the EPA as well as on the thorough economic and historical analyses by Steve Martinez of the Agricultural Research Service (ARS) of the USDA. See Neil Harl, "The Age of Contract Agriculture: Consequences of Concentration in Input Supply," *Journal of Agribusiness* 18, no. 1 (March 2000): 115–27; and Steve Martinez, "Vertical Coordination of Marketing Systems: Lessons from the Poultry, Egg and Pork Industries," Agricultural Economic Report No. AER-807, ARS, USDA, Washington, DC, May 2002.

p. 37: The OECD gives startling figures in its report on the growth of agricultural industry in the twentieth century in its *OECD-FAO Agricultural Policy Outlook* (Paris: OECD, 2011). The quote on intensification appears on p. ii.

pp. 40–41: For more on the changing relationship between humans and animals over time, see P. Jackson, N. Ward, and P. Russell, "Moral Economics of Food and Geographies of Responsibility," *Transactions of the Institute of British Geographers*, n.s., 34 (2008): 12–14.

pp. 43–47: There are parallels and differences between industrialization of broiler production and the organizational structures and practices known as Fordism. William Boyd provides a nuanced discussion of this topic, as well insights on the origins of the broiler industry within traditions of Southern agriculture, in his "Making Meat: Science, Technology, and American Poultry Production," *Technology and Culture* 42, no. 4 (October 2001): 631–64. I am grateful to Erica Schoenberger for pointing out the divergences, which are underscored by C. K. Kim and J. Curry in "Fordism: Flexible Specializations and Agri-Industrial Restructuring: The Case of the US Poultry Industry," *Sociologia Ruralis* 33 (1993): 61–80.

Several economists and many poultry growers I have talked with over the past fifteen years have noted the benefits of the integrated model. For the data on the economic impacts of biofuel production on animal feed prices, I relied on Donohue and Cunningham's "Effects of Grain and Oilseed Prices on the Costs of US Poultry Production" *Journal of Applied Poultry Research* 18, no. 2 (2009): 325–37, as well as analyses by M. Upton, "Scale and Structures of the Poultry Sector and Factors Inducing Change: Intercountry Differences and Expected Trends," in *Poultry in the 21st Century* (Rome: FAO, 2007). For the incursion of the outsourcing model into broiler production, I have read congressional testimony and various media, including from Food and Water Watch and online sources. See Shanker Deena, "Chicken Is Killing the Planet," *Salon*, September 16, 2013, http://www.salon.com/2013/09/16/chicken_is _killing_the_planet/, as well as Yanzhong Huang, "Should American Consumers Worry about Chicken Imported from China?," *The Atlantic*, September 30, 2013, http://www.theatlantic.com/china/archive/2013/09/should-american -consumers-worry-about-chicken-imported-from-china/280123/.

CHAPTER 3. IT ALL STARTED IN DELMARVA

p. 50: My main sources of information about the origins of the broiler industry in Delmarva come from conversations with colleagues at Salisbury University and the University of Maryland Eastern Shore, and William H. Williams's commissioned history of the Delmarva poultry industry. I also learned a good deal from my friendships with Senator Paul Sarbanes and the painter Glenn Walker, both born and raised in Delmarva. William Boyd, whose work is cited in chapter 2, has written one of the most complete histories of broiler production, weaving the historical themes of Southern agriculture into the development of this industry. Reverend Solomon Iyobosa Omo-Osagie wrote a remarkable dissertation for his PhD in history that provides a unique perspective from the black population of the region: "Commercial Poultry Production on Maryland's Lower Eastern Shore: The Role of African Americans, 1930s to 1990s" (Morgan State University, 2012). His insights were echoed by many of the workers I met while conducting health research in Wicomico and Accomack Counties.

Other notable sources for the history of Delmarva are from the Maryland Historical Society as well as the ecological histories by Grace Brush and her colleagues and the novels of John Barth, James Michener, and Christopher Tilghman. See Philip D. Curtin, Grace S. Brush, and George W. Fisher, eds., *Discovering the Chesapeake: The History of an Ecosystem* (Baltimore: Johns Hopkins University Press, 2001); James Michener, *Chesapeake* (New York: Random House, 1978); John Barth, *The Sot-Weed Factor* (New York: Doubleday, 1960); and Christopher Tilghman, *The Right Hand Shore* (New York: Farrar, Straus and Giroux, 2012).

For Mrs. Cecile Steele, the Sussex County, Delaware, historical society has a tribute to her part in the history and has preserved her house as a historic structure. The claim of primacy by the state of Arkansas can be found in the *Encyclopedia of Arkansas History and Culture*, available at http://www.encyclopediaofarkansas.net/.

p. 52: William Donald Schaefer, former mayor of Baltimore and governor of Maryland, referred to Delmarva in scatological terms, as recounted by C. Fraser Smith in his biography *William Donald Schaefer: A Political Biography* (Baltimore: Johns Hopkins University Press, 1999).

p. 53: Arthur Perdue's early career is described in William H. Williams's official history of the Delmarva poultry industry, *Delmarva's Chicken Industry: 75 Years of Progress* (Georgetown, DE: Delmarva Poultry Industry, 1998), and on the Perdue Company website, as well as in an "authorized biography" by Frank Gordy, *A Solid Foundation: The Life and Times of Arthur W. Perdue* (Salisbury, MD: Perdue Inc., 1976). There was also an episode on *Biography TV* about Purdue's early years, which seems to have disappeared from the Internet.

p. 54: Regarding the integrated model of poultry production, I rely on Steve Martinez's excellent history and analysis of the broiler industry here as in chapter 2. Doris Kearns Goodwin's biography of Roosevelt and Taft was published in time for me to benefit from her accounts of their response to Upton Sinclair and the politics of the pure food and drug legislation of 1906: *The Bully Pulpit: Theodore Roosevelt, William Howard Taft, and the Golden Age of Journalism* (New York: Simon & Schuster, 2013). Sinclair's regret concerned the failure of reform to extend to improving the lot of workers in food production, and I share his commitment to those who work in this industry.

p. 55: Herbert Hoover in 1928 promised a chicken in every pot, as cited by Roy Jenkins, "Europe and the Third World: The Political Economy of Interdependence," *Round Table: The Commonwealth Journal of International Affairs*, 68, no. 272 (1978): 304–14. I compare Norman Rockwell's iconic invocation of the industrially produced American turkey to a recent advertisement for the "new" chicken published in *Folha de São Paulo* and sent to me by Dr. Ana Carolina Almeida Lopes of the State University of Londrina. For Thomas Midgely and his contributions to refrigeration and automotive transport, I rely on the important book by Seth Cagin and Philip Dray, *Between Earth and Sky: How CFCs Changed Our World and Endangered the Ozone Layer* (New York: Pantheon, 1993).

pp. 57–59: On the history of crop liens, I consulted a number of sources on Southern history, including Jeffrey Kerr-Ritchie, who wrote about the transition from slave to share cropper agriculture in *Freedpeople in the Tobacco South: Virginia, 1860–1900* (Chapel Hill: University of North Carolina Press, 1999). On the early history of economic integration in broiler production and the ensuing legal battles, I drew on Boyd as well as Charles Brown's legal review, *"United States v. National Broiler Marketing Association:* Will the Chicken Lickin' Stand?," *North Carolina Law Review* 56, no. 29 (1978), available at www.nationalaglawcenter.org.

The Maryland lawsuit that successfully challenged the designation by Perdue that poultry house workers were independent contractors was won in 2002 by the Public Justice Center; this lawsuit served to introduce me to one of the plaintiffs, Patrick Harmon, a chicken catcher in Pocomoke City. Information on this case (*Trotter v. Perdue*) is available from the Public Justice Center at www.publicjustice.org.

p. 61: The USDA Census of Agriculture is my main source on the temporal trends in broiler production, with information on the national, state, and county levels. Their maps are worth more than a thousand words.

p. 63: I learned about Wilson, North Carolina, in 2011 when I was asked to speak at a local forum organized by the city council as part of their campaign to block the permit for a poultry processing plant. I learned of the relocation of the proposed plans by Sanderson when I was in Tar Heel in 2014.

CHAPTER 4. THE CHICKENIZATION OF THE WORLD

p. 64: The term *chickenization* comes from the USDA, and it is used to describe the global diffusion of industrial methods of food animal production. The application of poultry methods to swine production is well described in W. D. McBride and N. Key, "US Hog Production from 1992 to 2009," ERR-158, USDA, Economic Research Service, Washington, DC, 2013. For poultry, see James M. MacDonald, "Technology, Organization, and Financial Performance in U.S. Broiler Production," EIB-126, USDA, Economic Research Service, Washington, DC, June 2014.

Pierre Gerber's maps were published in "Geographical Determinants and Environmental Implications of Livestock Production Intensification in Asia," *Bioresource Technology* 96 (2006): 263–76.

p. 66: For the history of FAO, there is much material available on its website (www.fao.org). At a thrift shop in Cape Cod, I found a first edition of Dr. Josué de Castro's landmark book on the need for this organization, written in 1952: *Geography of Hunger* (London: Gollancz, 1952). Not everyone is happy with FAO's present status; one among many critical commentaries is by Brian Bolton, "Agribusiness and the FAO: A Critical Review," *Food Policy* (1977): 240, quote p. 241.

p. 68: Marcus Upton and others at FAO were valuable resources for me in writing this chapter. Pierre Gerber, Tim Robinson, Marius Gilbert, and Joachim Otte all encouraged me to write this book. Joachim was also strongly supportive of our work on the risks of industrialized broiler production related to avian influenza outbreaks in birds and humans, which we published together and which was posted as a research report on FAO's website. The joint report by FAO and the OECD is an encyclopedic resource on trends and projects regarding agricultural production and consumption: *OECD-FAO Agricultural Outlook 2013* (Paris: OECD, 2013), available at http://dx.doi.org/10.1787/agr_outlook-2013-en. For information on the specific production methods of countries, FAO reports and its database (FAOSTAT) and the USDA are rich sources with updated information.

p. 71: On Soviet agriculture, Robert Conquest's *Harvest of Sorrow* (Oxford: Oxford University Press, 1986) is an important source. For the role of food in US policy during the Cold War, the Office of the Historian at the US Department of State is a gold mine of information (https://history.state .gov/). The Congressional Research Service published a concise review of food aid programs from 1952 to the present: R. Schnepf, "International Food Aid Programs: Background and Issues," CRS Report 7-5700, Congressional Research Service, Washington, DC, 2015, available at http://fas .org/sgp/crs/misc/R41072.pdf. More critical reviews are also helpful; for example, M. B. Wallerstein, *Food for War—Food for Peace: United States Food Aid in a Global Context* (Cambridge, MA: MIT Press, 1980), and Polly Diven, "The Domestic Determinants of US Food Aid Policy," *Food Policy* 26 (2001): 455–74.

p. 72: Regarding country-specific information on the development of agriculture, in general, FAO and the Economic Research Service of the USDA were excellent sources of information and data. In addition, industry websites, such as that of Cobb-Vantress, were useful. I drew particularly on the two reports from FAO: on India, Rajesh Mehta and R. G. Nambiar, "The Poultry Industry in India," in *Poultry in the 21st Century* (Rome: FAO, 2007); on Thailand, S. Heft-Neal et al., "Supply Chain Auditing for Poultry Production in Thailand," ProPoor Livestock Initiative Research Report 08-09, FAO, Rome, 2008, available at http://www.fao.org/ag/againfo/programmes/en /pplpi/docarc/rep-0809_thaipoultrychain.pdf; along with other reports (see www.fao.org/ag/pplpi.html). Gregory C. Chow, "Economic Reform and Growth in China," *Annals of Economics and Finance* 5 (2004): 127–52, and David Burch, "Production, Consumption and Trade in Poultry: Corporate Linkages and North–South Supply Chains," in *Cross-Continental Agro-Food Chains*, ed. N. Fold and B. Pritchard (London: Routledge, 2004), 164–76, provided economic and social contextual analysis of events associated with the emergence of industrial methods, including national economic policy and interrelationships among companies in developed and developing countries.

p. 73: For Brazil, I also relied on information from EMBRAPA and the Economic Research Service of the USDA; see http://www.embrapa.br/english. Websites from Brazilian companies also provided information on recent developments in broiler production. Susanna Hecht, a longtime observer and engaged researcher of the Amazon, called out soybean production as the force that destroyed the Mid-Amazonian region. See S. Hecht and A. Cockburn, *The Fate of the Forest: Developers, Destroyers, and Defenders of the Amazon*, updated ed. (Chicago: University of Chicago Press, 2011).

The quotation from the President's Council of Advisors in Science and Technology comes from http://m.whitehouse.gov/sites/default/files /microsites/ostp/pcast_agriculture_20121207.pdf.

pp. 76–80: For Thailand and Charoen Pokphand, I was informed by J. Goss and D. Burch, "From Agricultural Modernization to Agri-Food Globalization," *Third World Quarterly* 22, no. 6 (2001): 969–86; S. Claessens, S. Djankov, and L. H. P. Lang, "The Separation of Ownership and Control in East Asian Corporations," *Journal of Financial Economics* 58, no. 1 (2000): 81–112; U. Pathmanand, "Globalization and Democratic Development in Thailand: The New Path of the Military, Private Sector, and Civil Society," *Contemporary Southeast Asia* 23, no. 1 (2001): 24–42; and P. Phongpaichit and C. Baker, *Thaksin: The Business of Politics in Thailand* (Copenhagen: Nordic Institute of Asian Studies, 2004), who covered the Thaksin Shinawatra government. For the impact of avian influenza on the Thai industry, I refer to research with Thanawat Tiensin and FAO; see J. P. Graham, J. H. Leibler, L. B. Price, J. M. Otte, D. U. Pfeiffer, T. Tiensin, and E. K. Silbergeld, "The Animal-Human Interface and Infectious Disease in Industrial Food Animal Production: Rethinking Biosecurity and Biocontainment," *Public Health Reports* 123, no. 3 (May–June 2008): 282–99.

For China, the history of agricultural intensification and Maoist policies came from REFS. FAO, the USDA Foreign Agricultural Service, and the OECD were sources of data on the current status of industrialization. There is a great deal of topical information in the media on environmental pollution in China and its impacts on surface water and crop production. Data on the EU come from FAO and the OECD. See M. Upton, "Scale and Structures of the Poultry Sector and Factors Inducing Change: Intercountry Differences and Expected Trends," in *Poultry in the 21st Century* (Rome: FAO, 2007).

p. 83: For India, work by FAO and Windhorst was again useful. Information on government policies was obtained from "Annual Report 2011–12," Department of Animal Husbandry, Dairying and Fisheries, Ministry of Agriculture, Government of India, New Delhi, available at http://www.dahd.nic.in/dahd /WriteReadData/Annual%20Report%20English%202011-12.pdf.

CHAPTER 5. THE COMING OF THE DRUGS

p. 89: I prefer the term *antimicrobials* over *antibiotics* because it is recommended by the WHO; for all practical purposes, the words are interchangeable. I also choose to continue using the term *growth-promoting* in the face of new coinage invented by the industry without objection from the FDA that the same use and conditions formerly known as GPAs can now be called "disease prevention" by the industry.

It is now widely understood that we are reaching the end of the antimicrobial era, with reports by the WHO and CDC laying out the current landscape. Brad Spellberg has written one of many readable accounts of this situation in *Rising Plague: The Global Threat from Deadly Bacteria and Our Dwindling Arsenal to Fight Them* (New York: Prometheus, 2009), but as in many books and too many government reports he fails to point the finger at agriculture.

p. 90: This chapter answers a rarely asked question: How did antimicrobial drugs really get into animal feeds? I discovered that much of the past writing on this topic was largely self-serving, written by Thomas Jukes and others claiming rights to invention. Current attempts to answer this question have not dug very deeply, for example, Marilyn Ogle's "Riots, Rage and Resistance: A Brief History of How Antibiotics Arrived on the Farm," *Scientific*

American, September 3, 2013. Others present the facts without the prologue, and also commingle the use of antimicrobials for preventing disease with promoting growth. See R. H. Gustaffson and R. E. Bowen (both employed by Cyanamid, the parent company of Lederle, where Jukes and Stokstad both worked), "Antibiotic Use in Animal Agriculture," *Journal of Applied Microbiology* 83 (2003): 531–41. The FDA promotes this confusion to this day, as discussed in chapter 7.

p. 91: Data on annual corn production and prices are available from the USDA Economic Research Division.

p. 92: I have published my own research on how lead got into and finally out of gasoline in "Preventing Lead Poisoning in Children," *Annual Review of Public Health* 18 (1997): 187–210; for a more complete account, David Rosner and Gerald Markowitz have written the authoritative story on the lead industry and government: "A 'Gift of God'? The Public Health Controversy over Leaded Gasoline during the 1920s," *American Journal of Public Health* 75 (1985): 334–75.

For the increased productivity of the poultry industry, as well as its relentless reduction of labor costs, I rely on William Boyd, whose work is cited in chapter 2.

p. 93: I intend in this book to resurrect Lucy Wills's importance in the history of nutrition research as well as to chart the real beginning of a history that ended with the rush to approve use of antimicrobials in animal feeds. The first trace I had of this remarkable scientist came through searching the literature on "animal growth factor," that holy grail of animal nutrition sought from the 1920s through the 1940s to solve the challenge of reducing the final cost of industrial production, as well as the time and feed needed to reach market weight. J. H. Martens, H. Barg, M. J. Warren, and D. Jahn describe the history of the confirmation of vitamin B12 as the animal growth factor in "Microbial Production of Vitamin B12," *Applied Microbiology and Biotechnology* 58, no. 3 (2002): 275–85. It was difficult to access information on Wills herself, as she has largely been erased from the history of nutrition sciences. Two sources were important: a biographical essay by Daphne Roe, "Lucy Wills," *Journal of Nutrition* 108 (1978): 1377–83, and an appreciation of her scientific accomplishments by A. V. Hoffbrand and D. G. Weir, "The History of Folic Acid," *British Journal of Haematology* 113 (2001): 579–89. From these leads, I was able to track down Wills's publications through Google Scholar.

p. 96: Thomas Jukes is the source of information about himself and his colleague, Robert Stokstad. See, for example, his article "Antibiotics in Animal Feeds and Animal Production," *BioScience* 22 (1972): 526–34, which also provides references to their earlier work. P. R. Moore, A. Evenson, T. D. Luckey, E. McCoy, C. A. Elvehjem, and E. B. Hart, "Use of Sulfasuxidine, Streptothricin, and Streptomycin in Nutritional Studies with the Chick," *Journal of Biological Chemistry* 165 (1946): 437–41, preceded them, as described by Gustaffson and Bowen, cited above.

On the history of penicillin, there are many scholarly and popular accounts. J. W. Bennett and K. T. Chung present this history from discovery through commercialization in their "Alexander Fleming and the Discovery of Penicillin," *Advances in Applied Microbiology* 49 (2001): 163–84.

p. 98: Regarding the rapid approval by the FDA of applications to use antimicrobials in animal feeds from 1946, see T. G. Summons, "Animal Feed Additives, 1940–1966," *Agricultural History* 42, no. 4 (1968): 305–13.

p. 99: There were early challenges to the acceptance of the flimsy evidence for the efficacy of antimicrobials in enhancing growth and reducing feed consumption, particularly by R. Braude, who first published on this topic in 1953 and again reviewed it in "Antibiotics in Animal Feeds in Great Britain," *Journal of Animal Science* 46 (1978): 1425–36. A revealing but unremarked upon summary of the paucity of data purporting to support claims of efficacy can also be found in an early report by US National Research Council, *The Use of Drugs in Animal Feeds: Proceedings of a Symposium* (Washington, DC: National Academies Press, 1969). This publication also reviews the many unsupported speculations on how antimicrobials could enhance growth, a topic covered more recently by J. J. Dibner and J. D. Richards, "Antibiotic Growth Promoters in Agriculture: History and Mode of Action Poultry," *Science* 84 (2005): 634–43. I have reviewed many of the applications submitted by industry to the FDA in support of registration of antimicrobials for growth promotion in food animals; the data are paltry. See chapter 7 for a fuller discussion of the microbiome.

p. 100: With growing interest in the microbiome, the first molecular studies on the effects of antimicrobials in feed were done by A. P. Neumann and G. Suen, "Differences in Major Bacterial Populations in the Intestines of Mature Broilers after Feeding Virginiamycin or Bacitracin Methylene Disalicylate," *Journal of Applied Microbiology* 119, no. 6 (2015): 1515–26. They reported relatively limited differences in the microbiomes of chickens fed different feeds, and no information on correlations with increased growth rates or decreased feed consumption. Regarding Libby and Shaible's finding of the secular trend in improved growth and feed conversion efficiency in poultry, see their "Observations on Growth Responses to Antibiotics and Arsonic Acids in Poultry Feeds," *Science* 121, no. 3151 (1955): 733–34. See also the USDA study on efficacy of antibiotic use in swine production in W. McBride, N. Key, and K. H. Matthews, "Subtherapeutic Antibiotics and Productivity in US Hog Production," *Review of Agricultural Economics* 30, no. 2 (2005): 270–88. The vastly superior study by Perdue is from H. M. Engster, D. Marvil, and B. Stewart-Brown, "The Effect of Withdrawing Growth Promoting Antibiotics from Broiler Chickens: A Long-Term Commercial Industry Study," *Journal of Applied Poultry Research* 11 (2002): 431–36, and our analysis of these data can be found in J. P. Graham, J. J. Boland, and E. Silbergeld, "Growth Promoting Antibiotics in Food Animal Production: An Economic Analysis," *Public Health* 122, no. 1 (2007): 79–87.

p. 103: The American Veterinary Medicine Association's 2015 statement can be found on their website: www.avma.org/KB/Resources/FAQs/Pages /Antimicrobial-Use-and-Antimicrobial-Resistance-FAQs.aspx.

p. 106: Both the Tyson announcement and the defiant stand by Sanderson were reported in *World Poultry* in 2015 (www.worldpoultry.net). David Gee has edited an important book on the delay between knowledge and action, *Late Lessons from Early Warnings* (Copenhagen: European Environment Agency, 2001); see www.eea.eu. Both editions of the book have included an essay on the failure to regulate antibiotic use in agriculture (including an essay I wrote written in 2013). Carl Cranor has written on the limitations of tort law to protect against public health harms in *Toxic Torts: Law, Science and the Possibility of Justice* (Cambridge: Cambridge University Press, 2008).

Starr and Reynolds published the first warning of the emergence of antimicrobial resistance in poultry production in 1951: "Streptomycin Resistance of Coliform Bacteria from Turkeys Fed Streptomycin," *American Journal of Public Health and the Nation's Health* 41 (1951): 1375–80.

p. 107: The FDA's current guidance—not regulation—is discussed more fully in chapters 7 and 9.

Dr. Margaret Chan, director of the WHO, was quoted on the end of the antibiotic era in J. Laurance, "Health Chief Warns: Age of Safe Medicine Is Ending," *Independent*, March 16, 2012, http://www.independent.co.uk/life -style/health-and-families/health-news/health-chief-warns-age-of-safe -medicine-is-ending-7574579.html. The equally dire report on antimicrobial resistance by the UK government, "Antimicrobial Resistance: Tackling a Crisis for the Health and Wealth of Nations," was published in 2014. In contrast, the US government has issued a halting series of statements, most recently a schematic that does not include agriculture. The tragic story of Synercid's first use in animal feeds is recounted in E. K. Silbergeld, M. Davis, J. H. Leibler, and A. E. Peterson, "One Reservoir: Redefining the Community Origins of Antimicrobial-Resistant Infections," *Medical Clinics of North America* 92 (2008): 1391–407.

p. 108: Carlo Cipolla's essential book on stupidity is *The Basic Laws of Human Stupidity* (Bologna: Mulino, 1976). It was first published in Italy in English because he considered it prudent to conceal his identity. Cipolla was also one of the most famous historians of public health and society. The quote from Thomas O'Brien is from D. C. Hooper, A. DeMaria, B. M. Limbago, T. F. O'Brien, and B. McCaughey, "Antibiotic Resistance: How Serious Is the Problem, and What Can Be Done?," *Clinical Chemistry* 58, no. 8 (2012): 1182–86.

CHAPTER 6. WHEN YOU LOOK AT A SCREEN, DO YOU SEE LATTICES OR HOLES?

p. 109: A former PhD student of mine, Dr. Megan Davis, was the first to apply the term *porosity* to the reality of industrial food animal production.

See M. F. Davis, L. B. Price, C. M. Liu, and E. K. Silbergeld, "An Ecological Perspective on U.S. Industrial Poultry Production: The Role of Anthropogenic Ecosystems on the Emergence of Drug-Resistant Bacteria from Agricultural Environments," *Current Opinion in Microbiology* 14, no. 3 (2011): 244–50.

p. 110: I along with my colleagues have written on the separation between infectious diseases from environmental health that developed with the establishment of the EPA. See B. J. Feingold, L. Vegosen, M. Davis, J. Leibler, A. Peterson, and E. K. Silbergeld, "A Niche for Infectious Disease in Environmental Health: Rethinking the Toxicological Paradigm," *Environmental Health Perspectives* 118, no. 8 (2011): 1165–72. John O'Neill's history of the EPA referred to its origins in the title, *Something New Under the Sun* (New York: W. W. Norton, 2000). The EPA's own history is available on its website: www.epa.gov.

p. 111: For more than twenty years, researchers and public health scientists have pointed out the limitations of current methods to assess microbial risks by testing only for "total coliforms." A comprehensive commentary comes from M. L. O'Shea and R. Field, "Detection and Disinfection of Pathogens in Storm-Generated Flows," *Canadian Journal of Microbiology* 38, no. 4 (1992): 267–76. Such limitations also affect the way we assess water safety at beaches; see C. S. Lee, C. Lee, J. Marion, Q. Wang, L. Saif, and J. Lee, "Occurrence of Human Enteric Viruses at Freshwater Beaches during Swimming Season and Its Link to Water Inflow," *Science of the Total Environment* 472 (2013): 757–66. In December 2015, EPA issued a new coliform rule, in which all samples testing positive for "total coliforms" must be retested for the presence of *E. coli* specifically. While this is an important advance, it falls short of providing information on the most dangerous strains of this bacterium (see http://www.epa.gov/sites/production/files/2015-10/documents/rtcrimplementation_guidance.pdf).

The conditions of work and life in communities with large numbers of industrial food animal production operations are well described by Sara Quandt, Tom Arcury, and Steve Wing, as discussed in chapters 8 and 9. Solomon Iyobosa Omo Osagie II offered an invaluable account of the history of the black community in Delmarva and the poultry industry in his

Commercial Poultry Production on Maryland's Lower Eastern Shore: The Role of African Americans, 1930s to 1990s (Lanham, MD: University Press of America, 2012). I am grateful to have learned of his published dissertation from a colleague at Morgan State University.

p. 112: For a description of the Monte Nero and the lead smelter in Torreón, Mexico, see G. G. Garcia-Vargas, S. J. Rothenberg, E. K. Silbergeld, V. Weaver, R. Zamoiski, C. Resnick, M. Rubio-Andrade, P. J. Parsons, A. J. Steuerwald, A. Navas-Acién, and E. Guallar, "Spatial Clustering of Toxic Trace Elements in Adolescents around the Torreón, Mexico, Lead-Zinc Smelter," *Journal of Exposure Science and Environmental Epidemiology* 24, no. 6 (2014): 634–42.

p. 113: Information on ventilation requirements for raising chickens and pigs in houses is available from the USDA; for the specific reference for the amount of heat and moisture generated, see R. A. Bucklin, J. P. Jacob, F. B. Mather, J. D. Leary, and I. A. Naas, "Tunnel Ventilation of Broiler Houses," Institute of Food and Agricultural Sciences, University of Florida, Gainesville, FL, 2012, available at http://edis.ifas.ufl.edu/pdffiles/PS/PS04100.pdf.

p. 114: The first news report of the rapidity of chicken deaths following loss of electrical power to a large house in August 2012 was published by the *Salisbury Times*; the accessible reference is http://usnews.nbcnews .com/_news/2012/08/28/13531163-sheriff-drunken-man-turns-off-power -on-poultry-farm-causes-death-of-70000-chickens.

p. 115: For information on highly pathogenic avian influenza in poultry houses, see J. H. Leibler, M. Carone, and E. K. Silbergeld, "Contribution of Company Affiliation and Social Contacts to Risk Estimates of Between-Farm Transmission of Avian Influenza," *PLoS One* 5, no. 3 (2010): e9888, and the later discussion of our study of HPAI in Thailand, J. H. Leibler, J. Otte, D. Roland-Holst, D. U. Pfeiffer, R. Soares Magalhaes, J. Rushton, J. P. Graham, and E. K. Silbergeld, "Industrial Food Animal Production and Global Health Risks: Exploring the Ecosystems and Economics of Avian Influenza," *Ecohealth* 6, no. 1 (2009): 58–70. For a report on porcine epidemic diarrhea, see J. Lowe, P. Gauger, K. Harmon, J. Zhang, J. Connor, P. Yeske, T. Loula, I. Levis, L. Dufresne, and R. Main, "Role of Transportation in Spread of Porcine Epidemic Diarrhea Virus Infection, United States," *Emerging Infectious Diseases* 20, no. 5 (2014): 872–74. See Jay Graham's study of flies as mechanisms of transporting antibiotic resistant pathogens from poultry houses into the environment: J. P. Graham, L. B. Price, S. L. Evans, T. K. Graczyk, and E. K. Silbergeld, "Antibiotic Resistant Enterococci and Staphylococci Isolated from Flies Collected near Confined Poultry Feeding Operations," *Science of the Total Environment* 407, no. 8 (2009): 2701–10.

p. 117: Jay Graham also gave an extensive review of animal wastes in J. P. Graham and K. E. Nachman, "Managing Waste from Confined Animal Feeding Operations in the United States: The Need for Sanitary Reform," *Journal of Water and Health* 8, no. 4 (2010): 646–70. On the lack of regulations, government websites reveal it all, as in the EPA's 2013 report on animal waste: http://water.epa.gov/scitech/cec/upload/Literature-Review-of -Contaminants-in-Livestock-and-Poultry-Manure-and-Implications-for -Water-Quality.pdf. Compare this to regulations on managing human biosolids, as reviewed by the National Research Council, *Biosolids Applied to Land: Advancing Standards and Practices* (Washington, DC: National Academies Press, 2002). That the FDA at least can promulgate regulations related to the use of animal wastes as manure use in organic farming is demonstrated in its recent regulations, FDA-2011-N-0921 and FDA-2011-N-0920; see http://www.fda.gov/Food/GuidanceRegulation/FSMA/ucm253380.htm.

p. 118: Information on cleanout practices in the poultry industry comes from conversations with growers and poultry scientists at the University of Maryland. Volkova and her colleagues identified this practice as a risk factor for the presence of pathogens in poultry flocks; see V. V. Volkova, R. W. Wills, S. A. Hubbard, D. L. Magee, J. A. Byrd, and R. H. Bailey. "Risk Factors Associated with Detection of Salmonella in Broiler Litter at the Time of New Flock Placement," *Zoonoses and Public Health* 58, no. 3 (2011): 158–68. Dr. Volkova also noted that poor management contributed to releases of pathogens from poultry houses via ventilation. For the lack of management requirements for swine waste, see http://www.epa.gov/oecaagct/ag101/porkmanure.html.

Information on Hurricane Floyd and the responses of politicians in 1999 comes from Peter T. Kilborn, "Hurricane Reveals Flaws in Farm Law as Animal Waste Threatens N. Carolina Water," *New York Times*, October 17, 1999.

C. W. Schmidt wrote a good review in "Lessons from the Flood: Will Floyd Change Livestock Farming?," *Environmental Health Perspectives* 108 (2000): A74–A77.

p. 119: Information on swine production is from W. D. McBride and N. Key, "US Hog Production from 1992 to 2009: Technology, Restructuring, and Productivity Growth," ERR-158, USDA Economic Research Service, Washington, DC, 2013, available at http://www.ers.usda.gov/publications/err-economic-research-report/err158.aspx.

The study of antibiotics found in rivers affected by land disposal of poultry waste was conducted by Dr. Judy Denver and others at the US Geological Laboratory in Delaware. Other publications have also documented this route of contamination, including H. A. S. Dolliver and S. C. Gupta, "Antibiotic Losses in Leaching and Surface Runoff from Manure-Amended Agricultural Land," *Journal of Environmental Quality* 37 (2008): 1227–37.

p. 120: For the story of Allied Chemical and its liability for inadequate waste management, see M. R. Reich and J. K. Spong, "Kepone: A Chemical Disaster in Hopewell, Virginia," *International Journal of Health Services* 13, no. 2 (1983): 227–46. A thoughtful commentary on the lawsuit against farmers over management of poultry waste in Maryland was written by Rona Kobell, "Wounds from Suit Filed by Waterkeepers to Take a While to Heal," *The Bay Journal*, http://www.bayjournal.com/article/wounds_from_suit_filed_by_waterkeepers_to_take_a_while_to_heal.

p. 121: On the failure of "composting" following USDA recommendations, see J. P. Graham, S. L. Evans, L. B. Price, and E. K. Silbergeld, "Fate of Antimicrobial-Resistant Enterococci and Staphylococci and Resistance Determinants in Stored Poultry Litter," *Environmental Research* 109, no. 6 (2009): 682–89.

p. 124: See Beth Feingold's pathbreaking study on environmental exposures to MRSA from livestock production in the Netherlands: B. J. Feingold, E. K. Silbergeld, F. C. Curriero, B. A. van Cleef, M. E. Heck, and J. A. Kluytmans, "Livestock Density as Risk Factor for Livestock-Associated Methicillin-Resistant *Staphylococcus aureus*, the Netherlands," *Emerging Infectious Diseases*

18, no. 11 (2012): 1841–49. See also our study on pathogens released from poultry transport trucks: A. M. Rule, S. L. Evans, and E. K. Silbergeld, "Food Animal Transport: A Potential Source of Community Exposures to Health Hazards from Industrial Farming (CAFOs)," *Journal of Infection and Public Health* 1, no. 1 (2008): 33–39.

CHAPTER 7. ANTIMICROBIAL RESISTANCE

p. 128: Antimicrobial resistance is the most significant impact of the industrial model of food animal production on global public health. As I indicated in the introduction to this book, antimicrobial resistance is the issue that drew me into over fifteen years of research and debate on food animal production. In this chapter I focus on the devastating consequences of this arguably ineffective and unnecessary use of the most precious resource of modern medicine. There's a common assumption that the biggest cause of antimicrobial resistance lies in the behavior of clinicians and patients—the first for overprescribing antibiotics and the second for demanding and improperly following treatment instructions. By the time you finish this chapter, I hope that you have become skeptical of these excuses as just another example of how it is difficult to see the reality of agriculture.

By taking on the microbiome, which is much vaster and more complex than our own world, and we have unheedingly disturbed the recent standoff between us and the bacteria. From my own research and education in the molecular world of bacteria, I have only become more astounded by the tragic mistakes we have accepted in return for the promise of cheap and available food. I likewise owe many people for their patience in educating me, including former students Lance Price, Jay Graham, Meghan Davis, and Amy Peterson; and colleagues Henrik Wegener, Frank Aarestrup, Tara Smith, Peter Collignon, Jan Kluytmans, Stuart Levy, and many others. Anthony van den Bogaard was a pioneer in much of the work I have done, and his extraordinary optimism and generosity remain an inspiration.

p. 130: In characterizing bacteria as sharing communities and means of communication, this chapter comes dangerously close at times to pathetic fallacy, or ascribing human emotions to nonhuman beings. I am less certain of the distinctions between us and the microbes; as Martin Blaser, professor of medicine at New York University Medical School, has pointed out, as organisms we are mostly made up of bacteria and we have been physically intertwined through the origin of species on earth. See his "Who Are We? Indigenous Microbes and the Ecology of Human Diseases," *EMBO Reports* 7, no. 10 (2006): 956–60.

p. 131: E. O. Wilson's famous book on the social life of insects is B. Hölldobler and E. O. Wilson, *The Superorganism: The Beauty, Elegance, and Strangeness of Insect Societies* (New York: W. W. Norton, 2008). *Superorganism* is also the term Rodney Dietert uses to describe the human:microbiome assembly; see "The Microbiome in Early Life: Self-Completion and Microbiota Protection as Health Priorities," *Birth Defects Research: Part B, Developmental and Reproductive Toxicology* 101, no. 4 (2014): 333–40. Lewis Thomas noted the superiority of bacterial communities in his preface to Lynn Margulis's *Microcosmos: Four Billion Years of Evolution from Our Microbial Ancestors*, reprint ed. (Berkeley: University of California Press, 1997). It is still common for biologists to consider bacteria silent and asocial organisms, as noted by Nicola C. Reading and Vanessa Sperandio, "Quorum Sensing: The Many Languages of Bacteria," *FEMS Microbiology Letters* 254 (2006): 1–11.

p. 132: There is a large area of research on our bacterial ancestors, following on Lynn Margulis with increasingly sophisticated methodologies. I only cite Dolezal and colleagues, who state that "the presence of similar translocase subunits in all eukaryotic genomes sequenced to date suggests that all eukaryotes can be considered descendants of a single ancestor species that carried an ancestral 'protomitochondria.'" We are among the most recently evolved of the eukaryotes; see P. Dolezal, V. Likic, J. Tachezy, and T. Lithgow, "Evolution of the Molecular Machines for Protein Import into Mitochondria," *Science* 313, no. 5785 (2006): 314–18. Owing to the contribution of bacteria to our mitochondrial genes, which are transmitted matrilineally in mammals, I take the liberty of calling out bacteria as the mother of us all. See J. N. Wolff, and N. J. Gemmell. "Lost in the Zygote: The Dilution of Paternal mtDNA upon Fertilization," *Heredity* 101 (2008): 429–34. The newly realized role of the microbiome in mediating our exposures to toxic agents in the environment and other xenobiotics is summarized by M. Klünemann, M. Schmid, and K. R. Patil, "Computational Tools for Modeling

Xenometabolism of the Human Gut Microbiota," *Trends in Biotechnology* 32, no. 3 (2014): 157–65. The extent to which the gut microbiome influences our behavior is discussed by A. Gonzalez, J. Stombaugh, C. Lozupone, P. J. Turnbaugh, J. I. Gordon, and R. Knight, "The Mind-Body-Microbial Continuum," *Dialogues in Clinical Neurosciences* 13, no. 1 (2011): 55–62.

p. 133: Dr. F. R. Blattner and colleagues have sequenced the genome of *E. coli*, which helps us to identify the pathogenic and commensal strains of this ubiquitous organism: F. R. Blattner, G. Plunkett III, C. A. Bloch, et al., "The Complete Genome Sequence of *Escherichia coli* K-12," *Science* 277, no. 5331 (1997): 1453–62. M. S. Donnenberg and T. S. Whittam have described how "good" strains of this organism evolve into highly toxic strains in "Pathogenesis and Evolution of Virulence in Enteropathogenic and Enterohemorrhagic *Escherichia coli*," *Journal of Clinical Investigation* 107, no. 5 (2001): 539–48. New members of the bacterial family are continuing to be identified; see S. Subashchandrabose, T. H. Hazen, D. A. Rasko, and H. L. Mobley, "Draft Genome Sequences of Five Recent Human Uropathogenic *Escherichia coli* Isolates," *Pathogens and Disease* (2013): doi:10.1111/2049-632X.12059. Of these, two of the greatest public health concerns relate to *E. coli* O157:7 and the recent and rapid global emergence of NDEC, which is resistant to multiple drugs, including our last and most critical antibiotics such as carbapenemase. See M. Berrazeg, S. Diene, L. Medjahed, et al., "New Delhi Metallo-beta-lactamase around the World: An eReview Using Google Maps," *Eurosurveillance* 19, no. 20 (2014): 20809.

p. 134: Parallels between the social networks of bacterial exchange communities and ours have been vividly described by R. McNab and R. J. Lamont, "Microbial Dinner-Party Conversations," *Journal of Medical Microbiology* 52, no. 7 (2003): 541–45, and by E. Skippington and M. A. Ragan, "Lateral Genetic Transfer and the Construction of Genetic Exchange Communities," *FEMS Microbiology Reviews* 35, no. 5 (2011): 707–35. Bacteria also communicate by dancing, like von Frisch's honeybees. Karl von Frisch was awarded the Nobel Prize in Physiology or Medicine for this research in 1973, but see Tania Munz's interesting account of the history of this idea in "The Bee Battles: Karl von Frisch, Adrian Wenner and the Honey Bee Dance Language Controversy," *Journal of the History of Biology* 38 (2005): 535–70. YouTube videos of bacterial dancing are available (see, for example, http://www.you-tube.com/watch?v=iFEoJIt8j2E), as well as serious studies of their complex movements; see, among others, D. B. Kearns, "A Field Guide to Bacterial Swarming Motility," *Nature Reviews Microbiology* 8, no. 9 (2010): 634–44.

p. 135: DNA-based computing was discussed in "Computing with Soup," *Economist*, March 3, 2012, http://www.economist.com/node/21548488. On the Mathusian principles of bacterial self-regulation of population size, I refer to C. S. Hayes and D. A. Low, "Signals of Growth Regulation in Bacteria," *Current Opinion in Microbiology* 12, no. 6 (2009): 667–73. Malthus wrote *An Essay on the Principle of Population*, on the social importance of restraining human population growth, in 1798. I have cited Carlo Cipolla's *The Basic Laws of Human Stupidity* (Bologna: Mulino, 1976) and thought about it throughout the writing of this book.

p. 137: The length of time for genetic adaptation through spontaneous mutation in humans is discussed by P. C. Sabeti, S. F. Schaffner, B. Fry, J. Lohmueller, P. Varilly, O. Shamovsky, A. Palma, T. S. Mikkelsen, D. Altshuler, and E. S. Lander, "Positive Natural Selection in the Human Lineage," *Science* 312, no. 5780 (2006): 1614–20, and the example of the evolution of genetic resistance to malaria in humans is discussed by T. N. Williams, T. W. Mwangi, S. Wambua, N. D. Alexander, M. Kortok, R. W. Snow, and K. Marsh, "Sickle Cell Trait and the Risk of Plasmodium Falciparum Malaria and Other Childhood Diseases," *Journal of Infectious Disease* 192, no. 1 (2005): 178–86. The genetic and phenotypic agility of bacteria has been called "bet-hedging" by Veening and colleagues, whereby bacteria can maintain linked genes so that the expressed protein is responsive to their situation. See Jan-Willem Veening, Wiep Klaas Smits, and Oscar P. Kuipers, "Bistability, Epigenetics, and Bet-Hedging in Bacteria," *Annual Review of Microbiology* 62 (2008): 193–210.

p. 138: The remarks on the limits on communication in nonhuman biota are from T. C. Scott-Phillips and R. A. Blythe, "Why Is Combinatorial Communication Rare in the Natural World, and Why Is Language an Exception to This Trend?," *Journal of the Royal Society Interface* 10, no. 88 (2013): doi:10.1098/rsif.2013.0520.

p. 140: References to Thomas O'Brien and others can be found in chapters 5 and 6. See our recent paper, Y. You and E. K. Silbergeld, "Learning from Agriculture: Understanding Low-Dose Antimicrobials as Drivers of Resistome Expansion," *Frontiers in Microbiology* 5 (2014): 284. To the official statements failing to give appropriate emphasis to agricultural use of antimicrobials in curtailing the resistance crisis, the President's Council of Advisors on Science and Technology added to the barriers to change by repeatedly calling for more research and monitoring in its "Report to the President on Combating Antibiotic Resistance," September 2014, available at http://www.whitehouse.gov/sites/default/files/microsites/ostp/PCAST /pcast_carb_report_sept2014.pdf. Statements by the American Veterinary Medical Association, discussed in chapter 5, also display and abet ignorance. This situation has been compellingly reviewed by the Infectious Diseases Society of America, the leading biomedical organization for clinicians and researchers on infectious disease. See Brad Spellberg, Robert Guidos, David Gilbert, John Bradley, Helen W. Boucher, W. Michael Scheld, John G. Bartlett, and John Edwards Jr., "The Epidemic of Antibiotic-Resistant Infections: A Call to Action for the Medical Community from the Infectious Diseases Society of America," *Clinical Infectious Diseases* 46, no. 2 (2008): 155–64. For the Animal Health Institute, a good example of their "science" is an article they commissioned, by Ian Phillips, Mark Casewell, Tony Cox, Brad De Groot, Christian Friis, Ron Jones, Charles Nightingale, Rodney Preston, and John Waddell, "Does the Use of Antibiotics in Food Animals Pose a Risk to Human Health? A Critical Review of Published Data," *Journal of Antimicrobial Chemotherapy* 53, no. 1 (2004): 28–52.

CHAPTER 8. COLLATERAL DAMAGE

p. 145: This chapter draws on material discussed in chapters 2 and 6, so I will not repeat citations here. Again I rely extensively on information from the USDA and FAO on trends in agriculture, including land use.

p. 146: The concept of dematerialization was introduced by Jesse Ausubel, among others in the field of industrial ecology. See Jesse Ausubel and Paul Waggoner, "Dematerialization: Variety, Caution, and Persistence," *Proceedings of the National Academy of Sciences* 105, no. 35 (2008): 12,774–79. I am not alone in my skepticism about this concept when applied to agriculture using metrics limited to acreage; see H. Steinfeld, P. Gerber, T. Wassenaar, V. Castel, M. Rosales, and C. de Haan, "Livestock's Long Shadow: Environmental Issues and Options," FAO, Rome, 2006, available at www.fao.org /docrep/010/a0701e/a0701e00.HTM.

p. 147: Susanna Hecht was an important influence on my research in the Amazon; her major book, written with Alexander Cockburn, on the ecological pressures on the Amazon is *The Fate of the Forest: Developers, Destroyers, and Defenders of the Amazon* (Chicago: University of Chicago Press, 1990; updated in 2011). The earlier edition did not mention soybeans. Her earlier research, like that of others, cogently argued that more comprehensive analyses of developing the Amazon for food animal production should include the value of smallholder traditional agriculture and ecosystem resources. See "Environment, Development and Politics: Capital Accumulation and the Livestock Sector in Eastern Amazonia," *World Development* 13, no. 6 (1985): 663–84. An international group of experts—Alicia Grimes, Sally Loomis, Paul Jahnige, Margo Burnham, Karen Onthank, Rocio Alarcón, Walter Palacios Cuenca, Carlos Cerón Martinez, David Neill, Michael Balick, Brad Bennett, and Robert Mendelsohn—wrote "Valuing the Rain Forest: The Economic Value of Nontimber Forest Products in Ecuador," *Ambio* 23, no. 7 (1994): 405–10.

pp. 148–49: The USDA characterization of the Mid-Amazonian region as "the soybean frontier" can be found in W. Jepson, J. C. Brown, and M. Koeppe, "Agricultural Intensification on Brazil's Amazonian Soybean Frontier," in *Land Change Science in the Tropics: Changing Agricultural Landscapes*, ed. A. Millington and W. Jepson (New York: Springer Science and Business Media, 2008), chap. 5. The incursion of agriculture into tropical forests is described by T. Wassenaar, P. Gerber, P. H. Verburg, M. Rosales, M. Ibrahim, and H. Steinfeld, "Projecting Land Use Changes in the Neotropics: The Geography of Pasture Expansion into Forest," *Global Environmental Change* 17, no. 2 (2007): 86–104. See also C. A. Klink and R. B. Machado, "Conservation of the Brazilian Cerrado," *Conservation Biology* 19, no. 3 (2005): 707–13.

p. 150: Regarding the ecological impacts of food animal wastes, see Jay Graham and Keeve Nachman, as referenced in chapter 6. For the legal background for the immunity of industrialized food animal protection from most liability, see chapter 3. Steve Sexton has written on economics of scale in terms of agricultural productivity; see Alan B. Bennett, Cecilia Chi-Ham, Geoffrey Barrows, Steven Sexton, and David Zilberman, "Agricultural Bio-technology: Economics, Environment, Ethics, and the Future," *Annual Review of Environment and Resources* 38 (2013): 249–79. Jules Pretty and others have written persuasively on the high price of externalized costs in industrial agriculture: *Regenerating Agriculture: Policies and Practice for Sustainability and Self-Reliance* (Washington, DC: National Academies Press, 1995). This topic is discussed more fully in chapter 11. Data on the adverse impacts of runoff on surface and coastal waters are available from www.fao.org/docrep/010/a0701e/a0701e00.HTM.

p. 153: Robert Kanigel describes the decline of the Blasket Island community in Ireland in his *On an Irish Island: The Lost World of the Great Blasket* (New York: Knopf, 2012). Information on the decline of farming and rural society in the United States comes from the USDA, specifically a publication by Cynthia Nickerson, Mitchell Morehart, Todd Kuethe, Jayson Beckman, Jennifer Ifft, and Ryan Williams, "Trends in US Farmland Values and Ownership," EIB-92, USDA, Economic Research Service, Washington, DC, February 2012.

p. 154: On agriculture and water in California, Mark Reisner's authoritative book *Cadillac Desert: The American West and Its Disappearing Water* (New York: Penguin, 1986) deserves rereading today.

p. 156: For more on intensive agriculture's effects on property values, see J. Kilpatrick, "Concentrated Animal Feeding Operations and Proximate Property Values," *Appraisal Journal* 69, no. 3 (2001), available at http://www.appraisalinstitutute.org, and K. Milla, M. H. Thomas, and W. Ainsine, "Estimating the Effect of Proximity to Hog Farms on Residential Property Values," *URISA Journal* 17, no. 1 (2005): 27–32.

Steve Wing coined the term "Broiler Belt" (see chap. 3); for the geographic coincidence, see the US maps of broiler production at http://www.ers.usda.gov/publications/eb-economic-brief/eb24.aspx#.UorJFsSkoXs. Steve Striffler, an associate professor of anthropology at the University of

Arkansas, wrote a firsthand account of working in poultry processing in *Chicken: The Dangerous Transformation of America's Favorite Food* (New Haven, CT: Yale University Press, 2005). Bill Satterfield's comment on the Latino workforce in Delmarva poultry processing plants was cited in a report on the Delmarva poultry industry published by the Department of Political Science at Salisbury University. The experiences of Carlisle, Pennsylvania, and Wilson County, North Carolina, come from my own interactions with local county executives in both places. For ag-gag laws, the media is the best source, such as the story by Cody Carlson, "The Ag Gag Laws: Hiding Factory Farm Abuses from Public Scrutiny," *Atlantic Monthly*, March 20, 2012, http://www.theatlantic.com/health/archive/2012/03/the-ag-gag-laws-hiding-factory-farm-abuses-from-public-scrutiny/254674/.

p. 158: On the cost of change for large operations, there is more discussion in chapter 12; my source is the World Bank's "Implementing Agriculture for Development," Washington, DC, 2013, available at www.worldbank.org/rural.

CHAPTER 9. HAVE A CUP OF COFFEE AND PRAY

pp. 159–60: I first heard "have a cup of coffee and pray" at a meeting at the headquarters of the United Food and Commercial Workers Union (UFCW). This chapter has been informed by my own experiences with workers through studying occupational health and safety in farmers, farmworkers, and slaughter and processing workers. Little of my work would have been possible without the strong engagement of the UFCW and their local offices in Maryland, North Carolina, and South Carolina. This engagement has been respectful of the need for independence in research as well as the obligation to report research findings to the community being studied. Work by Sandra Marquardt, Tom Arcury, Hester Lipscomb, John Dement, Melissa Perry, and Marc Linder has been influential throughout. Major reports on occupational health and safety in this industry have been published by the US Bureau of Labor Statistics, the Government Accounting Office, the Southern Poverty Law Center, and Human Rights Watch. All bear thoughtful reading; the Southern Poverty Law Center report is noteworthy for its firsthand accounts by workers: "Unsafe at These Speeds," Montgomery, AL,

2013, available at http://www.splcenter.org/sites/default/files/downloads
/publication/Unsafe_at_These_Speeds_web.pdf.

Tar Heel, North Carolina, is the site of the world's largest hog slaughter
and processing plant. The plant was opened in 1992 by Smithfield, which
was acquired by the Shuanghui Corporation in 2013. During our worker
health study, the plant processed about 32,000 hogs per day. After a fifteen-
year-long and bitter struggle, the United Food and Commercial Workers
Union succeeded in organizing the plant workforce in 2008. While the town
is miniscule, over seven thousand people work at the plant. Upon contacting
the company to inform them of our intention to conduct a health study with
funding from CDC, I was surprised when Dennis Treacy, vice president for
environmental health and safety, pointed out that we shared a common
past of working for the Environmental Defense Fund, a national nongovernmental organization that has focused on industrial agriculture in North
Carolina. Olga and the rest of the workers and union staff are all real people,
with names and some details changed in recognition of the charged atmosphere of labor relations in southern North Carolina. Our health study
was published in the leading scientific journal on environmental health:
R. Castillo Neyra, J. A. Frisancho, J. L. Rinsky, et al., "Multidrug-Resistant,
and Methicillin-Resistant *Staphylococcus aureus* (MRSA) in Hog Slaughter
and Processing Plant Workers and Their Community in NC," *Environmental
Health Perspectives* 122 (2014): 471–77. We completed a similar study at the
Columbia Farms poultry processing plant in Columbia, South Carolina,
in 2015.

p. 162: Dalits, Burakumin, and kosher slaughter are all examples of how
societies distance themselves from the unspeakable aspects of killing animals for human food. Augusto de Venanzi discusses the Burakumin and
the culture of outcasts, and Amy Fitzgerald extends the consideration of the
social anthropology of slaughter to the present day in terms of separation.
See Augusto de Venanzi, "Outcasts: The Social Construction of Exclusion,"
Revista Ven Anal. De Coyuntura 11 (2005): 117–37, and Amy Fitzgerald, "A
Social History of the Slaughterhouse: From Inception to Contemporary
Implications," *Human Ecology Review* 17, no. 1 (2010): 58–69.

Blaming workers for foodborne illness is often alleged, but usually poorly
supported, in the scientific literature. Are workers actually responsible for

introducing infectious pathogens in food preparation and service, or do they find themselves in the middle of the problem, which is often due to contaminated water, preparation surfaces, and rotten food. In other instances, workers in the food service industry, who often have little access to sick leave, work when they are sick because the alternative is no work at all. They get little sympathy from CDC and other health agencies. See L. R. Carpenter, A. L. Green, D. M. Norton, et al., "Food Worker Experiences with and Beliefs about Working While Ill," *Journal of Food Protection* 76, no. 12 (2013): 2146–54. Sadly, similar comments by academics (E. C. D. Todd, Judy D. Greig, Charles A. Bartleson, and Barry S. Michaels, "Outbreaks where Food Workers Have Been Implicated in the Spread of Foodborne Disease," *Journal of Food Protection* 70 [2007]: 2199–217) and even labor organizers like Melanie Forti blame workers in food animal production, both on the farm and in the slaughterhouse; see http://afop.wordpress.com/2012/08/01/first-defense -against-foodborne-illnesses/. The University of Florida report is available at http://ufdc.ufl.edu/IR00002283/00001. There is balance injected by Marc Linder in his searing article on conditions for workers in poultry plants: "I Gave My Employer a Chicken That Had No Bone: Joint Firm-State Responsibility for Line-Speed-Related Occupational Injuries," *Case Western Reserve Law Review* 46 (1995): 33–143. Karen Messing penned the study on stress-related dysmenorrhea in women workers: "Factors Associated with Dysmenorrhea among Workers in French Poultry Slaughterhouses and Canneries," *Journal of Occupational and Environmental Medicine* 35, no. 5 (1993): 493. A dry-as-dust report on the two deadly fires in poultry processing plants, in Hamlet, North Carolina, in 1999 and in North Little Rock, Arkansas, in 1991, was published by the Federal Emergency Management Administration: http://www.usfa.fema.gov/downloads/pdf/publications/tr-057.pdf. Eighteen of the twenty-five dead workers were women. As Irving Selikoff said about biostatistics, this is history with the human tears wiped away.

p. 165: My thinking about regulation has been informed by my experience as a staff scientist at the Environmental Defense Fund, as well as through continuing conversations with Drs. Paul Locke and Lynn Goldman. A good reference on EPA regulation is provided by N. Vig and M. Kraft, *Environmental Policy: New Directions for the Twenty-First Century* (Washington, DC: CQ Press, 2006). The concept of management-based regulation is well described by C. Coglianese and D. Lazer, "Management-Based Regulation: Prescribing Private Management to Achieve Public Goals," *Law and Society Review* 37, no. 4 (2003): 691–730, http://hdl.handle.net/2047/d20000315. The incisive characterization of regulatory deference to the regulated community is from Linder. In its extreme form, as in the case of OSHA, the FDA, and the USDA, this condition is called *agency capture*, by Casey and others, when the regulated industries essentially control the legislative agenda and enforcement. See D. Casey, "Agency Capture: The USDA's Struggle to Pass Food Safety Regulations," *Kansas Journal of Law and Public Policy* 142 (Spring 1998).

Information about HACCP and its history is available on websites of the FDA and the USDA, as well as the Codex Alimentarius; for example, Wallace F. Janssen, FDA Historian, "The Story of the Laws behind the Labels, Part I: The 1906 Food and Drugs Act," *FDA Consumer*, June 1981. Histories of HACCP have been penned by Peter Barton Hutt I and II (father and son) from the FDA perspective, and by Karen Hulebak from the USDA perspective. See P. B. Hutt and P. B. Hutt II, "A History of Government Regulation of Adulteration and Misbranding of Food," *Food, Drug, Cosmetic Law Journal* 39 (1984): 2–73, and Karen L. Hulebak and Wayne Schlosser, "Hazard Analysis and Critical Control Point (HACCP) History and Conceptual Overview," *Risk Analysis* 22, no. 3 (2002): 547–52. On HACCP, Dr. William Sperber is an interesting maverick. A scientist at Cargill, he has castigated HACCP for its opacity and lack of attention to prevention measures before the slaughterhouse. See his "HACCP and Transparency," *Food Control* 16 (2005): 505–9. Despite this stance, he also coauthored a laudatory history of HACCP in *Food Safety Magazine* for its fiftieth anniversary in 2010, praising its deliberate exclusion of product testing or lot acceptance criteria as "the timeless essence of HACCP, serving as a permanent testament to the vision of the HACCP pioneers."

p. 166: The regulatory proposal that stimulated my suspicions about HACCP was proposed by the USDA in 2012 and finalized in July 2014 (USDA proposal RIN 0583-2011-0012, Modernization of Poultry Slaughter Inspection, 77 Fed Ref 24,873 [April 26, 2012] and 77 Fed Ref 4,408 [January 27, 2012]). John Howard's letter to the USDA is described in an article by Kimberly Kindy, "Did USDA Mislead the Public, Congress about Injury Risks for

Poultry Workers?," *Washington Post*, April 14, 2014. HACCP is also discussed in chapter 10. For my enlightenment as to what HACCP really is, I have to thank my training in engineering and the clearest presentation I have found of HACCP, by J. K. Northcutt and S. M. Russell from the extension service at the University of Georgia, "General Guidelines for Implementation of HACCP in A Poultry Processing Plant," Department of Poultry Science, University of Georgia College of Agriculture, Athens, 2010, available at http://athenaeum.libs.uga.edu/bitstream/handle/10724/12487/B1155.pdf ?sequence=1 .

p. 173: Although the USDA referred to its pilot plant study in the proposal, a subsequent investigation by the GAO in 2013 concluded that this study was too flawed to support any claims about food safety by the USDA (see chap. 10 for more details). The ability of industry to evade regulations of line speed with its double-negative argument (no data, and even if there were data, no evidence for what line speed would be safe) is reminiscent of the same "gotcha" conditions of the law governing regulation of toxic chemicals by the EPA: if there are no data, then the agency cannot demand any data; if there are insufficient data, then no regulation. See E. K. Silbergeld, D. Mandrioli, and C. F. Cranor, "Regulating Chemicals: Law, Science and the Unbearable Burdens of Regulation," *Annual Review of Public Health* 36 (2015): 175–91.

p. 178: Many researchers have described the failure to control pathogen contamination in processing plants, including a combined or meta-analysis of many such studies. See, for example, O. Bucher, A. M. Farrar, S. C. Totton, et al., "A Systematic Review-Meta-Analysis of Chilling Interventions and a Meta-Regression of Various Processing Interventions for *Salmonella* Contamination of Chicken," *Preventive Veterinary Medicine* 103, no. 1 (2012): 1–15. Arunas Juska offered evidence identifying slaughterhouse contamination as a contributing cause of beef contamination by the highly dangerous strain of *E. coli* 0157:H7 in the United States. See Arunas Juska, Lourdes Gouveia, Jackie Gabriel, and Kathleen P. Stanley, "Manufacturing Bacteriological Contamination Outbreaks in Industrialized Meat Production Systems: The Case of *E. coli* 0157:H7," *Agriculture and Human Values* 20 (Spring 2003): 3–19. O. Hue, S. Le Bouquin, M. J. Laisney, et al., studying a poultry processing plant in France, offered a complete analysis of contamination through the workday: "Prevalence of and Risk Factors for *Campylobacter* spp. Contamination of Broiler Chicken Carcasses at the Slaughterhouse," *Food Microbiology* 27 (2010): 992.

p. 180: Studies by industry and government, as well as by academic researchers, confirm the high rates of injury and disability experienced by workers on the line in meatpacking and poultry processing. See the 2010 table of injuries, illnesses, and fatalities from the Bureau of Labor Statistics: http://www.bls.gov/iif/oshwc/osh/os/ostb2813.pdf; the industry-funded study is by D. J. Ortiz and D. E. Jacobs, "A Safety and Health Assessment of Two Chicken Processing Plants," Georgia Institute of Technology, Atlanta, 1990.

   The failure by occupational health and safety agencies around the world to pay attention to pathogen exposures in food animal production has motivated much of the research conducted by my former student Dr. Ricardo Castillo Neyra, among others. Ricardo assessed the failure to define pathogen exposure as a work-related risk by all occupational health and safety agencies in the world; see R. Castillo Neyra, L. Vegosen, M. F. Davis, L. Price, and E. K. Silbergeld, "Antimicrobial-Resistant Bacteria: An Unrecognized Work-Related Risk in Food Animal Production," *Safety and Health at Work* 3, no. 2 (2012): 85–91. This evaluation was confirmed at a meeting of the International Conference on Occupational Health in 2010.

p. 181: Our access to the OSHA 300 data on workplace injuries and infections in these industries was one of those extraordinary events that have illuminated my research over the years. With the cooperation of industry, OSHA undertook a study of worker health and safety in eighteen of the largest poultry processing and hog slaughter / processing plants in the United States from 2004 to 2009. OSHA collected thousands of reports from these industries and filed them in cardboard boxes, as there was no one willing to look at them. When OSHA decided to dispose of the boxes, an employee alerted the UFCW that some boxes would be in the hall outside the office for a few days if anyone cared to pack them up. The UFCW picked them up after I promised that one of our students would take on the task of examining them. Fortuitously, Dr. Emmanuel Kyeremateng-Amoah was at that time among our group of fellows in environmental health sciences and, like all of them, looking for a topic to fulfill his master's research requirement. With a background in occupational and preventive medicine as well as of high intelligence, he was well prepared to take on the task of analyzing these data and writing the paper describing our findings: E. Kyeremateng-Amoah, J. Nowell, A. Lutty, P. S. Lees, and E. K. Silbergeld, "Laceration Injuries and Infections among Workers in the Poultry Processing and Pork Meatpacking Industries," *American Journal of Industrial Medicine* 57, no. 6 (2014): 669–82.

p. 183: Staph infections were probably behind the lurid but not inaccurate description of hazards by Upton Sinclair in *The Jungle*, according to my colleagues in infectious disease. *S. aureus* was first named as the cause of skin infections by Sir Alexander Ogsten in 1882: "Micrococcus Poisoning," *Journal of Anatomy and Physiology* 16 (1882): 526–67; 17 (1883): 24–58.

p. 185: Regarding *Campylobacter*, CDC and others indicate the significance of this one pathogen as a cause of gastrointestinal infections. See R. L. Scharff, "Economic Burden from Health Losses Due to Foodborne Illness in the United States," *Journal of Food Protection* 75 (2012): 123. The FDA agreed with our studies on *Campylobacter* contamination of chicken products. See L. B. Price, E. Johnson, R. Vailes, and E. Silbergeld, "Fluoroquinolone-Resistant *Campylobacter* Isolates from Conventional and Antibiotic-Free Chicken Products," *Environmental Health Perspectives* 113 (2005): 557–60; T. Luangtongkum, T. Y. Morishita, A. J. Ison, S. Huang, P. F. McDermott, and Q. Zhang, "Effect of Conventional and Organic Production Practices on the Prevalence and Antimicrobial Resistance of *Campylobacter* spp. in Poultry," *Applied and Environmental Microbiology* 72 (2006): 3600–3607. Of course, only we could name names, which we did. We learned informally that the FDA study was ordered by the USDA to refute our findings, which were widely covered in the media. The Consumers Union study was reported in January 2010: http://www.consumerreports.org/cro/2012/05/how-safe -is-that-chicken/index.htm. The 2015 UK government study was conducted by the Food Safety Agency and reported by Food Safety News: http://www .foodsafetynews.com/2015/05/year-long-survey-finds-campylobacter-on -73-percent-of-uk-chicken/#.VW2XlM9Viko. On the prevalence of other pathogens in food, we and others have conducted studies while the FDA maintains periodic monitoring studies through the National Antibiotic Resistance Monitoring System.

CHAPTER 10. FOOD SAFETY

p. 186: Researching this chapter changed my mind about current methods of food animal production and food safety. Many of the sources for this chapter are the same as those in chapter 9. Through the serendipity of Internet searching, I found R. S. Adler's remarkable paper, from which I took the title for this chapter: "Redesigning People versus Redesigning Products," *Journal of Law and Politics* 11 (1995): 79. I also read in the literature on models of regulation, such as Julia Caswell's work on public–private partnerships (Marian Garcia Martinez, Andrew Fearne, Julie A. Caswell, and Spencer Henson, "Co-Regulation as a Possible Model for Food Safety Governance: Opportunities for Public–Private Partnerships," *Food Policy* 32 [2007]: 299–314) and the need for increased transparency and access to information on sources (Sébastien Pouliot and Daniel A. Sumner, "Traceability, Liability, and Incentives for Food Safety and Quality," *American Journal of Agricultural Economics* 90, no. 1 [2008]: 15–27).

p. 188: The illustration of the kitchen haunted by MRSA was the cover art for the issue of *The Lancet* in which Dr. Meghan Davis's article appeared: M. F. Davis, S. A. Iverson, P. Baron, A. Vasse, E. K. Silbergeld, E. Lautenbach, and D. O. Morris, "Household Transmission of Methicillin-Resistant *Staphylococcus aureus* and Other Staphylococci," *The Lancet: Infectious Diseases* 12, no. 9 (2012): 703–16.

The figures cited on foodborne illness were stated by Dr. Margaret Hamburger, commissioner of the FDA, and reported by Sabrina Tavernise, "FDA Says Importers Must Audit Food Safety," *New York Times*, July 26, 2013, http://nyti.ms/174xtd8. They have been updated as of 2015. More information on food safety, particularly related to risks of foodborne infection, is available in US and international sources, including CDC, "Antibiotic Resistance Threats in the United States, 2013," Atlanta, GA, 2013, available at www.cdc.gov, and WHO, "The Evolving Threat of Antimicrobial Resistance: Options for Action," Geneva, 2012, available from bookorders@who .int. These two reports contain data on disease burden and are notable for emphasizing agricultural use of antimicrobials as an important component of the global crisis in drug-resistant pathogens (see also chap. 7). Contrary to the perception of much of the public, foodborne microbial risks far outweigh foodborne exposures to pesticides and other chemicals in terms of morbidity and mortality.

p. 189: On the problems with managing unsafe food after it is detected, we have a long way to go, according to a report commissioned by Congress: GAO, "USDA and FDA Need to Better Ensure Prompt and Complete Recalls of Potentially Unsafe Food," GAO-05-01, Washington, DC, 2004. The limitations of current surveillance related to food safety are laid out in reports by the USDA, the FDA, and CDC; see US Department of Health and Human Services, "The National Antibiotic Resistance Monitoring System Strategic Plan, 2012–2016," Washington, DC, 2012, available from the FDA at http://www.fda.gov/AnimalVeterinary/SafetyHealth/AntimicrobialResistance/NationalAntimicrobialResistanceMonitoringSystem/default.htm. The Foster Farms outbreak was reported by the US nongovernmental organization New Mexico Public Interest Research Group: "Food Safety Scares 2013," Albuquerque, 2014, available at http://www.nmpirg.org/sites/pirg/files/reports/FoodSafetyScaresReport2013_nmpirg.pdf. In 2014, Foster Farms was involved in more recalls as a result of excessive salmonella contamination; see http://www.cspinet.org/new/201410011.html. The Rich Products outbreak of a highly pathogenic foodborne *E. coli* strain in chicken products in 2013 was reported by CDC; see http://www.cdc.gov/ecoli/2013/O121-03-13/index.html. Reports of similar foodborne illnesses and outbreaks can be found on CDC's website (www.cdc.gov), with some delay. News media are more rapid.

Data on monitoring of drug-resistant pathogens in animal, food, and human samples are the responsibility of the FDA, the USDA, and CDC through the National Antibiotic Resistance Monitoring System. Its inadequacies are plain to see in the NARMS reports.

pp. 190–91: There are examples of Guillain-Barré syndrome following *Campylobacter* infection and UTIs associated with toxigenic strains of *E. coli*. Both of these pathogens are commonly found in poultry, and there are strong associations between disease and consumption of poultry; see M. B. Batz, E. Henke, and B. Kowalcyk, "Long-Term Consequences of Foodborne Infections," *Infectious Disease Clinics of North America* 27, no. 3 (2013): 599–616. The costs of increasing drug resistance in these and other pathogens have been computed by CDC and others, for example, G. S. Tansarli, D. E. Kara-georgopoulos, A. Kapaskelis, and M. Falagas, "Impact of Antimicrobial Multidrug Resistance on Inpatient Care Cost: An Evaluation of the Evidence," *Expert Review of Anti-Infective Theory* 11, no. 3 (2013): 321–31.

The importance of refrigeration in food safety with respect to reducing gastrointestinal cancers is well known, as reviewed by P. A. van den Brandt and R. A. Goldbohm, "Nutrition in the Prevention of Gastrointestinal Cancer," *Best Practice and Research: Clinical Gastroenterology* 20, no. 3 (2006): 589–603.

pp. 192–93: The FDA's programs on food safety directed at consumers can be found at www.foodsafety.gov. The figure of the dangerous kitchen is available at www.safewise.com. The findings of the government survey on the effectiveness of labeling to prevent exposures to foodborne pathogens are available at http://www.cdc.gov/mmwr/preview/mmwrhtml/00054714 .htm. Dr. Julie Caswell noted in a 1998 article the effectiveness of labeling to provide consumer information and reduce foodborne hazards: "How Labeling of Safety and Process Attributes Affects Markets for Food," *Agricultural and Resource Economics Review* (October 1998): 151–58, available at http://ageconsearch.umn.edu/bitstream/31517/1/27020151.pdf. The story of Alar and how consumer pressure resulted in rapid abandonment by the food industry of this chemical in treating apples is well told by E. O. van Ravenswaay and J. P. Hoehn, "The Impact of Health Risk Information on Food Demand: A Case Study of Alar and Apples," in *Economics of Food Safety*, ed. J. A. Caswell (New York: Elsevier, 1991), 155–74.

Our study of the differences in contamination of poultry products by drug-resistant strains of *Campylobacter* was published in 2005: L. B. Price, E. Johnson, R. Vailes, and E. K. Silbergeld, "Fluoroquinolone-Resistant *Campylobacter* Isolates from Conventional and Antibiotic-Free Chicken Products," *Environmental Health Perspectives* 113 (2005): 557–60; our findings were confirmed by scientists at the FDA: T. Luangtongkum, T. Y. Morishita, A. J. Ison, S. Huang, P. F. McDermott, and Q. Zhang, "Effect of Conventional and Organic Production Practices on the Prevalence and Antimicrobial Resistance of *Campylobacter* spp. in Poultry," *Applied and Environmental Microbiology* 72 (2006): 3600–3607.

p. 194: The GAO reviewed the FDA's performance in issuing recalls for food products contaminated by pathogens and found it wanting; see http://www.gao.gov/products/GAO-05-51. The egregious example of Foster Farms as a repeat offender is well described by Wil S. Hylton, "A Bug in the System: Why Last Night's Chicken Made You Sick," *New Yorker*, February 2, 2014.

On postmarket drug recalls, see the 2014 Annual Report of the FDA's Center for Drug Evaluation and Research.

p. 195: The successful campaign by the pork industry to silence any official mention of H1N5 swine influenza during the 2009 outbreak was described in *National Hog Farmer*, April 30, 2009, http://nationalhogfarmer.com/swine-flu/0430-vilsack-stop-swine-flu. D. M. Souza Monteiro and J. A. Caswell have written on the conflicts among the various stakeholders with public and private interests—consumers, authorities, and food marketers—in terms of interests in information disclosure on food safety: "The Economics of Implementing Traceability in Beef Supply Chains: Trends in Major Producing and Trading Countries," Working Paper No. 2004-6, Department of Resource Economics, University of Massachusetts Amherst, Amherst, 2006, available at http://scholarworks.umass.edu/cgi/viewcontent.cgi?article=1209&context=peri_workingpapers&sei-redir=1&referer=http%3A%2F%2Fscholar.google.com%2Fscholar%3Fhl%3Den%26q%3DCaswell%2BJulie%26btnG%3D%26as_sdt%3D1%252C21%26as_sdtp%3D#search=%22Caswell%20Julie%22.

p. 196: Consumer attitudes and concerns about food vary around the world, as I learned from living in Italy. Surveys of US consumers include trade organizations and national polls, for example, the report that only 20 percent of Americans are "very confident" in food safety from the International Food Information Council Foundation (http://www.foodinsight.org/Content/3840/2012%20IFIC%20Food%20and%20Health%20Survey%20Report%20of%20Findings%20(for%20website).pdf) and the report "Nearly Three-Quarters of Americans Looking to Government for More Food Safety Oversight," Harris Poll, Rochester, NY, 2013, available at www.harrisinteractive.com. Some useful references indicating the differences between EU and US consumers include: T. M. Ngapo, E. Dransfield, J.-F. Martin, M. Magnusson, L. Bredahl, and G. R. Nute, "Consumer Perceptions: Pork and Pig Production. Insights from France, England, Sweden and Denmark," *Meat Science* 66 (2003): 125–34; Maria L. Loureiro and Wendy J. Umberger, "A Choice Experiment Model for Beef: What US Consumer Responses Tell Us about Relative References for Food Safety, Country-of-Origin Labeling and Traceability," *Food Policy* 32 (2007): 496–514; S. Van Boxstael, I. Habib, L. Jacxsens, M. De Vocht, L. Baert, E. Van De Perre, and A. Rajkovic, "Food Safety Issues in Fresh Produce: Bacterial Pathogens, Viruses and Pesticide Residues Indicated as Major Concerns by Stakeholders in the Fresh Produce Chain," *Food Control* 32, no. 1 (2013): 190–97.

p. 197: For life in Baltimore when housing discrimination was overt, Antero Pietila is an authoritative source; see *Not in My Neighborhood* (Chicago: Rowan and Littlefield, 2010). On neighborhood differences in food safety associated with differences in food access, see our study: Ellen K. Silbergeld, Jose Augusto Frisancho, Joel Gittelsohn, Elizabeth T. Anderson Steeves, Matthew F. Blum, Carol E. Resnick, "Food Safety and Food Access: A Pilot Study," *Journal of Food Research* 2, no. 2 (2013): doi:10.5539/jfr.v2n2p108.

pp. 199–201: As in much of this book, I found insights in the history of food and food regulation, particularly the writings of Sidney Mintz on food, Peter Barton Hutt I and II's history of food safety in the United States, and E. J. T. Collins's history of food safety in England. These two histories supported my sense of the waves of regulation and deregulation that followed on larger social and economic trends in food and agriculture. See S. Mintz, *Tasting Food, Tasting Freedom: Excursions into Eating, Culture, and the Past* (Boston: Beacon Press, 1996); E. J. T. Collins, "Food Adulteration and Food Safety in Britain in the 19th and Early 20th Centuries," *Food Policy* 18, no. 2 (1993): 96–126; and P. B. Hutt and P. B. Hutt II, "A History of Government Regulation and Misbranding of Food," *Food, Drug, Cosmetic Law Journal* 29 (1984): 3–72. The FDA's own history is also interesting; see W. F. Janssen, "The Story of the Laws behind the Labels," *FDA Consumer*, June 1981, http://www.fda .gov/AboutFDA/WhatWeDo/History/Overviews/ucm056044.htm. For the role of Quakers in improving the quality of goods in England, a probably biased account is given by Sir Adrian Cadbury, "Beliefs and Business: The Experience of Quaker Companies," http://www.leveson.org.uk/stmarys /resources/cadbury0503.htm. On the Progressive movement and Roosevelt's response to *The Jungle*, I relied on Doris Kearns Goodwin's *The Bully Pulpit* (New York: Simon & Schuster, 2013).

pp. 204–5: For information on outsourcing poultry processing and the lack of FDA inspection of imports, I cite the 2013 testimony by Patty Locavera of the Health Research Group, an NGO, which is available from Congress: http://docs.house.gov/meetings/FA/FA14/20130508/100807/HHRG-113 -FA14-Wstate-LoveraP-20130508.pdf. The effect of size on food safety problems is discussed by C. C. Hinrichs and R. Welsh, "The Effects of the Industrialization of US Livestock Agriculture on Promoting Sustainable Production Practices," *Agriculture and Human Values* 20 (2003): 125–44. The concerns of the WHO on this issue are similar as stated in http://www.who.int/food safety/publications/consumer/flyer_keys_eng.pdf. For aflatoxin in poultry and the work environments of farmers and farmworkers, the research by Susana Viegas and colleagues is important; see Susana Viegas, Luisa Veiga, Joana Malta-Vacas, Raquel Sabino, Paula Figueredo, Ana Almeida, Carla Viegas, and Elisabete Carolino, "Occupational Exposure to Aflatoxin (AFB1) in Poultry Production," *Journal of Toxicology and Environmental Health, Part A* 75, no. 22–23 (2012): 1330–40.

p. 206: For the section on nutrition, I obtained much of the data on current patterns of US food consumption from H. Stewart, N. Blisard, and D. Joliffe, "Let's Eat Out: Americans Weigh Taste, Convenience, and Nutrition," EIB-19, USDA, Economic Research Service, Washington, DC, 2006, available from ars.usda.gov; this is the source indicating that almost 20 percent of Americans eat out at least once a week, equally at full service and fast-food establishments.

p. 207: On revisions to the Food Pyramid in 1992, see M. Nestle, "Food Lobbies, the Food Pyramid, and US Nutrition Policy," *International Journal of Health Services* 23, no. 3 (1993): 483–96. A new plate was published in 2016.

p. 208: The observation on the incompatibility between efficient production and food safety is from Robert Kenner's 2009 interview with *Grist*; see http://grist.org/article/2009-06-26-food-inc-kenner/. For coverage on the debate over food safety from conventional or organic sources, a recent commentary comes from Jane Wells on CNBC, "Critics Question How Much Better Organic Really Is," available at http://www.cnbc.com/2015/11/06 /critics-question-how-much-better-organic-really-is.html.

CHAPTER 11. CAN WE FEED THE WORLD?

p. 214: Information on the aspects of feeding the world is available from national and international organizations, including FAO, the WHO, and the USDA. Reports on these topics have been published by the US National Research Council as well. For data on global food insecurity, FAO has statistics and the USDA Economic Research Service publishes frequent reports for the United States. A recent analysis of food insecurity in Maryland, downloaded in May 2015, is available from the local NGO Maryland Hunger Solutions at http://www.mdhungersolutions.org/food_insec_food_hardship.shtm. For a demonstration of the importance of nutrition, Dr. Alfred Sommer, former dean of the Johns Hopkins School of Public Health and the original supporter of this book, has pioneered studies on micronutrients in health and development among children in South Asia: A. Sommer and K. West, *Vitamin A Deficiency: Survival and Vision* (Oxford: Oxford University Press, 1996). Mickey Chopra has written on the global paradox of increasing obesity in the presence of hunger; see M. Chopra, S. Galbraith, and I. Darnton-Hill, "A Global Response to a Global Problem: The Epidemic of Overnutrition," *Bulletin of the World Health Organization* 80, no. 12 (2002): 952–58. Cecilia Tacoli, among many others, has noted the existence of inadequate incomes as a major factor in food insecurity, particularly among populations in rapidly expanding cities.

pp. 215–16: About the ethical value of food sovereignty, one of the most recent and most eloquently argued statements appears in "Project 2," in *7 by 5: Agenda for Ethics in Global Food Security* (Baltimore: Global Food Ethics Project, Bioethics Institute, Johns Hopkins University, 2015), available at http://www.bioethicsinstitute.org/wp-content/uploads/2015/05/7-by-5 -report_FINAL.pdf. I respect the ethical focus of this project, but I disagree with many of its conclusions, particularly in the context of this chapter. Much of the debate over food sovereignty has focused on issues of autonomy, such as the ethical issues of patent protections given to genetically modified organisms. See H. Wittman, A. Desmarais, and N. Wiebe, "The Origins and Potential of Food Sovereignty," in *Food Sovereignty: Reconnecting Food, Nature, and Community* (Winnipeg: Fernwood, 2001), chap. 1. On the conflicted interactions of food sovereignty with free trade in food, F. Mousseau presents a relatively balanced analysis. See *Food Aid or Food Sovereignty? Ending World Hunger in Our Time* (Oakland, CA: Oakland Institute, 2005).

Information on subsidies for agroecological farming in Sweden comes from L. Lohr and L. Salmonsson, "Conversion Subsidies for Organic Production: Results from Sweden and Lessons for the United States," *Agricultural Economics* 72 (2000): 133–46.

pp. 217–18: On agricultural development initiatives by the Bill and Melinda Gates Foundation, the website contains a link to work in this area; see www .gatesfoundation.org.

Advocates for emphasizing support for smallholder farming in Africa include Danielle Nierenberg, formerly with World Watch Institute, a US NGO, and Olivier de Schutter, formerly with the UN. See O. de Schutter and G. Vanloqueren, "The New Green Revolution: How Twentieth Century Science Can Feed the World," *Solutions* 2, no. 4 (2011): 33–44, and T. P. Tomich, S. Brodt, H. Ferris, et al., "Agroecology: A Review from a Global-Change Perspective," *Annual Review of Environment and Resources* 36 (2011): 193–222. Nikos Alexandratos and Jelle Bruinsma coauthored "World Agriculture towards 2030/2050," Agricultural Development Economics Division, FAO, Rome, 2006. The quote comes from N. Alexandratos, "Countries with Rapid Population Growth and Resource Constraints: Issues of Food, Agriculture, and Development," *Population and Development Review* 31 (2005): 237–58. Jonathan Crush, with Bruce Frayne and Wade Pendleton, has commented on these perspectives in "The Crisis of Food Insecurity in African Cities," *Journal of Hunger and Environmental Nutrition* 7, no. 2–3 (2012): 271–92. At the time Crush was also part of the African Food Security Urban Network, Cape Town, South Africa.

On the side of cities, there is a long literature that amply illustrates the draw of urban life in most countries. Dr. Chimedsuren Ochir's study of the impacts of rapid internal migration to the capital city was conducted for the Ministry of Health of Mongolia in 2009. Barney Cohen is an eloquent advocate for urban life; see his "Urbanization in Developing Countries: Current

Trends, Future Projections, and Key Challenges for Sustainability," *Technology in Society* 28, no. 1–2 (2006): 63–80.

p. 221: Edward Bernays was quoted by his biographer, H. L. Cutler, in *The Engineering of Consent* (Norman: University of Oklahoma Press, 1955). See also B. Bajželj, K. S. Richards, J. M. Allwood, P. Smith, J. S. Dennis, E. Curmi, and C. A. Gilligan, "Importance of Food-Demand Management for Climate Mitigation," *Nature Climate Change* 4 (2014): 924–29.

Trends in urbanization have been widely described and associated with changes in diet. Cecilia Tacoli and colleagues have connected these trends with changes with agricultural production in developing countries; see D. Satterthwaite, G. McGranahan, and C. Tacoli, "Urbanization and Its Implications for Food and Farming," *Philosophical Transactions of the Royal Society B* 365, no. 1554 (2010): doi:10.1098/rstb.2010.0136.

p. 222: Information on the robust but unequal growth in agricultural production comes from the Food and Agriculture Organization Statistical Reference (FAOSTAT). Global population growth data are available from the UN.

p. 226: Jules Pretty, among others, has evaluated the performance of what he has defined as sustainable intensification within agroecological methods in studies of farming projects in Africa and South America (reviewed by him in "Agroecological Approaches to Agricultural Development," World Bank, Washington, DC, 2008). I read his primary papers to evaluate the actual productivity of these projects and also benefited from e-mail correspondence with him. I am more persuaded by the work of H. C. J. Godfray, who advocates a more nuanced and complex toolbox of interventions; see "Food Security: The Challenge of Feeding 9 Billion People," *Science* 327, no. 5967 (2010): 812–18. The importance of agroecology as an ethical commentary and challenge to conventional methods is well expressed by the Global Food Ethics Project as well as by N. Alexandratos, both cited above, and M. A. Altieri, P. Rosset, and L. A. Thrupp, "The Potential of Agroecology to Combat Hunger in the Developing World," 2020 Brief 55, FAO, Rome, October 1998, available at http://www.fao.org/docs/eims/upload/207906/gfar0052.pdf.

p. 228: The argument over subsidies in agriculture may have started in biblical times. See John Hodges, "Cheap Food and Feeding the World Sustainably," *Livestock Production Science* 92, no. 1 (2001): 1–16. Today, this debate has both formal and less formal aspects. Less formal but often more inclusive analyses include those by Jules Pretty, cited above, as well by Tony Weis, "The Accelerating Biophysical Contradictions of Industrial Capitalist Agriculture," *Journal of Agrarian Change* 10 (2010): 315.

The role of subsidies in food supports, and the role of the USDA as a food agency, is demonstrated in its own statistics and the most recent federal budget for the agency (2015). The impact of national subsidies on agricultural production in poorer countries is asserted, but B. Hoekman, F. Ng, and M. Olarreaga provided a useful perspective on the potentially greater impact of protectionist tariffs erected by these countries; see their "Reducing Agricultural Tariffs versus Domestic Support: What's More Important for Developing Countries?," Policy Research Working Paper 2918, World Bank, Washington, DC, 2002.

p. 229: Although the structural readjustment policies and memories of neoliberalism may have faded, their deleterious impacts on health and hunger in developing economics are well described by D. E. Sahn, P. A. Dorosh, and S. D. Younger, *Structural Adjustment Reconsidered: Economic Policy and Poverty in Africa* (Cambridge: Cambridge University Press, 1999).

p. 230: Information on the economic sustainability of CSAs was discouraging, as was Laura DeLind's academic analysis and her firsthand experience as a supporter of the CSA concept. See her "Are Local Food and the Local Food Movement Taking Us Where We Want to Go?," *Agriculture and Human Values* 28, no. 2 (2010): 273–83, and "Close Encounters with a CSA: The Reflections of a Bruised and Somewhat Wiser Anthropologist," *Agriculture and Human Values* 16, no. 1 (1999): 3–9.

p. 231: Ben Smith's essay appeared in *New York Times Sunday Review*, August 9, 2014.

Dan Barber's comments come from his *The Third Plate* (New York: Penguin, 2014).

p. 232: My analysis of the success and sustainability of agroecology and organic farming as well as farmers' markets in the United States was informed by data from the USDA Census of Agriculture and its economic research service, NGOs, commercial sources, and some academic analyses. Overall, however, I was limited by sparse data as well as inconsistencies in measures for assessing these outcomes. One of the few academic sources was a report by the Center for Agroecology and Sustainable Food Systems at the University of California, Santa Cruz (Research Brief No. 4, 2004; available at http://casfs.ucsc.edu/documents/research-briefs/RB_4_CSA_farmers_survey.pdf). The size of the entire "organic" sector (as defined by USDA regulations) was estimated by a commercial marketing source (http://www.statista.com/topics/1047/organic-food-industry/), which seemed to me to be less biased than proponents of organic or industrial agriculture. Global figures came from World Watch, a proponent of agroecology.

p. 234: For more on the socioeconomic characteristics of CSAs, see S. M. Schnell, "Food with a Farmer's Face: Community-Supported Agriculture in the United States," *Geographical Review* 97, no. 4 (2007): 550–64.

CHAPTER 12. A PATH FORWARD, NOT BACKWARD

p. 235: Much of the material in this chapter draws upon the rest of this book, as the careful reader will have anticipated. Most of what I learned about policy tools that could be applicable to reforming industrialized agriculture came from my experience at the Environmental Defense Fund working with Karen Florini, now at the US Department of State. Specific references are provided below.

p. 238: Hesiod, the Greek poet who flourished before Homer, was cited in chapter 1; the quote here comes from an online reference to his works (http://www.sacred-texts.com/cla/hesiod/works.htm). The biblical quote is from Genesis 3:17 (King James Version).

p. 240: The latest revisions in food safety inspections were published on July 30, 2014, and can be accessed from the USDA at http://www.fsis.usda.gov

/wps/wcm/connect/00ffa106-f373-437a-9cf3-6417f289bfc2/2011-0012F
.pdf?MOD=AJPERES.

p. 242: The Perdue study of antibiotics in poultry feed is discussed more
fully in chapter 5 along with our analysis of the economics of this practice.

For the court decision concerning the FDA and antibiotic registrations,
see Ed Silverman, "FDA Doesn't Have to Ban Antibiotics Given to Food-
Producing Livestock," *Wall Street Journal*, July 24, 2014, http://blogs.wsj
.com/pharmalot/2014/07/24/fda-doesnt-have-to-ban-antibiotics-given
-to-food-producing-livestock. For the response of the Danish government
to relabeling the same use of antimicrobials in feeds as "prophylactic," see
P. R. Wielinga, V. F. Jensen, F. M. Aarestrup, and J. Schlundt, "Evidence-
Based Policy for Controlling Antimicrobial Resistance in the Food Chain in
Denmark," *Food Control* 40 (2014): 185–92. This extensive article provides
an excellent history of the rise of antimicrobial resistance in food and food
animals, as well as Denmark's enviably efficient monitoring system for
food safety.

p. 245: For a clear discussion of the environmental impact statement, its
origins, and its role in policy, see Thomas Sander's essay "Environmental
Impact Statements and Their Lessons for Social Capital Analysis," available
at http://www.hks.harvard.edu/saguaro/measurement/pdfs/sandereis
andsklessons.pdf.

p. 248: For Dow Chemical Company's failed legal attempts to block EPA
inspection of its facilities in Midland, Michigan, see the excellent review
and discussion of the legal issues involved published by the Legal Information Institute at the Cornell University School of Law: http://www.law
.cornell.edu/supremecourt/text/476/227. The citation of the case before the
Supreme Court is Dow Chemical Company, Petitioner v. United States etc.,
476 U.S. 227 (106 S.Ct. 1819, 90 L.Ed.2d 226).

For more on Wurster's efforts to establish the Environmental Defense
Fund, see Thomas Dunlap, *DDT, Silent Spring, and the Rise of Environmentalism* (Seattle: University of Washington Press, 2008).

p. 249: Nuclear power began, after several decades of experimentation, with the Atoms for Peace Program launched by President Eisenhower in 1953, followed by the 1954 Amendments to the Atomic Energy Act, which declassified US reactor technology and enabled development by the private sector.

pp. 250–51: Edward J. Blakely and Mary Gail Snyder's *Fortress America* (Washington, DC: Brookings Institution Press, 1997) is a penetrating sociological and political analysis of the rise of private solutions to public problems that threaten the concept of the community.

"Pink slime" and the impact of public outrage on the USDA and agribusiness are all well described by Joel Greene, "Lean Finely Textured Beef: The 'Pink Slime' Controversy," Congressional Research Service, Washington, DC, 2012, available at www.crs.gov.

p. 252: I referred to Tom O'Brien's comment on the global nature of antimicrobial resistance in chapter 7; the citation is to D. C. Hooper, A. DeMaria, B. M. Limbago, T. F. O'Brien, and B. McCaughey, "Antibiotic Resistance: How Serious Is the Problem, and What Can Be Done?," *Clinical Chemistry* 58, no. 8 (2012): 1182–86.

Index